Welcome to

THE
EVERYTHING
Family Guides ®

THESE HANDY, PORTABLE BOOKS are designed to be the perfect traveling companions. Whether you're traveling within a tight family budget or feeling the urge to splurge, you will find all you need to create a memorable family vacation.

Use these books to plan your trips, and then take them along with you for easy reference. Does Jimmy want to go sailing? Or maybe Jane wants to go to the local hobby shop. *The Everything® Family Guides* offer many ways to entertain kids of all ages while also ensuring you get the most out of your time away from home.

Review this book cover to cover to give you great ideas before you travel, and stick it in your backpack or diaper bag to use as a quick reference guide for the activities, attractions, and excursions you want to experience. Let *The Everything® Family Guides* help you travel the world, and you'll discover that vacationing with the whole family can be filled with fun and exciting adventures.

💼 TRAVEL TIP

Quick, handy tips

☂ RAINY DAY FUN

Plan ahead for fun

≡ FAST FACT

Details to make your ___ enjoyable

👥 JUST FOR PARENTS

Appealing information for moms and dads

THE
EVERYTHING
— Family Guides —

Dear Reader,

What a lucky author I am. Imagine getting the opportunity to write about your hometown when your hometown is New York City!

As a third-generation New York City resident and the former publisher of a Manhattan weekly newspaper, it is really exciting for me to be able to share the insider spots and family secrets about this incredible city that we have collected and shared over the years.

I am truly thrilled to write about my memories of this city as a child—there are parts of the American Museum of Natural History and the Metropolitan Museum of Art that remain unchanged. As a teenager, I discovered the hippest places to go shopping. As an art history student at New York University, I used to visit the wonderful art and museums of this cultural mecca. As a grown-up, I take pleasure in New York's wholesale outlet and sample sales and absolutely delight in the prospect of a second New York childhood—through the eyes of my son.

Enjoy!

THE
EVERYTHING®
FAMILY GUIDE TO
NEW YORK
CITY

SECOND EDITION

All the best hotels, restaurants, sites, and
attractions in the Big Apple

Lori Perkins

Adams Media
Avon, Massachusetts

To my son, Max Jimenez, who took me on a tour of his New York, sharing his favorite sites, such as the Museum of Television & Radio. For the sake of authenticity, Max also personally tasted every restaurant meal in here.

Publishing Director: Gary M. Krebs
Managing Editor: Kate McBride
Copy Chief: Laura MacLaughlin
Acquisitions Editor: Eric M. Hall
Development Editor: Julie Gutin
Production Editor: Jamie Wielgus

Production Director: Susan Beale
Production Manager: Michelle Roy Kelly
Series Designer: Daria Perreault
Cover Design: Paul Beatrice, Matt LeBlanc
Layout and Graphics: Colleen Cunningham,
Rachael Eiben, Michelle Roy Kelly,
John Paulhus, Daria Perreault, Erin Ring

An Everything® Series Book.
Everything® and everything.com® are registered trademarks of F+W Publications, Inc.

Published by Adams Media, an F+W Publications Company
57 Littlefield Street, Avon, MA 02322 U.S.A.
www.adamsmedia.com

ISBN: 1-59337-136-5
Printed in Canada.

J I H G F E D C B A

Library of Congress Cataloging-in-Publication Data
Perkins, Lori.
The everything family guide to New York City / Lori Perkins.– 2nd ed.
p.   cm.
(An everything series book)
ISBN 1-59337-136-5
1. Family recreation–New York (State)–New York–Guidebooks. 2. Children–Travel–New York (State)–New York–Guidebooks. 3. New York (N.Y.)–Guidebooks. I. Title. II. Series: Everything series.
F128.18.P365   2004
917.47'10444–dc22   2004011397

This publication is designed to provide accurate and authoritative information with regard to the subject matter covered. It is sold with the understanding that the publisher is not engaged in rendering legal, accounting, or other professional advice. If legal advice or other expert assistance is required, the services of a competent professional person should be sought.
—From a *Declaration of Principles* jointly adopted by a Committee of the American Bar Association and a Committee of Publishers and Associations

Many of the designations used by manufacturers and sellers to distinguish their products are claimed as trademarks. Where those designations appear in this book and Adams Media was aware of a trademark claim, the designations have been printed with initial capital letters.

Although the author has taken care to ensure that this book accurately sets forth information as of the time it was prepared, prices, practices, and policies at attractions may change at any time, and may be different from the information provided here.

Cover illustrations by Barry Littman / Manhattan and Central Park maps by Map Resources

Manhattan Subway Map, Manhattan Bus Map, and commuter railroad maps
for Long Island Rail Road and Metro-North Railroad
©Metropolitan Transportation Authority are printed with permission.

This book is available at quantity discounts for bulk purchases.
For information, call 1-800-872-5627.

Visit the entire Everything® series at www.everything.com

Contents

Acknowledgments

Richard Mintzer, who did an invaluable job of researching and pulling together an enormous amount of information, wrote the first edition of this book. Without his work, I would never have been able to give you this reorganized edition, which is now the product of two native New Yorkers.

New York City's fabulous tourism organization, NYC & Company, is one of the best resources any journalist could ever have in writing about this city. Arlene Kropf answered every one of my arcane questions swiftly and completely. She was a joy to work with and a fountain of knowledge.

Shelley Clark and Rachel Harris of Lou Hammond & Associates were tireless in their efforts to make sure that in addition to the must-sees, I reviewed some of the really creative and unusual restaurants.

My assistant, Aileen Chumard, researched, wrote up, and even visited many of these attractions as our deadline loomed. She kept me on my toes and on time for my appointments. This book would not exist without her help.

Dan Gold, a fellow journalist, reminded me about city restaurants I had forgotten and also helped me to remember that it is a privilege to write a book about my hometown.

And my editor, Julie Gutin, was smart and flexible and stepped up to the plate when two other editors wouldn't take the pitch. This edition of this book is as much hers as mine.

Top Ten Things to Do in N.Y.C.

1. Get up early on Thanksgiving morning, bundle up, and get a good spot on the Macy's Thanksgiving Day Parade route (usually along the Upper West Side).

2. Take the family to *The Phantom of the Opera* or *The Lion King*, and buy T-shirts afterwards for one and all.

3. Go to the top of the Empire State Building and ride the Skyride.

4. Splurge and take one of the ten-minute helicopter rides over Lower Manhattan.

5. Spend a day in Central Park—take pictures at the *Alice in Wonderland* and Balto statues, ride the carousel, float a wooden boat, ride a hansom cab, and eat lunch at Tavern on the Green.

6. Take the family to Times Square and actually ride in the Toys Я Us ferris wheel. Then see a movie in one of the megaplexes.

7. Have a meal in Chinatown, and stroll the streets examining the trinkets.

8. Go shopping at Macy's or Bloomingdale's, or in Greenwich Village, or along Fifth or Madison Avenues.

9. Take the ferry to the Statue of Liberty and visit the Tenement Museum and Katz's Deli on the way back.

10. In the wintertime, go ice-skating at the rink at Rockefeller Center, or at least have lunch at the American Festival Café and watch New Yorkers skate.

Introduction

NEW YORK is really the greatest city in the country, and everyone wants to visit. The Big Apple is the travel destination for more than 35 million visitors a year, and it's also the leading destination for foreign travelers. New York is a top family vacation destination because it truly has something for everyone, from the youngest to the oldest. No matter how many times you visit, there will always be something new and exciting, as well as familiar and rewarding to see.

I was lucky. I was born here, so I know this city inside out, from the parks and museums to the subways and all the discount shopping—and everything in between. I'm actually a third-generation New Yorker, so I have my grandparents' and my parents' stories about growing up in New York to guide me. I'm now a New York City parent and have my son's experiences to share, as well.

Most families come to New York to see the one-of-a-kind landmarks like the Statue of Liberty and the Empire State Building; to enjoy the entertainment industry and popular culture—New York City is home to Times Square, NBC Studios, and the *Late Show with David Letterman*; to see Broadway musicals like *The Phantom of the Opera* and *The Lion King*; and to shop, whether at flagship department stores, in shopping districts in Greenwich Village, or on Fifth Avenue.

But New York has even more to offer. It is the art center of the country (and some would say the world), with breathtaking museums and fabulous architecture. No visitor should miss the Metropolitan Museum of Art, which rivals the Louvre as one of the world's greatest museums. Add in the Guggenheim, the Whitney, and the Museum of Modern Art, and you'll be sure to see the latest in contemporary art.

New York is the premier city for both serious and popular theater and other performing arts. You can always see ballet, opera, and musical performances. It is also the culinary capital of this country, with some of the finest cuisine in the world in the most exquisite settings (Tavern on the Green and the 21 Club), and some of the most entertaining (Chinatown, hot dog street vendors, and pizza).

It is also rich in American history, something many visitors overlook. You can visit revolutionary and colonial homes, the preserved mansions of America's robber barons, a turn-of-the-century tenement, and some of the finest examples of corporate architecture, from the Art Deco style of the Chrysler Building to the International Style of the Lever House. On top of that, New York is a college town, with four major universities of its own and many more in the surrounding suburbs.

Because there is so much to see and do (and so many new museums and attractions opening every year), many people make New York a rotating spot on a variable list of vacation places and see a different side of the city each time they visit.

For families with children, New York is an oasis and a playground. Aside from the most obvious kid-pleasing attractions like the Bronx Zoo and the American Museum of Natural History, there are many other one-of-a-kind experiences. These range from the Museum of Television & Radio to Madame Tussaud's Wax Museum, or you can go off the beaten path on excursions to the Police and Fire Department museums. Kids who love the subway are always mesmerized by the Transit Museum, and never forget that the Brooklyn Museum has the country's finest collection of Egyptian art (and therefore mummies). No kid can resist a day in Central Park where there's fun to be had riding the carousel, sailing wooden boats, climbing on the *Alice in Wonderland* statue, and visiting the Central Park Zoo!

If it's your first visit to New York City, don't be shy. Do some planning, and make your reservations. Once you make one trip, you'll probably be back again and again.

CHAPTER 1

Welcome to New York

NEW YORK WAS (AND STILL IS) the first place that many travelers encountered as they headed west from Europe. For that reason, New York was able to grow rapidly. Geography accounts for the city's great ethnic diversity and explains why so many crafts from different parts of the world emerged into industries in New York.

To visit New York is to take in all the ambiance the present-day city has to offer. However, to fully appreciate what is today one of the largest, most significant cities in the world (financially, architecturally, and culturally), it's a good idea to become familiar with a brief history of New York, noting some of the many major events and contributions that went along with the city's growth. Many of the sights you will see in your travels around the city are part of the city's rich history; others are named for famous explorers, settlers, governors, and statesmen who helped define what the city became.

How It All Began

New York City's history is the history of the country on a smaller scale, but still larger than life. Discovered by Henry Hudson, after whom the mighty river to the west and the glorious Hudson Valley are named, the area was originally home to a plethora of Native American tribes. The first European settlers to arrive were the

Dutch, who allegedly bought Manhattan from a local tribe, the Canarsie Indians, for $24 worth of beads. The Dutch named their colony New Amsterdam. Later, the Dutch were supplanted by the English.

═FAST FACT

The Dutch colony had lots of problems with the Native Americans who lived in the area. In 1653, the governor, Peter Stuyvesant, ordered the construction of a wall in Lower Manhattan to guard against a possible Indian attack (and possible attack by the British settlers, who were not in harmony with the Dutch). By 1700, the wall had been torn down, but Wall Street is still in place today.

Battles were fought all over this city during the American Revolution, and there are parts of Lower Manhattan, Queens, and Long Island where you can still find colonial bullet casings. For a time, it was the nation's capital, before giving way to Washington, D.C.

The City Grows and Prospers

In the early nineteenth century, New York became the center of the fashion industry. Banking, commerce, and real estate were also thriving. Printing became a major industry in the city, and the book publishing world was already established, joined in the 1830s by newspapers like the *New York Evening Post* and the *New York Tribune*. The *New York Times* was first published in 1851. The arts also thrived in the 1800s, when going to the theater became the thing to do. Numerous artists settled in the city, and the first grand opera was staged, *The Barber of Seville*.

The settlements of Manhattan, which were initially located in the lower portion of the island, expanded north until the entire island was populated. The four other boroughs also grew as New Yorkers opted to move out to "the suburbs." Business, industry, and commerce grew rapidly, thanks to the harbor and little additions like the Erie Canal. Wall Street became the nation's financial center, Central Park became the city's place to play, and baseball became the game to watch. In 1886, the Statue of Liberty was unveiled to watch over the harbor and the city. And in 1891, Tchaikovsky conducted the opening night gala at Carnegie Hall.

A City of Immigrants

Throughout the nineteenth century, immigrants flocked to the city from Germany, Ireland, and the rest of Europe. Many settled on the Lower East Side, by the new Brooklyn Bridge. In 1898, New York united the five boroughs and became one city with a population of more than 3 million, making it the world's largest city.

As the twentieth century began, immigrants kept coming to the city. In 1902 alone, some half a million immigrants landed at the new home of immigration, Ellis Island. In 1907, Ellis Island set a new record for immigrants at more than 1.25 million. Great concern grew that the "outsiders" were taking over the city, and a great deal of anti-immigrant articles and propositions were bandied about.

RAINY DAY FUN

The Tenement Museum in Lower Manhattan re-creates the crowded slums of the Lower East Side at the turn of the century. At the time, nearly 70 percent of the city's population lived in tenements because there was just not enough housing to go around. The conditions were barely livable, but the immigrants flocking to a new land of freedom managed to make do.

Construction Projects

Before the twentieth century was even well underway, city workers were already busy building the underground maze of railways that would become the New York City subway system. The

Manhattan and Queensboro Bridges were also constructed and opened at the end of that first decade.

By 1910, there were more than eighty miles of subway below the New York City streets. The city continued to grow, with significant building projects such as Penn Station, which took six years to build and was completed in 1910, and the New York Public Library on 42nd Street, which cost some $9 million to build. Today, the library is still one of the foremost research centers in the world, and its striking architecture, protected by two giant lion statues in front, has become a national icon.

Despite troubles on Wall Street in 1907, the city continued to thrive as the financial center of the nation. Municipal services improved, automobiles replaced horse-drawn carriages on Fifth Avenue, and the immigrant population continued to grow. And in 1908, the *New York Times* kicked off what would become a long-standing New York City tradition, dropping the giant ball at Times Square to ring in the new year.

Fun and Games

And what did New Yorkers do for entertainment, besides visit the popular taverns and saloons? They went to see the Ziegfeld Follies; New York's dancing girls, or to the early silent films, many of which were shot in New York. The early twentieth century also saw the establishment of major league baseball—New York boasted three teams: the Yankees, Giants, and Dodgers.

Growing Pains

As the city grew—financially and in terms of population, which topped the 2-million mark—the second decade of the 1900s saw its share of tragedy as well. A 1911 fire at the Triangle Shirtwaist Company clothing factory killed 146 people. In 1912, families awaited the arrival of the greatest ocean liner ever built, the *Titanic,* but it never made it across the ocean. In 1915, the *Lusitania* set sail from New York, but it too never reached its destination. In 1916, a tragic subway crash killed 102 people.

The Triangle disaster sparked great debate over workers' safety, and over fifty reforms were instituted for factories. Unionization also became the talk of the town. In 1916, the city endured its first of many strikes that plagued the garment industry and the transit system.

While the unions were bringing workers together, the war brought New Yorkers together behind the troops who fought the Germans. Unlike other parts of the country, the German population in New York City was not subjected to ridicule, harassment, or violence. At the end of World War I, the city welcomed its war heroes home.

Roaring Twenties and the Depression

The Roaring Twenties brought in the postwar era of prohibition and speakeasies. It was a time of new hairstyles, nightclubs, flappers, jazz, and fun. Harlem became the hub of jazz in the city, with Duke Ellington and Louis Armstrong, among others, drawing crowds uptown, along with Paul Whiteman and a thirty-piece band, the Kings of Jazz. Establishments like the Cotton Club, Roseland on 52nd Street, and the Savoy Ballroom flourished. The Ziegfeld Follies were also going strong, having debuted in 1907. New Yorkers and the country were doing the Charleston and the city's playboy mayor, Jimmy Walker, was hitting hot spots all over town. Broadway shows were also the rage, including a classic, *Showboat,* which opened in 1927.

In addition to the music and dancing, the New York Yankees were the talk of the world, with a newfound hero, Babe Ruth, picked up from the rival Boston Red Sox. In 1927 he would set the home-run record with sixty homers, a record that stood until 1961. The Yankees would win twenty-five world championships throughout the century, far more than any other major league baseball team.

As if the Yankees weren't enough to celebrate, the city threw a ticker-tape parade through the streets of Lower Manhattan for Charles Lindbergh, who made the first-ever solo flight over the Atlantic Ocean, also in 1927.

Bottomed Out

The fun, dancing, and revelry that marked the decade of the 1920s came to a crashing halt when the stock market plummeted in 1929. Wall Street suffered through Black Thursday and then Black Tuesday, and the bottom dropped out of the stock market. The city fell into the Great Depression, which swept across the nation. People did whatever they could to get through the lean years, and the government tried to help by funding public projects that required lots of workers. As a result, the 1930s saw another construction boom.

When the Empire State Building was completed on April 11, 1931, it was the world's biggest office building. Soon after, work began on a proposed fourteen-building project called Rockefeller Center, and a massive hotel, the Waldorf Astoria. Very quietly, without any great fanfare, a small experimental television station—W2XAB—was set up by CBS. Nobody would realize the impact of that little station or the others like it for years to come.

The problem faced by the city, however, was that while it was surging forward in some respects (such as development), in others it was losing money. Even the Empire State Building could barely find tenants who could afford to rent office space. By 1932, the city was nearly $2 billion in arrears (which at that time was a lot of money), a debt not matched by the rest of the country put together. Nearly 2 million of the city's 7 million inhabitants were receiving relief of some type. Some 164 bread lines were not enough to feed the hungry in a very troubled city.

Mayor LaGuardia Steps In

The city needed a take-charge mayor, and in 1934 Fiorello LaGuardia stepped up to the plate. He was tough and ready to turn around the city he loved. He took over a $30-million deficit, with only $31 million left from a federal government loan that would run out just eight months after he took the oath. LaGuardia instituted sales tax and utility tax programs, just the beginning of measures that over the next several years would pull the city out of its financial crisis. He also cracked down on crime, starting with the arrest of the city's most notorious mobster, Lucky Luciano.

LaGuardia cleaned up the city, put welfare recipients to work, and made a better New York. He even closed down the famous Minsky's Burlesque, much the way Mayor Giuliani later cleaned up Times Square—a far more raunchy Times Square than the patrons of Minsky's could ever have imagined.

Construction Projects Continued

Despite the financial difficulties of the early 1930s, construction never stopped. Thousands of families moved into new housing projects, while the subway lines expanded and construction of New York City Municipal Airport began. The airport was later renamed LaGuardia.

Helping to build the city was the ever-aggressive Robert Moses, a parks commissioner with a mission. Despite coming under criticism for ousting the former tenants of the land, Moses would build 5,000 acres worth of parks and set up more than 250 playgrounds. One of the parks, Flushing Meadow in Corona, Queens, was created from a garbage dump, well worth the $600-million price tag. But Moses was preparing the site for the fabulous 1939 World's Fair, a huge economic boon for the city. To help make Queens and the World's Fair more easily accessible, the Triborough Bridge and Midtown Tunnel were constructed, and New York City Municipal Airport opened.

RAINY DAY FUN

E. L. Doctorow, a Pulitzer Prize–winning author and native New Yorker, wrote a wonderful novel about New York, *World's Fair*. You can read up on the career of Parks Commissioner Robert Moses in The *Power Broker: Robert Moses and the Fall of New York*, by Robert Caro, considered a classic tale of New York politics.

Surviving World War II

As splendid as the World's Fair was, the news from Europe wasn't encouraging. Germany had attacked Czechoslovakia, Poland, France, Britain, and Russia. The Japanese were expanding their empire in the Pacific. The United States tried to stay out of the war, but it became impossible when the Japanese attacked Pearl Harbor. Following the attack, security was increased on all bridges, tunnels, factories, and other significant points in New York City that were potentially prime targets for an attack.

Joseph Goebbels, Hitler's propaganda minister, reportedly wanted to destroy New York, which he called a "medley of races," none of which fit the Nazi ideal. During the war, the lights of the spectacular New York City skyline went dark or were dimmed. The lights of Broadway were also dimmed, as was the enthusiasm of the city as soldiers went off to war, leaving factories and production at a depleted level. While the mayor moved north into Gracie Mansion (originally built in 1804 and redesigned by Robert Moses), the people of the city watched and waited for news from overseas.

After the city welcomed its war heroes home with a rousing parade, New York continued the building expansion of the prewar era, and the Yankees just kept on winning pennants. Along with the city's renewed expansion was the controversial proposal to build the headquarters for the United Nations in Manhattan. Eventually, after much debate, a block of land purchased in 1946 by John D. Rockefeller became the home of the newly created United Nations. The focus of the world was on New York City as host to this new international organization.

The Boom of the 1950s and 1960s

After World War II, the city entered another period of boom. This was a time when the baby boomer generation was born. By the second half of the decade, New York City had nearly 8 million inhabitants, not much more than its current population. Postwar

New York saw a return to manufacturing, led by the successful garment industry. Another industry—television—also joined the fray, with early shows (including *The Honeymooners,* starring Jackie Gleason and shot in Brooklyn studios) being produced in the city.

≡FAST FACT

New York City became home to the first integrated baseball team in 1947, when Jackie Robinson broke the baseball color barrier by joining the Brooklyn Dodgers.

But while the city's economy was seemingly strong, with more than 100,000 retail stores selling billions of dollars worth of goods, there were other problems. New York continued to lure anyone who felt he or she could achieve the American Dream. As the population grew, housing became scarce; the city was in need of new dwellings. The 1950s would see numerous housing projects, including the massive Stuyvesant Town on the east side of Manhattan.

And Then Came the 1960s

The city entered the 1960s with new roadways, including the Throggs Neck Bridge, the Verrazano-Narrows Bridge, and the new second level of the George Washington Bridge. The New York Mets were born, taking the uniform colors of the recently departed Giants and Dodgers but gaining neither the trust nor the enthusiasm of those teams' old fans.

Lincoln Center, the most advanced and spectacular showcase for the cultural arts in the world, opened on Manhattan's Upper West Side, despite protests over its displacement of much-needed housing.

As if a new ball club and arts center were not enough, the city also got the thumbs-up to host the 1964 World's Fair, the second in twenty-five years at the same location, Flushing Meadow Park in Queens. Most exciting—to teenagers at least—was the American debut of the British phenomenon, the Beatles, who appeared on

The Ed Sullivan Show and later at a relatively new venue in the city, Shea Stadium.

In the summer of 1964, riots rocked Harlem, with hundreds of fires, several deaths, and a public outcry for help to stop the unrest. The 1960s were indeed turbulent times in the nation's largest city, where protests, sit-ins, walkouts, and strikes—including a newspaper strike that lasted for months and a transit strike that cost the city nearly a million dollars in revenue—set the city on a spiraling path. The city was already in financial trouble from government programs and efforts to solve the postwar housing crisis. Much of the tension came to a head when violent demonstrations broke out at the prestigious Columbia University on the Upper West Side of Manhattan.

At the end of the decade, the New York Jets pulled off an improbable Super Bowl upset, and the hapless Mets emerged from the depths to win the World Series. The United States had sent a man to the moon, but New York was still in trouble.

From Bad to Worse

While the tensions in the city eased somewhat in the early 1970s, the financial situation worsened. Much like the opening of the Empire State Building during the Great Depression, the new World Trade Center now towered over Manhattan while officials searched their pockets and the treasuries for enough money to keep the city from bankruptcy. By 1974 the Big Apple had hit rock bottom. The city was broke.

From newspaper employees to garbage collectors to doctors at city hospitals, everyone was walking out on strike, angered that they were feeling the effects of the city's plummeting financial situation. The police, who at one point also went on strike, issued warnings to tourists to stay away from "Fear City." Crime was up, and the city was falling apart. This was literally evidenced by a truck that fell through the West Side Highway, which was sorely in need of road repair.

Finally, when even the state could not bail out the city, New York turned to Washington and asked President Ford for help. The president snubbed New York, yielding the *Daily News* headline "Ford to City, Drop Dead."

But by the 1976 bicentennial, the city was back on its feet again, and the tall ships sailing the Hudson River celebrated not only the nation's 200th birthday but also the return of New York City. Broadway was revitalized, the struggling Yankees of the late '60s and early '70s returned to the top of the American League, and the city hosted a Democratic National Convention that would ultimately lead the party past Gerald Ford.

A Slow Comeback

It took a few years, but the city began to put itself back on track. Not all was smooth sailing, though. The city was terrorized in the summer of 1977 by a crazed killer, David Berkowitz, who called himself "Son of Sam." 1980 ended on a somber, chilling note as John Lennon was gunned down outside his Central Park West home, a crime that stunned the city and the world.

 JUST FOR PARENTS

Before you leave for New York, you might want to discuss the terrorist attack on the World Trade Center with your children. For children who watched this attack on television, visiting the site, which is currently under construction, might help bring a sense of security and forwardness to this difficult event in their childhoods, as they witness how the city is literally being rebuilt from its own ashes.

But with Mayor Koch at the helm, the city had hope for the 1980s. Things were slowly getting back on track, with tourists returning to a much-improved city. Financially, New York City was booming again. And the city resumed its place as the center of the art and music worlds.

A City Undefeated

New York is truly a city that's impossible to vanquish. It experienced another stock market crash in late 1987, only to re-emerge in the dot-com boom of the 1990s. This turnaround took place under the direction of hard-hitting Mayor Rudy Giuliani, who made New York a city where people once again felt safe.

The city and the nation were rocked by the second terrorist attack on the World Trade Center, and all of America watched in horror as the Twin Towers fell. But the city has risen, like a phoenix from those ashes. New Yorkers really came together as a result, and the city is thriving once again. According to NYC & Co., the local convention and visitors' bureau, New York City is the number-one tourist destination for families, safe for visitors and brimming with creativity and harmony.

CHAPTER 2

Planning Your Trip

NEW YORK IS A YEAR-ROUND, twenty-four-hour city, so it's always in full swing, offering "only in New York" sights and experiences any time you visit. You have a lot of options for scheduling your trip, including the time of year and mode of transportation for getting here.

When to Go

There is no "wrong" time to visit New York City, but your experience will vary depending on when you make your trip. Thanksgiving, Christmas, New Year's Eve, and the rest of winter are so special that many families visit every year; spring in the city can be as beautiful as it is in Paris; summer is an endless street fair with bustling beaches; and fall is a season of marathons and fashion under gorgeous falling leaves.

The Weather

From ample snowfall to sizzling summer heat, New York is a city with very distinct seasons and a wide range of temperatures. You can expect summer temperatures in the eighties, with high humidity coming into play in July and August. April and May are pleasant and mild, with temperatures around sixty-five degrees, and

September and October are perfect walking months, with a range of temperatures from the mid-sixties into the eighties. In November through March, temperatures are generally under fifty-five degrees, and late December, January, and February can be bitter and cold, in the single digits if you factor in the wind chill.

 TRAVEL TIP

The chilly temperatures of January and February may dissuade some travelers, but the hotel rates are lower during those two months, and there is always plenty to see and do.

New York sees an average of forty inches of rain annually, with no particular "rainy season." Annual snowfall is often around twenty to twenty-five inches, but the city has been known to get significantly more or less—for instance, nearly fifty inches of snow fell in the winters of both 2003 and 2004. Only Mother Nature knows for sure, but you can certainly expect at least one good snowstorm between December and March.

The summer can be quite hot, thanks to the humidity. However, Manhattan experiences a weekend exodus as the city dwellers head to Long Island and the Jersey shore to try to "beat the heat" and hit the beach. Thus, traffic can be lighter and hotels less expensive. Just make sure your hotel room is air-conditioned!

The Holiday Season

December is a joyous time in New York, with the glow of the Christmas tree at Rockefeller Center, the annual *Radio City Christmas Spectacular* and the traditional performance of *The Nutcracker,* as well as the incredible department-store windows. The city has a holiday spirit that's hard to match. The festivities end with the world-famous New Year's Eve party in Times Square. This is the peak tourist season, with high-priced hotel rooms that fill up fast. Following the holidays, tourism slumps a bit, which makes it easier to get great Broadway tickets or reservations at the best restaurants.

Spring and Fall

Spring and fall may be the best times to visit the city, if your schedule permits. In April and May, or September and October, you have the opportunity to enjoy most activities, from parks and zoos to baseball games to the Philharmonic and the opera. Temperatures are neither too hot nor too cold, and there are many festivals and special city events. Hotel rates are somewhere in between their highest and lowest points, tending to fluctuate from year to year.

 **TRAVEL TIP**

Shop around for your hotel room. With the development of the various Internet search engines, you should definitely go online and see if you can get a better rate. Always ask for a AAA discount or a weekend or package deal.

Make It a Road Trip

Once you've decided the time of your visit, consider your options for getting to the Big Apple. Driving to New York City will save you the cost of airfare and is certainly a popular choice when coming from nearby cities.

If driving seems like a good option, be sure you have a plan for what to do with your car once you arrive. Parking is at a premium in the city, so driving in means paying for garages. The average hotel parking fee is $25 a day, with some as high as $45 (like at the Waldorf). If you plan to use public transportation once you arrive—which is advisable in Manhattan—you can find a parking lot with a weekly rate, which will save you money.

Driving in and out of the City

Whether you're coming from Connecticut, New Jersey, or upstate New York, your options for entering the boroughs are the George Washington Bridge, Lincoln Tunnel, and Holland Tunnel. If you don't have an E-Z Pass, be sure to bring enough cash for the tolls.

The George Washington Bridge, which opened in 1931, has two levels of two-way traffic connecting Manhattan to Fort Lee, New Jersey, from 181st Street. Primary routes to the bridge are the Henry Hudson Parkway on the west side along the Hudson River, and Harlem River Drive, which becomes FDR Drive, along the East River.

The Alexander Hamilton Bridge connects the Cross Bronx Expressway directly with the George Washington Bridge, crossing into Manhattan. The bridge itself stands 200 feet above the Hudson River and is one of the most traveled bridges in the world. It connects easily with the Palisades Parkway, Route 80, the New Jersey Turnpike, and other major New Jersey roadways. You can also walk or bicycle across the bridge on outer walkways. The $6 toll is charged only to traffic entering Manhattan.

TRAVEL TIP

With the E-Z Pass, a prepaid toll card you mount on your car window, you can zip through the tollbooths instead of waiting in line to pay. If you don't have the pass, make sure you go through the "Cash Only" lanes. If you make a mistake and go through an E-Z Pass lane (marked by a purple and white sign), the system will trace you through your license plate and send you a bill.

The Lincoln Tunnel connects Manhattan from West 30th to 32nd Streets with Weehawken, New Jersey, and like the George Washington Bridge, intersects with most major Jersey routes. The tunnel has three connecting tubes that were completed in the late 1950s. Follow the signs for the Lincoln Tunnel carefully, as the lanes have been divided for use by trucks and cars. Some lanes are closed to passenger cars. Nearly 40 million cars, trucks, and buses use it every year. The toll is $6, charged only to traffic entering Manhattan.

The Holland Tunnel connecFts Lower Manhattan from Canal Street or Spring Street to Jersey City and provides easy access to Routes 1 and 9. The granddaddy of underwater travel, this tunnel dates back to 1927. There is a $6 toll for traffic entering Manhattan.

If you are traveling from Manhattan to or from Staten Island, catch the Staten Island Ferry. The ferry leaves every fifteen minutes from Whitehall Street next to Battery Park in Lower Manhattan and goes to the neighborhood known as St. George on Staten Island. The ride is free. The view from the third deck is quite pleasant. The 6.2-mile ride takes about twenty minutes. After a deadly accident in 2004 that killed thirteen people, it is no longer possible to transport your car on the ferry.

≡FAST FACT

Gas is significantly cheaper in New Jersey, and finding a gas station in Manhattan is not an easy task. If you're driving through the Garden State, go ahead and fill your tank. If you do find yourself running low and you're in Manhattan, look for gas stations on the far West Side, near access to the Westside Highway, or the East Side off FDR Drive.

If you're traveling from Queens into Manhattan, or vice versa, you can take the Queensboro Bridge, which connects Long Island City in Queens with First and Second Avenues in Manhattan at 59th and 69th Streets. Although the bridge has two levels, it is likely that one of those levels will be closed for repairs in at least one direction. Nonetheless, the bridge is free! It provides easy access to Queens Boulevard, Northern Boulevard, and, via Van Dam Street, the Long Island Expressway in Queens.

The Queens Midtown Tunnel is at the west end of the Long Island Expressway. The tunnel deposits you in the East 30s in Manhattan, between First and Second Avenues. The tunnel toll is $4 in both directions and is very busy during rush hour. The Triborough Bridge connects Queens from Grand Central Parkway to Manhattan at 125th Street, where you can easily go south onto FDR Drive or north onto Harlem River Drive. The elaborately designed bridge also connects Queens with the Bronx, and the Bronx (from the Bruckner

Expressway) with Manhattan. To confuse matters, the bridge also connects with Randalls Island. There is a $4 toll in all directions.

The Bronx connects with Manhattan at the Triborough Bridge and at other bridges, including the Willis Avenue Bridge, which connects the Harlem River Drive with the Major Deegan in the Bronx. The Willis Avenue Bridge (off the Harlem River Drive), Third Avenue Bridge (at 129th Street), the Madison Avenue Bridge (at 138th Street), and the Macombs Dam Bridge (at 155th Street) also connect the Bronx with Manhattan.

TRAVEL TIP

If you want to leave Manhattan for one of the four outer boroughs—the Bronx, Brooklyn, Queens, or Staten Island—it's probably best to go by car. Use the main parkways and expressways to get to your chosen section of the borough, and once you've exited carefully follow local street directions.

On Manhattan's west side, you can take the Henry Hudson Parkway North past the Cloisters and connect with Riverdale (part of the Bronx), which goes directly into the Henry Hudson Bridge. There is a $2 toll in both directions. The road will become the Saw Mill River Parkway and will head north to Westchester, where you can get the New York State Thruway and the Hutchinson River Parkway.

There are four routes connecting Brooklyn with Lower Manhattan. The famed Brooklyn Bridge will take you from Cadman Plaza or the Brooklyn Queens Expressway (BQE) into Manhattan, with easy access to FDR Drive or Park Row by City Hall. The Manhattan Bridge connects Atlantic Avenue or Grand Army Plaza in Brooklyn with Canal Street in Chinatown. The Williamsburg Bridge connects Metropolitan Avenue or the BQE with Delancey Street in Manhattan. All of these bridges are free.

The Brooklyn Battery Tunnel connects West Street in Manhattan—with easy accessibility from the FDR Drive or Henry Hudson Parkway (through elaborately designed tunnels at the lower tip of Manhattan)—to the Gowanus Expressway in Brooklyn. The tunnel toll is $4 in both directions.

Be Prepared

The best way to plot your course, both in getting to the city and once you are there, is with an online mapping service like Mapquest (✑ *www.mapquest.com*). Many of New York's streets are one-way or have limited access (especially with new traffic laws during weekday work hours that restrict turns in midtown Manhattan between Sixth and Park Avenues). Mapquest will show you the best way of reaching your destination and will give you directions based on the address. Another option is to contact the Automobile Association of America (AAA), which provides maps and driving directions to members.

If You Prefer to Fly

Since New York City is truly a city that never sleeps, you can fly into one of the three major airports, get a cab, and check into a hotel at any hour. However, if you arrive after midnight, you might have to wait for a cab. Since the shuttle services stop running at a certain time, have the number of a car service handy. Also, make sure the hotel knows ahead of time when you plan to arrive. (Otherwise, they may make you wait for your room, which can be exhausting when you are traveling with kids.) If it's not inconvenient, flying at night is a good way to avoid crowds at the airports and traffic en route to Manhattan.

Give yourself plenty of time to get to the airport and for check-in. Passengers have been known to get bumped from overcrowded flights because they showed up too late! Youngsters may enjoy watching planes take off and land while you relax before your flight, perhaps reading up on New York City. It's also important to arrive early to get through the added security checkpoints at airports. Don't forget to bring two IDs, including a photo ID such as your driver's license.

New York airports have completely revised their check-in procedures as a result of the terrorist attacks of September 11. You must arrive an hour ahead of time for a domestic flight, and two hours early for an international flight to or from New York City. You may be asked to remove your belt and/or shoes when going through the metal detector, as well as those of your children, so dress accordingly. All passengers are expected to have photo ID at check-in, so pack identification for yourself and the kids.

RAINY DAY FUN

Before you head toward the city, let the kids draw a map of how you will get there. Point out the landmarks you'll be passing on the way, such as the George Washington or the Brooklyn Bridge. These may be their first, and therefore most memorable, glimpses of the city.

Major Airlines

Every major airline and most of the smaller ones offer frequent flights to New York City. It's always best to check with several carriers to find the best deals. These are the major airlines with service to New York City:

Air Canada
✆ 1-800-776-3000
🖰 www.aircanada.com

American Airlines
✆ 1-800-433-7300
🖰 www.americanairlines.com

America West Airlines
✆ 1-800-235-9292
🖰 www.americawest.com

British Airways

☎ 1-800-247-9297

✎ www.britishairways.com

Continental Airlines

☎ 1-800-523-0280

✎ www.continental.com

Delta Airlines

☎ 1-800-221-1212

✎ www.delta.com

Jet Blue

☎ 1-800-538-2583

✎ www.jetblue.com

Midwest Express

☎ 1-800-452-2022

✎ www.midwestexpress.com

Northwest Airlines

☎ 1-800-225-2525

✎ www.nwa.com

United Airlines

☎ 1-800-241-6522

✎ www.united.com

US Airways

☎ 1-800-428-4322

✎ www.usairways.com

Virgin Atlantic

☎ 1-800-862-8621

✎ www.virgin.com

Try to make your reservations ahead of time. Airlines generally give better deals if you book at least twenty-one days in advance. Check prices on various airlines, and look for advertised specials. If your schedule permits, you'll almost always get a better airfare if your stay includes a Saturday night. If you're planning your visit around a major holiday, you need to book far in advance. Tickets do go quickly during the holidays, particularly around Thanksgiving and Christmas. Airfares vary widely depending on where you are flying from, what type of seats you are purchasing, and when you purchase them. On an airplane, everyone on board may have paid a different ticket price.

TRAVEL TIP

One of the ways to save money on a flight to New York is to fly into one of the lesser-known airports—White Plains in Westchester County or MacArthur in Long Island. Since few people know about these airports, there are often seats available during the more crowded times. However, this only saves you money if you are renting a car or have someone who will pick you up at the airport. Otherwise, a cab ride to Midtown will run you at least $100.

JFK International Airport
📞 718-244-4444
🖃 www.jfkairport.com

JFK International Airport is one of the world's busiest. Opened as Idlewild International Airport in 1948, its name was changed in the 1960s in honor of John F. Kennedy. All major carriers land at JFK. Transportation information-counters are located on the lower level near baggage-claim carousels, and taxis, buses, shuttles, and limousines pull up just outside. Car rental facilities are also nearby and can be reached by rental company shuttle buses.

Although the airport is located some fifteen miles outside of Manhattan in Queens, travel by taxi to Manhattan takes about forty to sixty minutes—longer during very busy times. Taxis charge a flat rate of $45 plus tolls and tips, so don't let them tell you otherwise! The tip should be 15 percent, more or less, depending on service.

LaGuardia Airport

✆ 718-533-3400

✎ www.panynj.com

Smaller than JFK but larger than airports in many other major cities, the 680-acre LaGuardia Airport handles all of the primary carriers and offers mostly domestic flights. Originally opened commercially in 1939 as New York City Municipal Airport, the name was later changed to commemorate former Mayor Fiorello LaGuardia. Located less then ten miles from Manhattan, the trip from this Queens-based airport can be anywhere from twenty minutes during the off hours to an hour during heavy traffic. Taking a cab that charges by the meter will cost around $30 plus tolls and tips. Cabs are easy to find at any number of taxi stands.

≡FAST FACT

Are you confused about which airport to choose? All three city airports are about the same distance from Manhattan. Finding the best fares may help you choose your airport. If you're staying in Brooklyn, Queens, or the Bronx, Newark Airport would be a less desirable choice, since the other two airports are located close by.

Newark International Airport

In nearby Newark, New Jersey, Newark International Airport is some thirty to forty minutes from Manhattan (more during rush hour) by car or bus. New Jersey's largest commercial airport, Newark has enjoyed major renovations over the years, including monorail service from terminal to terminal. If you're heading to the west side of Manhattan, you might consider flying into Newark, as with the other airports you'll enter the city from the east. Also,

Newark is generally less crowded than Kennedy or LaGuardia because some consider it farther away. Without traffic it can seem closer. Taxis cost $60 to $85 plus tolls and tip.

Airport Transportation

If you think a cab isn't a great option for your family, you still have plenty of options.

If you need information about ground transportation from any of New York's three major airports, you can call the Port Authority Ground Transportation Hotline, at ✆ 1-800-247-7433. They also provide information on parking at the three major airports.

JFK Airport

Shuttles run from the airport to Grand Central, Penn Station, and the Port Authority on 42nd Street, as well as to some midtown hotels. During the day and early evening, this is a good way to save on cab fare. However, if you are traveling with a large family, a cab might be cheaper because you'll pay a flat fee rather than a per-person charge, as you would on a shuttle.

 TRAVEL TIP

Most luggage mix-ups are quickly resolved. However, you should always report lost luggage immediately. File a complaint with the carrier, and include your flight and time of arrival. You can also call the U.S. Department of Transportation at ✆ 202-366-2220 or write to them at ✉ C-75, Room 4107, Washington, D.C., 20590.

Bus or Shuttle

New York Airport Service goes directly to the east side of Manhattan at Grand Central Station between 41st and 42nd Streets on Park Avenue. Another bus goes to the west side, to the Port Authority Bus Terminal at 42nd Street and Eighth Avenue. Buses are

$13 per person, and a round trip ticket costs $23. Call ✆718-875-8200, or find information online at ✐ *www.nyairportservice.com.*

Super Shuttle provides a blue van on twenty-four-hour call to all destinations in Manhattan. They charge $19 to go from JFK to any of their regular stops, but they will drop you off at a residential address for an additional fee. For more information, call ✆212-964-6233 or visit ✐ *www.supershuttle.com.*

Driving

If you rent a car, you can get to Manhattan from JFK by taking the Van Wyck Expressway to the Long Island Expressway. Head west to the Midtown Tunnel, which will deposit you in the East 30s in Manhattan. You can also take the Grand Central Expressway and proceed over the Triborough Bridge—but watch the signs because the bridge also goes to the Bronx—and follow the signs for Manhattan/FDR Drive. You can also take the Belt Parkway around Brooklyn to the Brooklyn/Queens Expressway and go over the Brooklyn Bridge to Lower Manhattan. Or follow signs to the Gowanus Expressway and take the Battery Tunnel into Lower Manhattan, but be ready to pay a toll.

Airtrain JFK

New York City has finally joined other international cities in offering train service. Airtrain JFK is a cheap, relatively efficient way to get from the airport to Midtown. With service made available again in 2004, this forty-five-minute ride from JFK to Midtown will take $5 off your subway fare card, called a MetroCard (plus a regular $2 subway fare). During rush hour, it is definitely the way to go. It runs twenty-four hours, seven days a week, and is heated in the winter and air-conditioned in the summer. For more information, call ✆ 1-877-JFK-AIRT or visit ✐ *www.airtrainjfk.com.*

LaGuardia

From LaGuardia, take the shuttle offered by the New York Airport Service (✆ 718-875-8000, ✐ *www.nyairportservice.com*).

Tickets run between $10 and $15. Super Shuttle blue vans run to Manhattan, and these will drop you off at a residential address for a little extra (about $14). For more information, call ✆ 1-800-258-3826, or visit ✍ *www.supershuttle.com.*

If you rent a car, you can get to Manhattan from LaGuardia by going west on Grand Central Parkway, which will take you to the Triborough Bridge—but watch the signs, because the bridge also goes to the Bronx! Look for the sign for Manhattan/FDR Drive. If you're going to Lower Manhattan, you can also get the Brooklyn/Queens Expressway from Grand Central Parkway and head to the Williamsburg or Brooklyn Bridge.

TRAVEL TIP

Taxi drivers are not allowed to solicit fares. Always wait in the taxi stand line when catching a cab from an airport. If a cab driver or anyone else meets you in the terminal and offers you a ride—even at a "low rate"—refuse it. So-called "gypsy cab" drivers are not legal and are not authorized by the city. Don't take chances. Get taxis at designated taxi stands and buses at designated bus areas.

Newark International Airport

If you prefer public transportation, take AirTrain Newark (✆ 888-397-4636, ✍ *www.airtrainnewark.com*), an elevated train that, with connections to New Jersey Transit and Amtrak, can get you to Penn Station in twenty minutes for $11.15.

The New Jersey Transit Airlink (✆ 973-762-5100, ✍ *www.njtransit.com*) is a twenty-four-hour bus service that leaves for Penn Station, Newark (*not* Penn Station in Manhattan), every fifteen minutes (or every half hour between 1 and 6 A.M.). The fare is $4 per person, and be sure you have exact change. From Penn Station, Newark, you can catch a PATH train into Manhattan.

Another option is to take a privately run bus. Olympia Trails Express buses leave for Port Authority every fifteen minutes from

4 A.M. to 12:45 P.M. and cost $11. Call ☏ 212-964-6233 or ☏ 908-354-3330, or visit ✍ *www.olympiabus.com.*

If you rent a car, you can get to Manhattan from Newark by following the airport exit signs to the New Jersey Turnpike (95) North. Take the turnpike, following signs for the Holland Tunnel, the Lincoln Tunnel, or the George Washington Bridge. The Holland Tunnel goes into Lower Manhattan, the Lincoln Tunnel goes into midtown Manhattan, just south of 42nd Street, and the George Washington Bridge enters the city near the upper tip of Manhattan, around 178th Street.

Take the Bus

If you don't live very far away, taking the bus is an affordable option. Greyhound, Trailways, and other carriers offer service to Port Authority Bus Terminal on Eighth Avenue between 40th and 42nd Streets in Manhattan. The largest bus terminal in the country, Port Authority sees buses coming from and heading to all points in the continental United States, plus Canada and Mexico.

The following bus companies offer service to New York City:

Adirondack Trailways
☏ 1-800-225-6815
✍ *www.trailways.com*

Bonanza Bus Lines
☏ 1-800-556-3815
✍ *www.bonanzabus.com*

Greyhound Lines
☏ 1-800-231-2222
✍ *www.greyhound.com*

Martz Trailways
☏ 1-800-233-8604
✍ *www.martztrailways.com*

New Jersey Transit
☏ 973-762-5100
✍ www.njtransit.com

Peter Pan Trailways
☏ 1-800-343-9999
✍ www.peterpanbus.com

Shortline
☏ 1-800-631-8405
✍ www.shortline.com

Vermont Transit
☏ 802-864-6811
✍ www.vermonttransit.com

To contact Port Authority, call ☏ 212-564-8484 or visit ✍ www.panynj.gov.

 TRAVEL TIP

Here are a few tips for driving in New York. Unless a sign specifies otherwise (a rarity), you cannot make right turns on a red light in New York City. People frequently cross against the light in Manhattan, so watch out for pedestrians. Do not leave your car unattended unless it is parked and locked.

Ride the Train

Amtrak is the leading rail carrier of passengers to and from points across the country in and out of New York City. For Amtrak information, call ☏ 1-800-USA-RAIL (872-7245), or visit their Web site at ✍ www.amtrak.com. Trains pull into Penn Station on the west side of Manhattan between Seventh and Eighth Avenues just below 34th Street. From there, you'll easily be able to take a taxi or bus to your hotel. Penn Station is very busy and crowded, so be sure to keep an eye on your property at all times. Cabs are easily found on surrounding streets.

For travel north and south, to and from other points in New York State, and even as far as Connecticut, you can travel via the Metro-North Commuter Railroad, which departs from the Grand Central Terminal on East 42nd Street at Park Avenue. For schedules and information, call ✆ 212-340-3000 or visit ✎ *www.mta.nyc. ny.us/mnr.*

Working with a Travel Agent

You can make your travel arrangements and hotel plans all at once through a travel agent. With the help of his or her connections, a travel agent can often put a package together for less money. This can save you both time and cash. Travel agents are terrific to work with, but you must still make sure all the details are to your liking. So ask questions about the flight and the room arrangements, as you would if you were making plans yourself. Also find out ahead of time what to do if you are dissatisfied with the accommodations and need to change them. Flexibility is important!

It's a good idea to read up on accommodations at various hotels so that you have an idea of what you are looking for. Then ask the travel agent about rates or discounts at those specific hotels. Also, if you are not renting a car, ask about arrangements or at least details for the shuttle service to and from the airport. Good travel agents can also arrange transportation.

Deal with reputable travel agents, and be careful about any too-good-to-be-true deals advertised on the Internet or anyplace else. To check on a travel agent, you can call the American Society of Travel Agents (ASTA) at ✆ 1-800-965-2782, or visit their Web site at ✎ *www.astanet.com.* As is the case when hiring anyone to look out for your best interest, try to establish a good rapport with your travel agent, or get a referral from someone you know and trust.

Packing Tips

First and foremost, bring comfortable clothes and shoes. The primary means of getting around Manhattan is walking, so be prepared. A good pair of walking shoes can make the difference between a fun-filled, action-packed day and an all-out exhausting one.

Also be prepared for varying temperatures. Wearing layers of light and warm clothing will help keep you comfortable and happy while touring the city. The four seasons have the same characteristics you'd find anywhere, but the weather within those seasons can sometimes be unpredictable.

Watching the Weather Channel or checking the weather section of the paper will give you an idea of the climate as you plan for your trip. It's a good idea to have at least one small folding umbrella, since there's always the chance of a shower—particularly a late-afternoon thundershower, if you're visiting in the summer months.

 JUST FOR PARENTS

While the finer restaurants may require sport jackets and a tie for men, most restaurants, particularly those with family fare, do not have strict dress codes. Nonetheless, it's a good idea to pack some dressy clothes along with your casual attire.

If you plan to stay in New York City for ten days or less, it's to your advantage to bring two weeks' worth of clothes, since doing laundry in many Manhattan hotels can be expensive. Midtown Manhattan does not have many Laundromats, although they are plentiful once you leave the Midtown area for Chelsea or the Upper West Side.

Other than these tips, there's not much else to add. If you forget something at home, don't worry! The multitude of shops and twenty-four-hour stores in New York City will allow you to buy whatever you might need. However, the city is pricey, and you don't want to have to buy items you could have brought along with you just as easily. So make a list before packing.

Stay Safe

Make sure all bags have zippers or clasps that can be closed for security. If you are planning to carry bags onto an airplane, limit them to two per person. Try to arrange for one person to have a free hand. Remember to label all bags so that they are easily identifiable at the airport luggage carousel.

TRAVEL TIP

When approaching New York City, you might tune in to WINS (at 1010 on your AM radio dial) or CBS-AM (880 on your AM radio dial). These are New York's all-news radio stations, and they have regular traffic updates.

If you bring things to do on the plane, tuck them away before you land so that you're not carrying anything but your suitcases. Keep cameras tucked safely away until you are settled in your hotel. Unfortunately, there are some people in every major city who will try to take advantage of tourists, so be alert and don't accept offers of rides, tours, currency exchanges, or anything else from anyone you just happen to meet at the baggage claim area or on the streets of the city. Don't let anyone hold or guard your things for you. Exercise common sense at all times.

CHAPTER 3

Getting Around the City

NOW THAT YOU'RE HERE, how do you get from your hotel to the Empire State Building? The Metropolitan Museum of Art? Yankee Stadium? Jones Beach? If you are staying in Manhattan, the simple rule of thumb is that you use mass transit, take a taxi, or walk. Outside of Manhattan, you can drive (unless you're going to one location in the heart of Brooklyn or Long Island City in Queens) or take an express bus.

The Street System

Manhattan is pretty easy to figure out. The numbered streets start with First Street in Lower Manhattan and end with 220th Street at the top of the island, right before the Bronx starts. The island is laid out on a grid, with numbered cross streets running east and west and avenues running north to south.

≡FAST FACT

The Bronx continues Manhattan's numbered streets—from 221st Street until 260th Street, where Yonkers (a different municipality) begins. Broadway runs from Lower Manhattan through the Bronx and into Yonkers in a fairly straight line.

Here are the primary avenues on the east side, starting at the East River and going west:

- **York Avenue** runs both ways between 53rd Street and 96th Street.
- **First Avenue** runs north.
- **Second Avenue** runs south.
- **Third Avenue** runs north, with two-way traffic below 24th Street.
- **Lexington Avenue** runs south to 22nd Street.
- **Park Avenue** runs both ways.

Fifth Avenue, which runs south, is the line that divides the east and west sides of Manhattan. All cross-street addresses are designated "East" or "West," and they proceed in ascending order from Fifth Avenue. Therefore, 12 East 59th Street will be just east of Fifth Avenue, and 12 West 59th Street will be just west of Fifth Avenue. Always specify east or west when taking down an address on numbered streets.

Here are the primary avenues on the west side:

- **Sixth Avenue,** also known as Avenue of the Americas, runs north to Central Park.
- **Seventh Avenue,** also known as Fashion Avenue, runs south from Central Park.
- **Eighth Avenue** runs north and becomes Central Park West at 58th Street.
- **Ninth Avenue** runs south and becomes Columbus Avenue above 59th Street (Columbus Circle).
- **Tenth Avenue** runs north and becomes Amsterdam Avenue above 59th Street.
- **Eleventh Avenue** runs two ways above 42nd Street and south below it; it becomes West End Avenue above 59th Street.
- **Twelfth Avenue** runs north, and ends at 59th Street.

- **Riverside Drive** runs both ways from 72nd Street to the George Washington Bridge (between 178th and 179th Streets). When the Henry Hudson Parkway is congested, Riverside Drive is often the best alternate route.

Franklin Delano Roosevelt Drive (known as the FDR to New Yorkers) runs along the East River. It becomes the Harlem River Drive above the Triborough Bridge. On the west side is the West Side Highway, which becomes the Henry Hudson Parkway as you head north from Lower Manhattan. It runs the length of the island, with great views of the Hudson River, the George Washington Bridge, and the New Jersey Palisades.

 **TRAVEL TIP**

When the Rockefellers donated the land in Upper Manhattan where the Cloisters was built, they also donated the land across the river in New Jersey. They stipulated that no commercial development ever be made, leaving us an unobstructed view of the New Jersey Palisades from Upper Manhattan, much like Henry Hudson might have seen hundreds of years ago.

Both FDR Drive and the West Side Highway run uptown and downtown with narrow entrance and exit ramps. When not crowded, they are the quickest ways of getting uptown or downtown, but watch out for potholes!

Exceptions to the Rule

When navigating Manhattan, the grid of numbered cross streets and primary avenues runs from Greenwich Village to Harlem and is relatively easy to follow (as you'll see on any city map). Washington Heights, at the far northern end of the island, is the narrowest part of the city. It's easy to navigate because you're never too far from either the Harlem River Drive to the east or the Henry Hudson Parkway to the west.

All bets are off, however, once you get into Greenwich Village (the widest part of Manhattan). This is particularly true in the West Village, where narrow streets cross and turn in all directions. The East Village, also known as Alphabet City, brings you to avenues A, B, C, and D, in a new grid leading to the Lower East Side.

The Lower East Side, SoHo, TriBeCa, Little Italy, Chinatown, and the Financial District, which are all essentially part of Lower Manhattan, require careful navigation and good directions and/or map-reading skills. Church Street, Center Street, Broadway, and Bowery are your primary north/south avenues; major cross streets include Houston (pronounced HOWS-ton), Canal, Delancey, and Church Streets (in the financial district). Wall Street is a well-known street in this area, but it isn't a major thoroughfare.

Car Rentals

Renting a car in New York City is expensive. If you are flying in, your best bet is to pick up a car at the airport, and try to get a package air/car deal. Also try the Internet for rates. From $70 a day to over $400 a week, a car in the city can be costly, with tolls, gas, and parking costs added to your rental expense. There is also insurance to worry about, which can run an additional $15 to $20 per day if you are not covered under your own policy or the credit card you rent the car with. And finally, there is a 13.25 percent tax on car rentals!

 JUST FOR PARENTS

There are two weekly publications for New York parents. You might want to call and ask for a copy of *Big Apple Parent* ✆212-889-6400 or *New York Family* ✆914-381-7474 before you arrive, especially if you have young children. Issues of the publications can usually be found free in banks and kid-related stores once you arrive.

A Good Way to Explore Beyond Manhattan

Knowing that driving in the city can be difficult and that parking is hard to come by, you might want to rent a car for part of your stay if you want to venture outside of Manhattan. Make those rental arrangements before you arrive, and use AAA or any other memberships for discounts on rental cars. You should also book in advance and be careful to reserve your pick-up for a time you are fairly sure you can make—many Manhattanites don't have cars, so they rent on weekends, which means that New York City car rental companies do not hold cars past the scheduled pick-up time, especially on weekends in the summer. Be sure to choose a major rental company with a good reputation and a good service record. Here are a few suggestions:

Alamo
✆ 1-800-327-9633
✐ www.alamo.com

Avis
✆ 1-800-331-1212
✐ www.avis.com

Budget
✆ 1-800-527-0700
✐ www.budget.com

Dollar
✆ 1-800-800-4000
✐ www.dollar.com

Hertz
✆ 1-800-654-3131
✐ www.hertz.com

National Car Rental
✆ 1-800-227-7368
✐ www.nationalcar.com

You must be at least eighteen to rent a car (or to drive) in New York City. Many rental companies will not rent to anyone under twenty-five, so call to check on this policy if any of the drivers are between those ages. You also need a major credit card. Children under five, or under forty pounds, are required to ride in car seats, which you can rent from the rental car company (usually $5 to $8 extra per day). Have your reservation number ready when you get to the rental car window at the airport or at the rental car office. Don't let them talk you into a host of unnecessary extras.

 **TRAVEL TIP**

If you can, fill the gas tank in advance (if the deal offered is a good one) rather than agreeing to the traditional "return the car with a full tank" routine, since finding gas stations in Manhattan is difficult. If you plan to pick up the car at one location and deposit it at another, arrange this with the rental car company ahead of time, particularly if you are traveling to another city. Sometimes there are drop-off charges.

Limos and Car Services

For those who want to travel in style, a number of popular limousine services in New York offer standard cars as well as stretch limos. Rates start at about $50 for standard cars, not much more than a taxi. Major city limousine companies and car services include the following:

Allstate Car & Limousine
☎ 212-741-7440

Bermuda Limousine International
☎ 212-249-8400

Carey
☎ 212-599-1122

Concord
✆ 1-800-255-7255

Gotham
✆ 1-800-385-1033

Fugazy
✆ 212-661-0100

London Towncars
✆ 212-988-9700
✑ www.londontowncars.com

Mirage
✆ 212-744-9700

Sabra
✆ 212-777-7171

Safeway
✆ 212-826-9100

Tel Aviv
✆ 212-777-7777
✑ www.telavivlimo.com

You can usually charge these trips on a credit card—in fact, many companies prefer it. Either way, always tip your driver. Also be sure to ask the company whether they have limousines, if that is what you are looking for. Some companies are limo services, and others are not. It is not always implied by the title.

Mass Transit

The New York City subway system runs throughout four out of five boroughs (excluding Staten Island) and buses run everywhere the trains don't. Both the subway and the bus system are run by the Metropolitan Transit Authority (*www.mta.nyc.ny.com*), where you can find information about fares as well as maps and suggested routes.

In Manhattan, the quickest way to travel is by subway. Buses, while slower, will get you where you want to go while giving you some views of the city. Bus and subway fare is $2 per person.

▊ TRAVEL TIP

You need a subway map that you can carry in your purse or pocket. You can always ask for one at a token booth, but if you can't get one there, you can pick up a MetroCard-sized folding one at one of the NYC & Company offices at ✉810 Seventh Avenue. Call them at ✆1-800-NYC-VISIT, visit them on the Web at *www.nycvisit.com*, or order one before you arrive.

Get MetroCards for Everyone

You really need a MetroCard to ride the subway—and buses take MetroCards or exact change (coins—no dollar bills). Buses offer free transfers for one trip on an adjoining bus—simply ask the driver for a transfer—but you cannot get a transfer to the subway. There is a free transfer on your MetroCard, but you must spend a minimum of $4 to get a MetroCard (that's one round trip). Transfers and MetroCard transfers are good for two hours from the time issued.

If you expect to be traveling by mass transit (buses and subways), you will need a MetroCard for each member of the family. There are no discounts for students, and every person over age 5 pays full fare. You can buy MetroCards at automatic kiosks outside every token booth, where you can use cash or charge them to your credit card, or you can buy them at the token booth, newspaper stands, supermarkets, or candy stores. A seven-day unlimited-use MetroCard will run you $21, or you can buy a single-day unlimited card—the "fun pass"—for $7. You can also buy a card in $10 increments, with one free trip for every $10 you spend.

Taking the Bus

New York City has numerous buses (more than 3,500), all equipped for passengers with disabilities. There are also privately operated express buses to the outer boroughs (✑ www.liberty lines.com or ✑ www.nybus.com) with fares of $4 each way. (They take single dollar bills in their fare machines.) Before you get on a bus, read the sign on the front that tells you where it is going. It's easy to get on the wrong bus, so ask if you are not sure. New Yorkers, in general, will be helpful. Drivers, although sometimes curt, will usually answer if you ask where the bus is going.

The concierge at your hotel, or someone at the front desk, can help you plan your route for the day and tell you which bus or subway will take you where you are headed. Also, watch for "limited" buses in Manhattan. These are buses that stop only at major intersections. If you find yourself at an express bus stop, you're in luck. When there is no traffic, limited buses can get you where you want to go in a hurry, provided they stop near your destination. "Limited" buses are designated as such in the front window.

≡FAST FACT

The last subway token was used at some time around midnight on April 13, 2003. It was known as the "five-borough pentagram" token, because it had a cut-out pentagram at its center. It cost the rider $2.

The Subway System

The New York City subway system is an intricate maze of underground tracks covering more than 700 miles and zigzagging under four of the five boroughs. Initially constructed in the early 1900s, the subways carry nearly 4 million passengers daily in some 6,000 subway cars that stop at 469 stations. It is still the quickest and easiest way to get around. The most popular station is Grand Central Station, at 42nd Street and Lexington Avenue in Manhattan; it sees nearly every train that heads into the borough.

Transferring from one train to another is free, provided the two trains connect at some point. Subway maps tell you the stations where multiple trains stop.

A free copy of the subway map is readily available at any subway station booth and in many hotels. During morning and evening rush hours (6:00 to 10:00 A.M. and 5:00 to 7:00 P.M.), the trains are very crowded, so try to travel at other times.

You can plan numerous connections to take you where you want to go. Be aware, and follow the signs carefully. Finding your connection can be confusing at busy stations such as 42nd Street or Union Square (14th Street) in Manhattan. Subway entrances often indicate "uptown only" or "downtown only," meaning you need to cross the street and look for the train going in the other direction. If you pay attention, you won't join the many visitors (and New Yorkers, for that matter) who have taken the wrong train—it happens.

RAINY DAY FUN

A visit to the New York City Transit Museum is a unique experience for anyone who really loves trains. It has all the dirt on how the 100-year-old system was built, as well as great antiques and artifacts. There is also one of the best museum shops where you can get the signature subway map on a tie or even a shower curtain. Subway token jewelry is also available. Visit the museum Web site at *www.mta.nyc.ny.us/mta/museum.*

Subway Lines of the City

New York City subway lines are designated with either a letter or a number. They cover four of the five boroughs; Staten Island has its own Staten Island Railway system. Here are some popular destinations and the subway routes you can take to get there:

- Brooklyn Bridge, South Street Seaport, or City Hall: Take the 4, 5, 6, J, or M train.
- Central Park West and the American Museum of Natural History: Take the B or the C train.
- Grand Central Terminal or East 42nd Street (closest to the United Nations)—take the 4, 5, 6, 7, or S train (cross-town shuttle).
- Lincoln Center—take the 1 or the 9 train.
- Macy's, 34th Street area—take the B, D, F, Q, N, or R train.
- Metropolitan Museum of Art—take the 4, 5, or 6 train and walk two blocks west.
- Rockefeller Center—take the B, D, Q, or F train.
- Shea Stadium—take the 7 train from Grand Central, or pick it up at Queensboro Plaza.
- Times Square—take the 1, 2, 3, 7, 9, N, R, or S train (cross-town shuttle).
- Upper East Side of Manhattan or East Harlem—take the 4, 5, or 6 train.
- Upper West Side of Manhattan or Washington Heights—take the 1, 2, 3, or 9 train.
- Yankee Stadium—take the B, D, or 4 train.

Keep in mind that you can transfer for free at stations where the lines intersect. A complete and updated map is provided on the inside cover of this book.

Going on Foot

In Manhattan, one of the best ways to get around is to walk. Whether it's window shopping along Fifth Avenue or strolling the narrow streets of the Wall Street area or Little Italy, walking is a marvelous way to enjoy the sights and sounds of New York City. It also beats sitting in traffic.

One thing you must remember when walking is to look very carefully when stepping off a curb. Just because the light has changed does not mean a cab driver is going to stop—many take red lights as a mere suggestion. Bicycle messengers do not adhere to traffic laws and have been known to hit pedestrians. Always wait a moment before crossing, or follow the crowds of people at a busy intersection.

Walking through New York City can be exhilarating. Times Square, Greenwich Village, Broadway, Fifth Avenue, Wall Street, the Upper East or West Sides—they all offer a host of stores, restaurants, street vendors, and excitement found nowhere else in the world. People-watching is often half the fun. From a film crew to a clown or mime, you can spot just about anything on the streets of New York.

For those interested in architecture, the city is a paradise, mixing cultures and periods from corner to corner. An ornate nineteenth-century church standing next to a sleek black-glass skyscraper is not at all uncommon. When you walk around the city, you can truly appreciate that New York City indeed has it all!

 TRAVEL TIP

It's generally not advised to ride the subways past 11:00 P.M., particularly if you're alone. If you are at a rather quiet, unoccupied subway station, once you enter through the turnstiles, stand near the token booths or in the yellow designated "waiting area" toward the center of the platform. The city does have transit cops; however, there are more stations than cops, and more often than not the transit cops are busy watching the turnstiles rather than the platform.

Taking a Taxi

The best thing about taxis is that they are plentiful, at least in Manhattan, where more than 10,000 cabs drive zealously in pursuit of their next fare. They are available at all hours and get you places quickly. Taxi fares currently begin at $2.50 and increase $.40 for every $1/5$ mile. There is a $1.00 surcharge between 4:00 P.M. and 8:00 P.M.

How to Hail a Cab

Outside of Manhattan, you need to call to get a taxi or car service. In Manhattan, however, you can get a taxi through the concierge at your hotel, at a taxi stand, or, most commonly, by standing on the corner and signaling with your arm up and extended.

Be aggressive when hailing a cab, particularly in busy areas—watch how New Yorkers do it; it's an art. The toughest times to get a taxi are during rush hour, in the rain, or at 4:00 P.M., which is shift-change for cabbies. Many of them are anxious to get home after a twelve-hour day and will not pick up passengers.

When a cab stops to pick you up, do not tell the driver where you are going until you are seated and the door is closed. Once inside, they cannot turn you away. If they do, you can take down their number and report them to the Taxi and Limousine Commission, or call a police officer to intervene.

Clearly explain to the driver where you are going. Giving street coordinates, such as "34th Street and Fifth Avenue, please" is usually the best way to get where you want to go, better than giving a street address. If you are going to a well-known building, you can give him that information, such as "I'm going to Macy's." As you would in any other car, make sure you and your children are secured in seat belts.

At the End of the Ride

Have your money ready as you approach your destination. The driver gets the amount on the meter plus a tip (usually 15 percent). He or she may not ask for more, except for tolls incurred. Trips to JFK Airport are charged at a flat rate ($45). Rules and rates are posted clearly in the back of the cab.

Watch carefully when getting out of a cab; the driver may leave you off in a busy area, and bike messengers think nothing of zipping past a taxi on the passenger side. Look before getting out.

Check to make sure you take your belongings. When you pay, you should ask for a receipt—not only for your travel expense records, but also so you'll have the taxi ID number in case you leave something behind in the cab. Call the New York City Taxi and Limousine Commission at ✆ 212-302-TAXI or ✆ 212-676-1000 (or find them on the Web at ✍ *www.ci.nyc.ny.us*) if you need to track down a lost article left in a taxi or if you need to complain.

☰FAST FACT

In 2003, SUV cabs were introduced to the city. Still yellow, and still the same price, they carry up to six passengers. By law, regular cabs can only carry four passengers, and one person has to sit in the front with the driver.

For People with Disabilities

New York, like the rest of the country, has become more and more accessible for people in wheelchairs. All newer buildings, and many of the older ones, are wheelchair accessible, and city buses pick up wheelchair passengers at the curb by lowering the steps in the back-door stairwell.

Most hotels, major tourist sites, and theaters provide access for wheelchairs or anyone who cannot climb stairs. It is advisable to call ahead and ask where the entrance is and how to navigate once inside. Facilities like Madison Square Garden and other arenas, theaters, and stores have elevators. When booking your hotel, you should inquire about accessibility as well as in-room facilities such as hand railings in the shower or bathtub, and so forth. Newer hotels are more likely to meet the needs of people with disabilities than older ones.

One significant program that is designed to assist travelers with disabilities is called the Access Project. It is associated with Big Apple Greeters, a volunteer program that connects visitors to the city with residents of the city for three- or four-hour personalized visits/tours. The Access Project works in conjunction with the New York Convention and Visitors' Bureau and the Mayor's Office for

People with Disabilities and other organizations, plus the MTA, to provide information and easy access to the sights, hotels, theaters, and transportation of New York City to people with a wide range of disabilities and mobility problems. The Access Project at Big Apple Greeter can be reached at ✆ 212-669-3602. They help make New York accessible to all visitors.

Other resources for travelers with disabilities include the following:

MTA (subway and bus) twenty-four-hour access hotline
✆ 718-330-1234
TDD ✆ 718-596-8273

MTA NYC Transit, Access-a-Ride, Paratransit
✆ 212-632-7272
TDD ✆ 212-333-3147

RJV Transport Ambulette
✆ 516-867-1900

Wheelchair Getaways (accessible vans with lifts)
✆ 1-800-379-3750

The Lighthouse (national service organization for the blind)
✆ 212-821-9200

New York Society for the Deaf
V and TDD ✆ 212-777-3900

Able Newspaper
✆ 516-939-2253

New Mobility
✆ 1-800-543-4116

Travelin' Talk Network (for travelers with disabilities)
☎ 615-552-6670

We Magazine
☎ 1-800-WEMAG26

Mayor's Office for People with Disabilities
☎ 212-788-2830

The Andrew Heiskill Library for the Blind and Physically Handicapped
☎ 212-206-5400

Disability Rights
☎ 1-800-514-0301
TDD ☎ 1-800-514-0383

For a more detailed list, including options for sightseeing in New York, contact the Access Project at ☎ 212-669-3602.

≡FAST FACT

At one point in time, there were eight daily newspapers in New York City. Today, there are four major players: the *New York Times*, the *Daily News*, the *New York Post*, and the *Wall Street Journal*. Also published daily are the *New York Observer* and *Newsday*. There is a free weekly newspaper, the *Village Voice*, which is published on Wednesdays (so it's very hard to find by Friday, when you need it) and offers an excellent events calendar.

CHAPTER 4

New York Tours

NEW YORK HAS TOURS for every interest and level of adventure. While bus tours are probably the most popular, especially the hop on/hop off variety, walking tours let you set your own pace, and they are often quicker when you take traffic into consideration. There are also customized tours, ethnic tours, food tours, multilingual tours, water tours, and even helicopter tours available.

Gray Line New York Sightseeing Tours

✉ 777 Eighth Avenue
☎ 1-800-669-0051
🖰 *www.graylinenewyork.com*
The main offices of this busy and popular bus-tour operation are on Eighth Avenue between 47th and 48th Streets. Another branch is located inside the Port Authority. It's a good idea to drop in and see what they have to offer, as they are the leader in the city bus-tour field. You can always visit their Web site, but the brochures and displays will give you a better overview, and the personnel will tell you where to pick up buses and at what time.

In business since 1910, Gray Line is the bus-tour sightseeing leader. One of its many tour offerings combines a double-decker bus ride around Manhattan and a trip to the Empire State Building observatory. From their two-and-a-half-hour Holiday Lights tours to their eight-and-a-half-hour Manhattan Comprehensive, Gray Line has a host of tours to offer with professional tour guides to lead the way on motor coach and double-decker buses.

 **TRAVEL TIP**

> News reports that keep up on traffic and weather are very important in this crowded city. Turn your radio dial to 1010 or 880 AM. There is also a weather and traffic channel on every local cable system. Ask your concierge for the channel in your hotel, as there are different systems in different parts of the city.

There's also a four-loop tour ($71 for adult and $50 for kids) that you can use over a forty-eight-hour period. It gives you a tour of Lower and midtown Manhattan, Manhattan at night, Brooklyn, and Harlem, and is a great package for the first-time visitor or someone who has never ventured outside of downtown. There are jazz and gospel tours as well as an all-day Broadway tour that combines the NBC and Radio City tours with a behind-the-scene tour of the New Amsterdam Theatre, home of *The Lion King,* and lunch at Planet Hollywood ($89 per person).

There are also a number of two-hour tours or separate loops. In addition, the Gray Line runs day trips to Woodbury Commons (an incredible outlet shopping area about ninety minutes outside the city), and offers special packages that combine land and sea (in association with Circle Line tours) or land and air (helicopter tours). Major credit cards are accepted.

Boat Tours

Manhattan is an island, which makes boat touring a good alternative to the bus tours. You have several options to choose from, from straightforward tourist venues to specialty tours.

Circle Line Tours

✆ 212-563-3200

✎ *www.circleline42.com*

For over fifty years, Circle Line has been sailing the waters around Manhattan, pointing out the sights along the way. You will see and learn from an educated tour guide about key attractions including the Statue of Liberty, Ellis Island, the World Trade Center site, Yankee Stadium, and many other sights of the city as you sail under the Brooklyn Bridge, George Washington Bridge, and past the piers and South Street Seaport. Take a sweater or jacket, as it can get breezy. Three-hour sightseeing tours are $26 for adults, and $13 for children under 12.

Various other tours are offered, including music and DJ tours, a Seaport Liberty Cruise, Semi-Circle Cruises (shorter versions of the Circle Line full tour), Cruises to Bear Mountain, as well as holiday cruises on the Fourth of July and for fall foliage. Food and drink, including snacks, sandwiches, and hot dogs, are available on board. Ships sail from 42nd Street at Pier 83.

 TRAVEL TIP

For those who want to see the sights with a bit more excitement and in only thirty minutes, Circle Line offers "The Beast," a speedboat that takes up to 145 passengers on a fun-filled ride around the harbor (at forty knots, or about forty miles per hour). Adults pay $16, and children under 12 pay $10.

Chelsea Screamer

✆ 212-924-6262

✎ *www.chelseascreamer.com*

A speedboat, "The Screamer" takes off at forty miles per hour from Pier 62 at Chelsea Piers on West 23rd Street and takes you on an exhilarating wind-in-your-hair trip around Lower Manhattan, past the Statue of Liberty, and then up the Hudson for a look at the *Intrepid* (the floating seaside museum). Chelsea Screamer speedboats run from May through October and cost $15 for adults and $8 for children under 12.

Spirit Cruises

✆ 212-727-2789

✎ www.spiritcruises.com

From Pier 61 at 23rd Street, you can set out on one of several lunch or dinner cruises around Lower Manhattan, in a climate-controlled environment with large glass windows, an outdoor deck, and a sumptuous menu. Dancing and entertainment cruises are also offered. From $34 to $70, you can set out for a two- or three-hour cruise.

New York Waterways

✆ 1-800-533-3779

✎ www.nywaterways.com

Primarily a commuter ferry service between Hoboken, New Jersey, and Lower Manhattan, New York Waterways also offers sightseeing cruises. The Yankee Clipper and Met Express Baseball cruises take riders from Manhattan and New Jersey to Yankee Stadium in the Bronx and Shea Stadium in Queens ($14 round trip). The baseball cruises include a hot dog, a beverage, and a souvenir to get you in the mood for the game; after the game, they bring you back to Manhattan. It's a great way to see a game. They also go to West Point, Hudson Valley, the beach, and Tarrytown.

World Yacht Dining Cruises

✆ 212-630-8100

✎ www.worldyacht.com

Since 1984, the World Yacht has been setting sail with its offerings of luxurious, romantic dining experiences at sea. The ship sails down the Hudson River, past the Statue of Liberty and Ellis Island, as musicians play and dinner is served. It's a highly recommended, very special dining, sailing, and sightseeing experience for visitors and New Yorkers alike. Three-hour cruises depart at 7:00 P.M. from

Pier 81 at West 42nd Street (passengers board at 6:00 P.M.). Cruises cost $67 per person Sundays through Thursdays, and $75 on Fridays and Saturdays. Brunch cruises also run during part of the year. Jackets are required for men on the dinner cruises. There are special cruises for Mother's Day, Christmas, New Year's Eve, and other holidays.

 ## JUST FOR PARENTS

World Yacht's sunset dinner cruise or the Sunday-morning brunch cruise are romantic experiences. There's even music and dancing. Get a baby-sitter or have the in-laws look after the kids, and treat yourself to a memorable night out. Be sure to book ahead.

Helicopter Tours

Many say that a helicopter tour of New York City is the ultimate New York experience. You have two good options: Helicopter Flight Services and Liberty Helicopters.

Helicopter Flight Services, Inc.
✆ 212-355-0801
🖥 *www.heliny.com*

Since these sky-high tours only accommodate two guests at a time, advance reservations are required. Tours run from $109 per person to $159 per person, depending on the length of the flight. Tours leave from Twelfth Avenue and 30th Street or from the downtown heliport at Pier 6 and the East River. Call ahead to make reservations.

Liberty Helicopters
✆ 1-800-542-9933
✆ 212-967-6464
🖥 *www.libertyhelicopters.com*

An award-winning company for helicopter safety, Liberty has some ten choppers offering flights (Mondays through Fridays) from Twelfth Avenue and 30th Street or downtown heliport at Pier 6 and the East River. A variety of tours (routes) are available, ranging from five to twelve minutes. Tours cover numerous sights and cost from $56 to $101 per person. Call ahead for schedules and more information.

Walking Tours

Walking is a good way to meet Manhattan, and you'll find a variety of walking tours of the city to choose from.

Citywalks

✉ 410 West 20th St.

✆ 212-989-2456

Citywalks offers a private tour guide and features tours of downtown, the Lower East Side, Greenwich Village, and more. John H. Wilson conducts private tours for two people starting at $100 or for groups of around ten for $250. In a corporate world, Citywalks offers old-fashioned, personalized service. Call for more information.

92nd Street Y

✆ 212-996-1100

✐ www.92ndsty.org

The 92nd Street Y offers a wide selection of walking tours of different areas of the city and outer boroughs. The tours include journeys to areas of historic, social, artistic, and cultural importance. Some walking tours available are Castles in New York, Governor's Island and Battery Park, Jewish Harlem, and Gracie Mansion. The tours run from two to four hours and cost $15 to $25. If you register for five or more tours, you will receive a 10-percent discount. All tours meet in the neighborhoods visited. Call for more information and to register.

≡FAST FACT

Other walking tours are run by the Municipal Arts Society (✆212-935-3960) and Harlem Your Way! Tours Unlimited, which offers customized tours of Harlem, including gospel and jazz tours. Call them at ✆1-800-382-9363.

Additional Options

You have more eclectic tour options available. You can schedule a personal tour with a Big Apple Greeter, go on a tour of parks with an urban park ranger, or take a biking tour of the city.

New York Southerland Hit Show Tours

✆ 1-800-221-2442

This package tour company specializes in Broadway and off-Broadway packages and is celebrating its fiftieth year in the business. Packages include two, three, or four nights at a range of hotels, with tickets to a Broadway or off-Broadway show, tours of the city, and dinners. Call for more information.

Big Apple Greeters

✆ 212-669-8159

✑ www.bigapplegreeter.org

This organization provides free personal tours by New Yorkers themselves who, as volunteers, show you around a neighborhood on a one-to-one basis. It's a marvelous way to get a feel for a neighborhood while enjoying a personalized experience, as opposed to a boilerplate tour. You might also enjoy meeting a Big Apple Greeter as the perfect complement to a "grand" tour of the city. Contact the organization to make reservations at least two weeks in advance.

Doorway to Design

✆ 718-339-1542

✎ *www.doorwaytodesign.com*

Doorway to Design offers tours of the fashion and art world, architectural tours with an architectural historian, as well as shopping tours to New York's wholesale district and private discount shopping in Manhattan.

Urban Park Rangers

✎ *www.nycgovparks.org*

The rangers are a part of the New York City Department of Parks. They provide free tours of the many parks in New York City, with an emphasis on plant life, bird watching, wildlife, and geology. Call ✆ 311, the general New York Information number (✆ 212-NEW-YORK from outside the city), for more information or to request a schedule.

 TRAVEL TIP

New York has a great general information phone number. Just call ✆ 311 from any phone in the city, and an operator will transfer you to the department you need—whether it has to do with city parks or taxis and limousines. Outside the city, call ✆ 212-NEW-YORK.

Central Park Bike Tours

✆ 212-541-8759

A bike tour is a marvelous way to see a great park and get exercise at the same time. Two-hour tours are $35 for adults and $20 for children 15 or younger, and prices include bike rental. Tours leave at 10:00 A.M., 1:00 P.M., and 4:00 P.M. from 2 Columbus Circle. You can also rent bikes at a rate of $20 for two hours or all day for $35, which includes a lock and a map of Central Park. Credit cards are accepted.

CHAPTER 5

The Neighborhoods of Manhattan

WHEN YOU LOOK AT MANHATTAN from across the Hudson or East River, you see a spectacular skyline. But when walking, driving, or touring the streets of Manhattan, you'll discover that it's a blend of distinctive neighborhoods with their own characteristics. You'll see the nooks and crannies, the parks, the playgrounds, and the architecture. You'll encounter the local merchants, read the signs, and see the storefronts that characterize the overall flavor of each neighborhood.

Home Is Where the Heart Is

New Yorkers define themselves by their neighborhoods. Each one is unique and splendid, with its own sites and history, cuisine and lore. This is why Manny Ramirez always comes back to his roots in Washington Heights, why Spike Lee opened his store in Brooklyn, and why Yoko Ono still lives at the Dakota.

New York is an immigrant city as well, where cultures have blended and created some of the most incredible food and arts imaginable. Where else could you find Cuban Chinese food or a gourmet Japanese/Italian restaurant?

There's a definite pulse to the city found in the subcultures that meld and merge from one part of town to another. Even the beat changes slightly, from the frantic pace of Chinatown to the slower saunter of Bleecker Street in the Village. With the exception of parts of Midtown, you'll find residential buildings like brownstones, old brick apartment buildings, and sleek, modern, high-rise glass buildings. Historical sights, special events, and the people you'll pass on the street will tell you what part of town you're in. Buildings from different eras often share the same block, and a ten-block stroll can take you into an entirely different socioeconomic and ethnic neighborhood.

TRAVEL TIP

It should be no surprise that the shrine of the patron saint of immigrants, Mother Cabrini, can be found in New York City. The shrine of this founder of the Order of the Sacred Heart is in Upper Manhattan, at ✉701 Fort Washington Avenue and about 190th Street. Mother Cabrini's body is enshrined in a glass coffin, just yards away from the Cloisters, where European saint reliquaries are on display as part of the Metropolitan Museum of Art's medieval collection.

You'll also find a variety of manufacturing centers throughout parts of Lower and midtown Manhattan. The Upper West 20s, for example, is called the flower district; it leads to the fur district, around 30th Street and Seventh Avenue. The West 30s are home to the garment industry, and in the West 40s you'll find electronics on one block and jewelry on another, in the "diamond district." And these areas aren't subtle. You'll see a row of jewelry stores lining a city block on West 47th Street between Fifth and Sixth Avenues.

A Quick Overview

In Manhattan alone, there are more than twenty distinct neighborhoods, and at least as many more in each borough. As a point of reference, here are the neighborhoods of Manhattan as they run from north to south:

- Inwood, from 220th Street to approximately 190th Street
- Washington Heights, the area from 155th Street to 190th Street
- Harlem, 110th Street to about 135th Street
- Morningside Heights, the area around Columbia University
- The Upper East Side, everything east of Central Park from 59th Street to about 99th Street
- The Upper West Side, west of the park from 99th Street to 59th Street
- Midtown (including the theater district of the West 40s and Hell's Kitchen), from 34th Street to 59th Street
- Murray Hill, a residential area above Gramercy Park, from about 23rd to 34th Streets on the east side;
- Chelsea, on the west side of town from 14th to 30th Streets
- Gramercy Park, a private park on the east side in the 20s and the neighborhood that surrounds it
- Union Square, the neighborhood around 14th Street and Fifth Avenue
- Greenwich Village, from Broadway to the Hudson River from about 8th Street on down
- The East Village, Broadway to the east, from about 8th Street down to 1st Street
- SoHo, the area **so**uth of **Ho**uston Street
- TriBeCa, the **tri**angle **be**low **ca**nal Street
- Chinatown, the East River side of Canal Street
- Little Italy, the area around Mulberry Street
- The Lower East Side, the far east side of Manhattan below 1st Street
- Wall Street/Battery Park City, everything south of Canal Street

It would take an entire book to give you the history and an overview of each neighborhood. The rest of this chapter covers a few of the more commonly frequented neighborhoods in greater detail.

💼 TRAVEL TIP

In New York City, signs that read "Tow-Away Zone" or other ominous warnings really mean business—your car will be towed if you leave it unattended. When you park, be sure to read the signs and pay the meter, if required. If your car is towed, you'll find it in the police lot on the west side of Manhattan. You'll have to pay a steep fine to get it back.

The Lower East Side

It is hard to find a neighborhood more diverse in culture than Manhattan's Lower East Side. The first settlement for millions of immigrants who came to Ellis Island from Europe, the Lower East Side has been, for more than a century, home to tenement housing with sparsely furnished apartments.

From 1892 to 1934, more than 25 million men, women, and children took their first steps onto American soil at Ellis Island. The next stop from the tiny island for a great number of these immigrants was the small pocket of land near the Brooklyn Bridge along the East River, Manhattan's Lower East Side. In the early 1900s, the neighborhood was the most overcrowded in America. On what had been farmlands, builders started erecting three- and four-story row houses that barely fit on the narrow strips of land that had been sectioned off for single-family dwellings. These Lower East Side tenements were quickly filled and then overcrowded, housing more people than they were designed for. Many ethnic groups lived together in the area, including an enormous Jewish population, immigrants from Eastern Europe, and large contingencies from Ireland and Italy.

Many New York celebrities grew up on the Lower East Side, including Robert DeNiro, Zero Mostel, James Cagney, George Burns, and Jimmy Durante. The Marx Brothers, George Gershwin, and others honed their skills in the burlesque houses, Yiddish theaters, and (in later years) the settlement houses there. One of New York's most famous gangsters of the 1930s, Lucky Luciano, and one of the city's most renowned mayors, Fiorello LaGuardia (who would later put Luciano behind bars), were also born in the neighborhood.

Today, the population of the neighborhood is mainly Latino, but it is still mixed with various ethnic groups. There is still a Jewish presence, with Katz's and Ratner's Delicatessens and various discount shopping stores along Orchard Street. Trendy shops are now sprinkled in among the old storefronts.

A Brief Itinerary

To get to the Lower East Side, take the F or the V train to Delancey Street. When you visit, stroll along Orchard Street and along Delancey Street for some great bargains. From vintage clothing to hip-hop wear and designer clothes, plus shoes and inexpensive packs of underwear, you can pick up plenty of good bargains here. For many years, vendors took their wares out to the streets on Sunday along these popular shopping locales. Some still do so today.

Visit the Lower East Side Tenement Museum for a guided tour through an 1863 tenement at 97 Orchard Street. The furnishings give an idea of the daily existence of the thousands of immigrants who lived there. The unique museum is a tribute to urban housing.

Get a bite to eat at either Ratner's Restaurant or Katz's Delicatessen, where the portions are big, the décor isn't fancy, and the traditional Jewish-style food is still first rate.

≡FAST FACT

Don't order what you would at home. New York's delis are the birthplace of delicatessen around the country, so try something authentic: pickles straight from a barrel, homemade coleslaw, potato salad, and pickled peppers. Get pastrami on rye, a knish or two, and try the matzo ball soup, a hot dog or two with sauerkraut, and a blintz with applesauce. Seltzer goes well with everything. If they have it, and you have any room left, the apple strudel is always good.

Stop by the Elridge Street Project, which has converted the site of the nation's first Orthodox synagogue, built in 1887, into a cultural center and gift shop.

For those who like kosher wine, visit Shapiro's House of Kosher and Sacramental Wines on Rivington Street. You can visit this working winery on Sunday (closed Saturday for the Sabbath). It's a family-run business where they still make thirty-two flavors of wine in the cellar.

New York's Chinatown

Chinatown and Little Italy are neighbors, located just blocks from the city's courthouses, City Hall, the municipal buildings of Lower Manhattan, and the Lower East Side. To get to Chinatown, take any of the A, C, E, 1, 9, 4, 5, or 6 trains to Canal Street.

For years, Chinatown has been the place to go for New York's best Chinese food. But it is much more than a neighborhood of restaurants. It is a full-blown hustling, bustling community, home to more than 100,000 members of New York City's Chinese population. Since the early settlers came to the neighborhood from China in the 1870s, the area has been growing, now extending beyond its original boundaries into Little Italy and even across Canal Street. For years, immigrants worked in factories, restaurants, and local shops. Many locals still do.

The neighborhood houses garment factories and numerous shops. Many of the shops sell food, and you'll see roasted ducks hanging in many windows. Noodles, seafood, and vegetables are abundant inside and outside the jam-packed little shops that line the tiny streets. Clothing, electronics, souvenirs, and all sorts of goods are for sale here beneath Chinese signs. You'll even see a few pagoda-style roofs. But the area is not a tribute to Chinese culture; it is an authentic and very busy neighborhood that moves at a frantic pace. If you stroll the main business streets, Canal and Mott, you'll find yourself smack in the middle of the frenzy.

A visit to Chinatown should include a stop at the Museum of Chinese in the Americas on Mulberry Street. Also shop—or at least stroll along—the stores on Mott Street, and be sure to stop by at Quong Yuen Shing & Company, a classic neighborhood retailer for more than 100 years. Once you've worked up an appetite, have lunch and/or dinner at one of the 300 restaurants in the neighborhood. Here are a few recommendations:

- Bo Ky, on Bayard Street between Mott and Mulberry
- Canton, on Division Street between Bowery and Market
- Hunan Garden, on Mott by Worth
- Jing Fong, on Elizabeth between Bayard and Canal
- Mandarin Court, on Mott between Bayard and Canal
- Nam Wah Tea Parlor, on Doyers between Bowery and Pell
- Oriental Garden, on Elizabeth by Bayard
- Peking Duck House, on Mott between Park Row and Pell Street
- Sweet 'n Tart Café, on Mott by Canal
- Wong Kee, on Mott between Canal and Hester

RAINY DAY FUN

Drop into the Museum of Chinese in America, at ✉ 70 Mulberry Street, or call them at ✆ 212-619-4720. Founded in 1980 as the New York Chinatown History Project, the museum was chartered in 1992. It is currently the only museum in the United States dedicated to documenting and interpreting the history and culture of Chinese-Americans. Included in the exhibits are photos, documents, sound recordings, textiles, and more. Admission is $3 for adults and $1 for students and seniors; children under 12 are free.

Another option is to stop at Fung Wong's on Mott Street to buy rice cakes, roast pork buns, egg rolls, and other delights to take back to your hotel. And definitely visit the Chinatown Ice Cream

Factory on Bayard Street by Mott for a taste of lychee, papaya, or some other exotic flavor of ice cream.

While there aren't many traditional "sights" found in Chinatown beyond the museum, the neighborhood is worth a visit. And if you love Chinese food, it is the place to go!

The Chinese New Year is celebrated in grand style in Chinatown, with dragon parades and all sorts of festivities. It's very crowded, but if you're in town in late January or early February, when the Chinese New Year falls, you might head on down and check out the excitement. Take note: Although the city has outlawed the use of firecrackers, you should still be careful—they are very popular in Chinatown around this time of year.

Little Italy

Smaller and slightly less bustling than Chinatown, Little Italy has narrow streets and turn-of-the-century buildings with restaurants and shops below. For many years, it was the first stop for the city's numerous Italian immigrants. In the early twentieth century, many of the half-million Italian immigrants to the city lived in this area extending from the Lower East Side. In the past fifty years, however, neighborhoods in the other boroughs, such as Bensonhurst (in Brooklyn), Belmont (in the Bronx), along with the suburbs of New Jersey, now house the lion's share of Italian-Americans.

The neighborhood is home to a bevy of first-rate old-fashioned Italian restaurants and bakeries, along with some trendy newer shops mixed in. E. Rossi & Company is still at Grand and Mulberry, selling everything from Italian cookbooks to embroidered postcards to pasta-makers and bocce balls. Also in the area you'll find Old St. Patrick's Cathedral on Mulberry Street and San Gennaro Church on Baxter Street, which hosts one of the city's best festivals.

A visit to Little Italy should include a stop at Ferrara's to buy incredible pastries (especially a cannoli, if you've never had one) on Grand Street between Mott and Mulberry. Have lunch or dinner at one of a number of local favorites including the following:

- Angelo's of Mulberry Street, between Grand and Hester
- DaNico, on Mulberry between Grand and Broome
- Il Cortile, on Mulberry by Canal
- Taormina of Mulberry Street, near Grand
- Umberto's Clam House, on Mulberry

If you happen to be in town during the second week of September, you must take the family to the Feast of San Gennaro that lines Mulberry Street from Canal to Grand. The smells are delicious from the food offered by street vendors, such as sausage and peppers, fried dough (zeppoli), and candied fruits (even chocolate-dipped strawberries!), but you can also sit outside and have a meal at one of the fine Italian restaurants, such as Umberto's, as the throngs pass you by. The street teems with outdoor games, music, and fun.

RAINY DAY FUN

If your kids liked the street-vendor zeppoli at the San Gennaro Festival, you can make them at home. Heat about an inch of oil in a large skillet. Take frozen crescent-roll dough and make it into balls. Drop into the oil and fry for about a minute or two. When brown, remove from oil and blot on a paper towel. Roll the zeppoli in confectioner's sugar.

Greenwich Village

Greenwich Village and its close neighbor, East Village, are located below 8th Street. If you're planning to meander around the Village, it's best to get down there by public transportation. Greenwich Village is very popular, and parking is at a premium. To get there, take the A, D, or F train to West 4th Street, or the 1, 2, 3, or 9 to Christopher Street. The nearest subway stop in the East Village is Astor Place on the 4 and 5.

A Little History

The Dutch settlers of New Amsterdam ventured north in the early 1600s and discovered a large portion of land where they could plant crops. Until then, the land had been inhabited by Native Americans. When the English took over in the later 1600s, the neighborhood became a country setting—a suburb of sorts. By the 1700s, the West Village by the Hudson River was a major area for fishing and growing produce. Room was set aside for a public gallows in the center of the city; that area is now Washington Square Park.

In the early 1800s, more and more settlers moved north to escape the epidemics—smallpox, yellow fever, and cholera—that plagued the city. They moved primarily to the area below Houston Street. The Village began to grow with farms, shops, markets, and various businesses. Finer, more fashionable homes were built, particularly at the foot of Fifth Avenue around Washington Square Park.

≡FAST FACT

One of the Village landmarks musicians flock to but that is rarely pointed out in guidebooks is the Electric Lady Studio, off West 8th Street. This was the first recording studio ever owned by a recording artist. It was founded in 1970 by Jimi Hendrix and has been the site of major recording contracts for David Bowie, the Beastie Boys, and many other artists from the 1970s to the present. In 1997, its signature curved brick arch was demolished and replaced with a glass front.

The nineteenth century also saw the birth of New York University and the emergence of galleries and establishments where the literary community gathered. An upscale community throughout much of the nineteenth century, the neighborhood began to change toward the turn of the century. The elite moved further north, and a more bohemian culture settled into the area. Small theaters and galleries sprung up, and diverse local magazines were published, along with irreverent books by small local publishers.

The Village blossomed into New York City's home of up-and-coming writers, artists, and musicians. Edgar Allan Poe, Walt Whitman, and Mark Twain lived in Greenwich Village in the 1800s, and Sinclair Lewis, Eugene O'Neill, Jackson Pollock, and Norman Rockwell were among the many to be part of the Village in the twentieth century. The Beat poets of the 1950s gave way to the folk singers of the early 1960s, including Bob Dylan, Arlo Guthrie, and Peter, Paul and Mary. By the late 1970s, the East Village was home to punk rock.

Whatever the artistic trend, the Village captures it in art and music. Outdoor art shows flank the park twice a year, and clubs like the Webster Hall present the hottest up-and-coming and established performers. Off-Broadway and avant-garde theater became part of the local artists' own brand of self-expression many years ago, and it remains a significant part of Village culture today. Stores and galleries have displayed the latest trendy paraphernalia of each new generation, and the fads and fashions are evident in the area around Washington Square Park.

≡FAST FACT

Movements and social causes have also been an important part of Village life, from the antiwar protests of the 1960s to activities championing the rights of gays and lesbians in recent decades. The Village has become a place where the gay and lesbian community can thrive and flourish.

In terms of aesthetics, little has changed in Greenwich Village over the past thirty years. The redbrick townhouses with cozy little courtyards still line the streets. Restaurants, shops, and galleries are still busy at night; only the latest merchandise changes with the times.

The East Village

The neighboring East Village was a drug-infested, seamy neighborhood in the 1970s. Today, it has seen an economic and social resurgence, with trendy clothing shops, boutiques, and popular restaurants. Over a dozen relatively inexpensive Indian restaurants can be found on East 6th Street (between First and Second Avenues); several theaters featuring rising talent are busy on East 4th Street; and trendy shops are in vogue on St. Marks Place. The East Village has emerged as the alternative to the alternative, especially for those interested in escaping the more commercial Greenwich Village. Don't be fooled, however—some of the East Village shops have Fifth Avenue prices.

A Quick Itinerary

Stroll through Washington Square Park. Note the Memorial Arch built in 1889 to celebrate the 100th anniversary of George Washington's inauguration. You can watch street-performers, chess and checker players, and artists drawing or sketching.

Go for a shopping spree on 8th Street in the more popular mainstream stores, on Bleecker Street for more trendy shopping, or on St. Marks Place in the East Village for even more trendy shopping or some thrift shopping at Love Saves the Day. You can also get great gourmet food at Balducci's on Sixth Avenue by 10th Street or the absolute best in pastries and desserts at Veniero's on 11th Street between First and Second Avenues. If you want first-rate tea or coffee, try McNulty's Tea & Coffee Company on Christopher by Bleecker.

See a play at the Actor's Playhouse, Cherry Lane Theater on Commerce Street, the Minetta Lane Theater, or Astor Place Theater on Lafayette (East Village). Or find out what is playing at the Joseph Papp Public Theater on Lafayette Street between 4th Street and Astor Place, where musicals such as *Hair* and *A Chorus Line* had their first performances.

Check out the nineteenth-century houses of Grove Court between Bedford and Hudson Streets or Gay Street between Waverly and Christopher. You might also look at 75 Bedford Street (go slowly so you don't miss it)—it's only 9.5 feet wide and was built in 1873—and 77 Bedford Street, which is now some 200 years old.

Browse the Forbes Magazine Galleries, featuring items from the Forbes personal collections, including hundreds of toy boats, thousands of toy soldiers, old Monopoly games, rare Fabergé eggs, plus numerous trophies and awards. There are also changing exhibits at the gallery on 62 Fifth Avenue in the Forbes Building.

Have a drink, or at least a look, at White Horse Tavern on Hudson Street at Eleventh Avenue. The 120-year-old saloon was the drinking home of poet Dylan Thomas, as well as O. Henry, who has a booth named after him here, among other writers, poets, and artists.

JUST FOR PARENTS

Go to a concert at Webster Hall (formerly the Ritz) on East 11th Street, where Duran Duran got their U.S. start and Cyndi Lauper plays on New Year's Eve. There's also the longtime home of folk music, the Bitter End, on Bleecker. You can also find plenty of jazz if you visit legendary clubs like the Blue Note, Village Vanguard, or Visions. Perhaps you'll drop by the former punk haven CBGBs in the East Village, where you can still hear the hot new bands.

Stroll down narrow Minetta Lane, and stop in to see the former speakeasy Minetta Tavern at Minetta and MacDougal. You might also stop at a great people-watching locale and longtime favorite Village hangout, Le Figaro Café, on the corner of Bleecker and MacDougal.

Admire the Gothic Revival architecture of the Grace Church (1846) or the Church of the Ascension (1841), the Romanesque architecture of Judson Memorial Church (1892), or the more recent copper-domed St. George's Ukrainian Catholic Church (1970s).

Have dinner at one of the many village restaurants, including the following:

- Café Loup, on West 13th Street between Sixth and Seventh Avenues
- Ennio & Michael, on LaGuardia between Bleecker and West 3rd Street
- James Beard House, on 12th Street between Sixth and Seventh Avenues
- Il Mulino, on 3rd Street between Thompson and Sullivan
- La Ripaille, on Hudson between Bethune and West 12th Street
- Mesopotamia (serving Belgian food in the East Village), on Avenue B between Sixth and Seventh Avenues
- Pearl Oyster Bar, on Cornelia between Bleecker and West 4th Street

The spring and fall art shows are enjoyable, but the Village always has so much activity that it's always easy to get caught up in the atmosphere that makes this New York City's most eclectic, yet earthy, neighborhood. Anything goes in the village.

Times Square and 42nd Street

Brownstones, narrow streets, bohemian coffee shops, blue jeans, and a quiet subtlety have characterized much of Greenwich Village for years. But go less than two miles north and you'll find the bright neon lights, mega-hotels, and anything-but-subtle tourist shops and restaurants that define Times Square. Like the billboards that look down from the rooftops above, everything is grand and bright in the lights of Times Square. If you are heading into the area, do not drive. All major transportation goes to Times Square and cabs are plentiful, but parking is not. Take the A, B, C, D, E, 1, 2, 3, 9, or 7 train. It's best not to visit Times Square late at night.

A Historical Overview

From as far back as the early part of the twentieth century, the area around Times Square has been home to numerous theaters.

It was the place to go for entertainment, and as the city grew—with people living all up and down the east and west sides of Manhattan—it became a central focal point. Since 1913, all Manhattan subways have stopped at 42nd Street, Grand Central Station. The Port Authority bus terminal brought visitors to the city, and passenger ships docked at piers on the west side of town. In short, it was the first stop for numerous visitors to the city.

A focal gathering point, advertisers saw it as a place for grand-style billboards, and theater owners made sure to have dazzling marquees. By 1904 it had become known as "the Crossroads of the World." It was the place the ball was dropped on New Year's Eve, with large crowds flooding the streets below, a tradition that began early in the twentieth century.

Times Square and 42nd Street went largely unregulated in many respects. Primarily a nonresidential neighborhood, the area around West 42nd Street became a haven for anyone who could do business with the visitors coming into the city, from merchants to prostitutes. Always a home for the latest trend in cinema, 42nd-Street movie houses would run into competition as theaters were built in neighborhoods throughout the boroughs after World War II.

Times Square fell on hard times through the late 1990s, but with the beginning of the new millennium, Disney has been a leader in getting the area completely rehabilitated. The neighborhood was radically overhauled with new stores, and many of the old theaters were revamped.

Walking around Times Square and 42nd Street today, you'll see the usual big, bright, and brassy giant neon lights—"the lights of Broadway." Don't stop and look up without stepping into an alcove, or you might get knocked over, as the streets are very crowded. Thousands of people work in the large office buildings around the area, including much of the media—from the *New York Times* (the reason it's called Times Square) to HBO, *Billboard,* and MTV.

Times Square itself is where Broadway and Seventh Avenues cross as Broadway slants its way down the city from the west side toward the east side. Standing in the actual Square (really a triangle), you can see a bevy of massive billboards, huge storefronts, major hotels, marquees, fast-food eateries, and hordes of people, not to mention constant traffic.

Suggested Itinerary

Times Square and 42nd Street are always full of activity. There's a lot to do, so choose carefully. To start, visit the actual Times Square between 42nd and 47th Streets, and Broadway and Seventh Avenue, to look up at the myriad immense billboards, some of which move. Look at the new Times Square Studio on 44th Street and Broadway. From behind those glass windows, *Good Morning America* is broadcast live every weekday morning. If you get there early enough, you can watch them do the show.

Get tickets to see a Broadway show. From 42nd to 54th Streets, you'll find nearly thirty shows at spectacular old theaters. You can stop at the TKTS booth on 47th Street and Broadway. They sell tickets at half price (plus a service charge) for many of the Broadway shows, as posted on a board behind the ticket window. Chapter 14 covers Broadway performances in greater detail.

RAINY DAY FUN

The flagship Toys Я Us store on 44th and Avenue of the Americas is a must-see. Young children should take a spin on the giant Ferris wheel, with its fourteen different cars modeled after famous toys, but there's also the roaring T-Rex from *Jurassic Park* and an entire Empire State Building made of LEGOs. Girls love the two-story Barbie dollhouse, and the life-size Candyland candy store is always a big hit too.

Check out some of the remodeled, reopened theaters, such as the New Amsterdam on West 42nd Street. The 1903 theater was the original home of the Ziegfeld Follies and was remodeled and reopened by Disney in 1997. The art deco facade was added in the 1940s and remains on this architecturally stunning theater. The New

Victory Theater, dating back to 1900, was restored a few years earlier. This was a former home to numerous productions in the early part of the twentieth century, before becoming a popular burlesque house in the 1930s. For many years, these theaters were "dark" (with no performances) and did nothing but deteriorate amid the decadence that was 42nd Street. Today they are worth seeing, at least from the outside, and if you are fortunate you'll get tickets for a show there. The New Victory Theater hosts many types of shows, often for kids, including acrobatic acts and other fun events.

Stop by the New Ford Center for the Performing Arts, which opened in 1998 with the hit show *Ragtime*. Built to reflect the architectural elements of two New York landmark theaters, the Lyric and the Apollo, this is one of the biggest and most dazzling theaters in the city. Tours are available; call ✆ 212-556-4750.

Test your gamesmanship at the multilevel entertainment complex, XS New York, on Broadway between 41st and 42nd, featuring state-of-the-art video games and virtual reality. You can also check out similar space-age games at Lazar Park on West 46th Street by Seventh Avenue.

There's plenty of shopping to do here. Be forewarned that many of the smaller places sell overpriced junk; don't get suckered. But you can shop at one of the many huge stores including Disney and the Virgin Megastore (for tapes and CDs).

You can head west and check out the *Intrepid* Sea, Air & Space Museum, off Pier 86 in the Hudson, or head east to Fifth Avenue and visit the incredible New York Public Library, between 40th and 42nd Streets.

Take a stroll through Bryant Park, a seven-acre park that was recently renovated and now sports lovely gardens, interesting statues, plenty of chairs for outdoor concerts or fashion shows, and a grill. The park is situated behind the library (and over stacks of thousands of books stored underground) on Sixth Avenue between 40th and 42nd Streets.

If you have time, stroll down West 46th Street between Eighth and Ninth Avenues and check out Restaurant Row, with its wide selection of first-rate dining (and entertainment in several of the establishments). Another option is to dine at the theater crowd's longtime favorite, Sardi's, on 44th between Broadway and Eighth Avenue.

RAINY DAY FUN

If it gets rainy and cold, take a break from the elements and check out some of the incredible hotels in the area, including the Marriott Marquis, Millennium Broadway, the brand-new Time Hotel, or the classic Algonquin.

Harlem

North of 110th Street, the neighborhood of Harlem covers some six square miles and has been one of America's pre-eminent African-American communities for decades. Divided by Fifth Avenue into Harlem and East Harlem, the overall neighborhood, which also includes Spanish Harlem, has a long history that has seen its share of both high and low points. To get to Harlem, take the A, D, 1, or 9 train to 125th Street. The 2 and 3 also stop at Lenox Avenue.

Harlem's Dutch Roots

Originally a Dutch settlement back in 1658 (called Nieuw Haarlem), the area grew into an affluent section of the city in the 1800s, with estates, farms, and even plantations. If they became successful, immigrants from the Lower East Side commonly moved north to this rapidly growing area.

It was thought that the new subway lines of the early 1900s would further the growth of this area by making Harlem more easily accessible from the rest of the city. With that in mind, developers began constructing more apartment buildings throughout the neighborhood. The buildings, however, did not fill up. A developer named Phillip Payton bought up many of these empty properties and began turning them over to hundreds of black families, hard pressed for housing in the city. By 1915, nearly a quarter of a million black families had moved in, and an equal number of white families had moved out.

By the 1920s, Harlem was the largest black community in the United States. It was at that time that the Harlem Renaissance began. Harlem was filled with popular nightspots, including the famous Cotton Club, and jazz greats could be seen and heard performing all over the neighborhood. White audiences traveled north to hear the likes of Count Basie, Duke Ellington, and Cab Calloway. Literary legends like Langston Hughes and James Baldwin also grew up in this thriving, exciting community. Jazz flourished in the 1940s.

It would, unfortunately, take some thirty more years before the rebirth of Harlem would begin. The famed Apollo Theater returned, and restaurants, clubs, parks, and new housing finally began to emerge again in Harlem in the 1990s. While the area is still in the throes of re-establishing itself, there is definitely a sense that Harlem is back. Today, Harlem is a busy, growing community once again.

A Visit to Harlem

Stop at the classic Apollo Theater on 125th Street between Seventh and Eighth Avenues. It's one of the neighborhood's greatest landmarks and has seen a long list of legendary performers in its nearly ninety-year history. Catch a show (particularly on Amateur Night) or take the tour. Another option is to see a production at the National Black Theater on Fifth Avenue between 125th and 126th Streets.

Browse the Studio Museum; it features a history of Harlem on Lenox Avenue between 125th and 126th Streets. Stop at the Schomburg Center for Research in Black Culture on Lenox Avenue at 135th Street.

Have a weekend gospel brunch at the new rendition of the old Cotton Club on West 125th Street, or enjoy the finest soul food in town at Sylvia's, on Lenox and 126th Streets.

Take a trip west to Riverside Drive at 120th Street and visit Riverside Church, with its 400-foot carillon tower and a spectacular view looking out over the Hudson River.

Take a tour featuring the gospel music of Harlem. (There are now, after many years, a significantly growing number of points of interest highlighting the neighborhood, starting with the Dana Discovery Center.)

TRAVEL TIP

Harlem has become a major shopping area, with branches of Old Navy, Gap, HMV, and Models stores lining 125th Street, as well as the ever-popular street vendors offering music, incense, dashikis, and African sculpture. The Malcolm Shabazz Harlem Market, which features fabulous African wares, can be found at ⊠52 West 115th Street off Lenox Avenue. Some of the vendors even take credit cards, but bring cash.

CHAPTER 6

Must-See Attractions

THERE'S SO MUCH to see and do in New York City that you really have to go through the list of must-see attractions and decide what you can do in the number of days you have allotted for your visit. Of course, the age and interests of your vacation party and the time of the year will determine some of your choices.

This chapter includes a few of the most-popular, most-visited sights New York City has to offer. Most of the sights on this list will take several hours to visit, with travel time and waiting in line figured in. However, if you plan ahead, you can arrange it so that you can see a group of them more efficiently, such as Rockefeller Center, Radio City Music Hall, and St. Patrick's Cathedral.

▮ TRAVEL TIP

Some of the most significant sights are the city's museums. If you plan to mix one of the major museums into your itinerary, you'll need to plan accordingly. For instance, the American Museum of Natural History will take at least three hours, as will the Metropolitan Museum of Art.

Central Park

☎ 212-366-2726

✐ *www.centralpark.org*

Central Park is more than 150 years old, and it is the heart of Manhattan. This 843-acre plot of land is the green space and front yard to more than half the island's inhabitants, who come to run, walk their dogs, listen to free concerts in the summer, and watch their children play in the twenty-one different playgrounds within the larger park. It truly is an oasis in the middle of the city, exactly what the designer, Frederick Law Olmsted, had in mind when he conceived the idea in the tradition of the great parks of Paris and London.

There is so much to see and do in this green haven that you really should put aside at least an afternoon to tour it, no matter what time of the year you visit. (See Chapter 8 for a full guide to the park.)

Young children will want to visit the statue of Balto, the famous Alaskan sled dog, play on the giant *Alice in Wonderland* statue, float and race boats, and ride on the carousel. Everyone will want to visit the small zoo, famous for its polar bears, seals, and petting zoo. In the winter, there's outdoor ice-skating, and in the spring and summer there are boat rides. Those true romantics will want to eat a meal at the fabulous Tavern on the Green or take a carriage ride through the park. There are also free concerts around the band shell in the summer, a Shakespeare-in-the-Park series, as well as one or two fabulous events (such the Diana Ross or Simon and Garfunkel reunion concert). And no one can go through the park without passing Strawberry Fields, the green space Yoko Ono dedicated to her slain husband, John Lennon.

Location and Hours

The park is right in the middle of Manhattan, from 59th Street and Columbus Circle to 125th Street. You can reach it by subway on the A, D, C, B, 1, and 9 trains (59th Street entrance), as well as on the B, C, 1, and 9 trains (all entrances between 59th Street and 125th Street). Even though the park is a wonder during the day, no one should enter after sunset. There are free daily walking tours throughout the park. Call the park for a schedule.

Ellis Island

✆ 212-363-3200

✍ *www.ellisisland.com*

Starting in the early 1890s and for about the next sixty years, Ellis Island was the first stop on American shores for immigrants who entered from Ireland, Italy, Germany, Poland, and many other nations (nearly 16 million of them). Their first stop was the federal immigration facility. Today, that facility is the Ellis Island Immigration Museum, a major tourist attraction, redesigned and reopened in 1990 as a testament to the people who made America their new home.

 TRAVEL TIP

Details are always subject to change, so you should call to confirm your options before setting out for the day. Most major sights are open between 9 A.M. and 5 P.M. every day, but tour hours do change, as do gift shop and restaurant hours. Be aware that most museums are closed on Mondays.

Today, more than 100 million Americans, nearly 40 percent of the nation's population, can trace their roots back to these immigrants. Located just north of the Statue of Liberty, the Ellis Island Immigration Museum combines photos and items from the past with modern technology, including computers that help visitors trace their heritage.

Ellis Island attractions include the following:

- An Immigrant's Living Theater Presentation called *Ellis Island Stories* features re-enactments of the immigrants' stories performed by actors.

- Two small theaters feature *Island of Hope, Island of Tears*, which recounts the history of the famed island.
- A spacious gallery houses photos and items from the immigrants.
- A learning center helps children learn about their roots.
- The American Immigrant Wall of Honor contains the names of over half a million immigrants, from the great-grandparents of George Washington to those of Jay Leno.
- The American Family Immigration History Center, a brand-new resource for immigration history, featuring state-of-the-art computer technology. Visitors can trace their roots and receive a printout of family background information.
- An outdoor restaurant on the premises offers a breathtaking view of the New York City skyline.

Ellis Island should be part of your visit to the Statue of Liberty. They are right next to each other, just off the foot of Manhattan in the harbor between New York and New Jersey.

Location and Hours

Tickets go on sale at 8:30 A.M., and the museum is open from 9:30 A.M. to 3:30 P.M. daily. Prices are $7 for adults, $6 for seniors, and $3 for children and teenagers from 3 to 17. You can get to Ellis Island by ferry. The ferry runs every thirty minutes and costs $7. The ferry leaves Castle Clinton Monument in Lower Manhattan. Call ✆ 212-269-5755 for ferry information.

Statue of Liberty

✆ 212-363-3200

✎ *www.nps.gov/stli*

After the terrorist attacks of September 11, the interior of the Statue of Liberty was closed to tourists for over two years, but it reopened to the public in the summer of 2004. However, the torch tower is considered too fragile for visitors and has been closed indefinitely. The outside grounds and exhibits are all open, as well as the gift shop. Liberty Island also has an outdoor café and a large gift shop full of Liberty souvenirs.

You can always view this national icon by circling Manhattan on a boat tour, such as Circle Line (call ✆ 212-269-5755 for more info).

The History

In 2000, 6 million people visited the Statue of Liberty. Along with the Empire State Building, Lady Liberty was the city's premiere tourist attraction of the twentieth century. Officially named *Liberty Enlightening the World,* the statue was built in France in 1875. More than 180 cities throughout France raised some $250,000 so that Frederic-Auguste Bartholdi could design and construct the statue, with its framework by Alexandre Eiffel, as a gift to the United States. The statue was transported in 350 pieces, and it took nearly a decade for New York to get the proper pedestal approved and constructed so Lady Liberty could stand high above the Hudson River. The Statue of Liberty was officially dedicated in 1886. With pedestal, she towers some 305 feet above the waters, and she has welcomed ships into the land of liberty for more than 100 years. In 1986, Lady Liberty received a full facelift and makeover, just in time for her 100th birthday.

Location and Hours

The Statue of Liberty stands at the gateway to the harbor, just off the tip of Manhattan on Liberty Island, a stone's throw from neighboring Ellis Island. You'll have a tremendous sense of what America, freedom, and democracy are all about after spending a day visiting these two sites.

A round-trip ferry ride costs $10 for adults, $8 for seniors, and $4 for children over 3; it's the only transportation to and from the statue. For advance ferry tickets, call ✆ 1-800-388-2733. The ferry leaves Castle Clinton Monument in Lower Manhattan starting at 9:30 A.M. (9:15 A.M. during the summer months).

Because it draws huge crowds, it's a good idea to set out for the statue in the morning. Waiting in line can be very hot in the summer, so dress accordingly. Bring sunscreen, and wear a hat. If possible, go on a weekday rather than a weekend, when the lines are simply too long.

Due to increased security measures, all bags and knapsacks are searched and there is a bit of a wait to get through security. Bring your camera for some terrific shots of the statue. Consider visiting both Ellis Island and the Statue of Liberty on the same day.

≡FAST FACT

The Staten Island Ferry is a fun boat ride that heads from the southern tip of Manhattan into New York harbor. It provides a terrific view of the Statue of Liberty (so take a camera) before it reaches Staten Island. You can then make the return trip. The ride is free. No vehicles are allowed on the ferry. The Staten Island Ferry leaves from South Street and Peter Minuit Plaza. It operates twenty-four hours a day, so you can travel by moonlight too!

Empire State Building

✉ 350 Fifth Avenue
✆ 212-736-3100
✍ www.esbnyc.com

The famed "Eighth Wonder of the World" was first opened in 1931, and for many years was the tallest building in the world. The Empire State Building is one of the city's icons, immortalized in such films as *King Kong* and *Sleepless in Seattle*, when Tom Hanks finally meets Meg Ryan atop its observation deck. Its upper floors are adorned with lights that change colors for special occasions (such as red and green for Christmas), casting a glow over the vast skyline that surrounds it. The view from the top is one you'll never forget.

Nearly 4 million people visit this signature landmark annually, and more than 100 million have visited it in almost seventy years. The observatories, one on the 86th floor (1,050 feet high and outdoors) and the other on the 102nd floor (1,250 feet high and glass enclosed), offer a breathtaking view that on a clear day extends well beyond the city, into New Jersey and even into Pennsylvania. Tickets are sold on the concourse level, just above the ornate marble lobby.

A snack bar, ground-floor restaurants, and a well-stocked gift shop are also part of the New York City landmark. The best time to visit the Empire State Building is on any clear day.

The Skyride

☎ 212-736-3100

✍ www.skyride.com

An additional attraction for children in particular is the New York Skyride, an interactive flight-simulated tour of New York City. The eight-minute "wild" ride is located on the second floor of the building. Pregnant women and children under 4 are not allowed on the ride.

Location and Hours

The Empire State Building is at 350 Fifth Avenue, between 33rd and 34th Streets. To reach it by subway, take the D, B, F, N, or R train to 34th Street. Observatory prices are $11 for adults and $6 for children ages 6 to 12, and $10 for seniors and youths between 12 and 17; children 5 and under are free. There are discount rates for groups of ten or more. The observatory is open from 9:30 A.M. to 11:30 P.M. The Skyride is open from 10 A.M. to 10 P.M. daily. Tickets costs $17 for adults, $14 for children over 12 and for seniors, and $12 for children 5 through 12. Four-year-olds and under are free.

Combination tickets are available for the Skyride and Observatory, and both the Observatory and Skyride are part of the CityPass package (see page 152 for more information on the CityPass).

American Museum of Natural History

✉ 81st Street and Central Park West

✆ 212-769-5200

✐ *www.amnh.org*

Founded by Theodore Roosevelt in the late 1800s, this museum is one of the city's gems. It's a must-see attraction for visitors of all ages, especially children. Currently, it houses more than 32 million specimens and has a research staff of 200. It will take at least a half a day to visit the museum with the new and improved Rose Center and Hayden Planetarium, the IMAX theater, and four floors of dinosaur bones, preserved animal specimens, gems, and scientific displays about life on this planet.

 TRAVEL TIP

Remember to bring a student ID card or a card showing that you qualify for senior rates (generally, those over age 62). Almost all sights have lower prices for seniors, and many do for students. There are often discounts for AAA members.

One of the most wonderful things about this museum is how little it has changed. You can show your kids your favorite exhibits, such as the nearly century-old model of a giant mosquito or the felled trunk of the 1,300-year-old Mark Twain tree—and yet there are always new wings and exhibits. The museum recently added an indoor butterfly exhibit open in the winter months, reorganized the entire gem collection, and reinstalled the ninety-four-foot giant blue whale suspended over the redone Hall of Ocean Life.

While exhibits change, some of the permanent exhibits to catch include the new Earth Event Wall, which delves into computer-generated earthquakes, volcanoes, and other natural occurrences. Also check out the Center for Biodiversity and Conservation on the first floor, where you can step into a re-created rain forest and also see a twenty-odd-pound New Jersey lobster from the turn of the century, while you learn about the changing environment and extinction.

≡ FAST FACT

Hardly anyone realizes that world-famous anthropologist Margaret Mead's office within the American Museum of Natural History is still intact, although it is not open to the public for viewing.

Other halls include African Mammals, Primitive Mammals, Human Biology and Evolution, Fossils (including two dinosaur halls), and Reptiles and Amphibians. Several exhibitions feature the people and culture of the world, including the Hall of African People, Margaret Mead Hall of Pacific Peoples, and the Asian and South American Peoples Hall. For children ages 5 through 12, there is the Discovery Room, where they can touch and re-create many of the objects they've seen in the museum itself.

Some of the museum highlights include the following:

- An actual skeleton of a dodo bird, extinct for more than 300 years
- The Cape York meteorite, discovered by Admiral Perry on one of his Arctic explorations
- The Star of India, the world's largest blue star sapphire, as well as one of the world's finest dinosaur specimens—a Corythosaurus, with a nearly complete skeleton and large areas of skin impression
- The Willamette meteorite—at fifteen tons, the largest meteorite ever discovered in the United States

Location and Hours

The museum is located on 81st Street and Central Park West, accessible via the B and C trains. Admission to the museum is by suggested contribution, but it is hard to get in the door without paying the strongly suggested contribution of $12 for adults, $7 for children, and $9 for seniors and students. A combination ticket to the Rose Center is $19 for adults, $11 for children, and $14 for seniors and students. You can also use the CityPass at the American Museum of Natural History (see page 152 for more information on CityPass). You can purchase tickets over the phone or online.

≡FAST FACT

The Cape York meteorite is the largest meteorite on display in the world (thirty-four tons), so big that it has to be supported by beams planted in the bedrock beneath the museum. It was once an object of reverence for the Inuit Indians, who come to the museum annually for a private ceremony. It is believed to be 4 billion years old.

Rockefeller Center

✎ 212-664-7174

✐ www.rockefellercenter.com

Since 1934, Rockefeller Center has stood tall in the midst of all the change and growth of the city around it. The nineteen buildings that make up the eleven-acre complex house numerous corporations, including some of the leaders in media and communications. Recently renovated, Rockefeller Center remains one of the most popular tourist stops in New York City.

Named for John D. Rockefeller, who initiated the construction of what was originally designed as three office buildings and the Metropolitan Opera, the complex continued to grow. The focal point of the complex, and the building most associated with Rockefeller Center, is the GE building, also known as "30 Rock."

Take a Tour

The towering art deco structure is best known for the many television and radio programs that have been taped inside. *Late*

Night with Conan O'Brien, the old *Late Night with David Letterman,* and numerous other programs including talk shows and game shows have been recorded in the famed building. A one-hour NBC studios tour has been a highlight for many years and still provides you with a glimpse of television past and present. NBC's *Today Show* operates from a storefront glass-enclosed studio across the street from 30 Rock, in another of the many buildings in the complex. If you arrive early, you can watch from the sidewalk as Katie Couric and Matt Lauer do their show every weekday morning.

While touring 30 Rock and its neighbors, you'll find an abundance of fine art including sculptures, murals, and mosaics. The designers developed a motif for the artwork, called "New Frontiers and the March for Modern Civilization," which expresses the vision behind the new venture. Among the great works of art at 30 Rock are two murals, one featuring Abe Lincoln and Ralph Waldo Emerson, and one called *Time* that depicts the past, present, and future.

Beautifully landscaped roof gardens adorn several of the buildings in Rockefeller Center. Unfortunately, they are only open to employees of the buildings. You can, however, check out *Atlas,* the statue on Fifth Avenue directly across from St. Patrick's Cathedral. Since 1936, the art deco gold statue has been holding up the world in front of the skyscraper at 650 Fifth Avenue.

Outside the GE Building, take time to stroll the promenade from Fifth Avenue to the Channel Gardens, where nearly 20,000 varieties of plants can be found. Just before the gardens meet the skyscraper, you'll find the famed ice-skating rink, which by summer becomes the outdoor seating for the American Festival Café and the Sea Grill Restaurant. The Channel Gardens were given their name by journalists, who noted that the promenade was set between the French and English buildings.

Overlooking the skating rink is *Prometheus,* an eighteen-foot-tall, eight-ton gilded bronze statue. The mythical Greek figure sits below a gold leaf and is shown stealing fire from the gods as a gift for man. Every year since 1936, from early December through early January, the famous Rockefeller Center Christmas tree is set up overlooking the rink. The tree-lighting ceremony, complete with a bevy of entertainers, draws thousands of onlookers. Thousands more visitors will stop by to see the dazzling tree during the holidays.

JUST FOR PARENTS

High atop 30 Rock sits the famous Rainbow Room restaurant. Opened in 1934, the Rainbow Room has long been a fashionable and romantic place for fine food and a spectacular view. A revolving dance floor, fabulous views through big glass windows, and an orchestra add to the ambiance. It is now open to the public on a limited basis—currently Friday dinner and Sunday brunch (call ✆212-632-5000 for reservations), but men must wear a dark jacket or tuxedo and women must wear a dress or evening gown.

Essentially, the entire area is replete with stunning artwork and period architecture. Shops are also abundant around the GE Building, as are a few restaurants, including (as previously mentioned) the American Festival Café and Sea Grill Restaurant.

A long way down below 30 Rock, underground walkways connect most of the buildings, allowing visitors and the nearly 300,000 people who work in Rockefeller Center to stay warm and dry during inclement weather as they head to the maze of subways below.

Location and Hours

Rockefeller Center covers the area from 48th to 51st Streets between Fifth and Sixth Avenues. It is accessible by subway on the D, F, B, V, N, or R train (Rockefeller Center station) or the 1 or 9 (50th Street station). Tours leave from the main floor of the GE Building every fifteen minutes from 9:30 A.M. to around 4:30 P.M., sometimes later on weekends. Tours cost $10. Children under 6 are not permitted, and there are no bathroom facilities available on the one-hour tours. Call for more tour information and scheduling changes. The NBC Studio tour costs $17.75, or $15.25 for seniors and children over 6. You can take a combination Rockefeller Center/NBC Tour package for $21.

Times Square

✍ *www.timesquare.com*

Once the seediest part of Manhattan, Times Square has been completely revitalized in the past decade. Now it is a fun New York day and/or night spot that is a family favorite. Everyone loves just walking through the bustling streets and looking at the glowing billboards while street vendors offer their wares, from pastel portraits to your name in hand-painted decorative letters. Every year, 26 million people visit Times Square.

≡FAST FACT

Times Square has just celebrated its 100th anniversary under its current name. In 1904, when the new *New York Times* building opened (once the second-tallest structure in New York City), the square around it was renamed after the famous newspaper. To inaugurate this change, the Times dropped the first ball on New Year's Eve. Today, more than a million people watch the ball drop on New Year's Eve from Times Square.

The Times Square neighborhood is located between 44th to 42nd Streets from Eighth to Sixth Avenues. The best way to get there is the subway. Take the A, C, E, 1, or 9 train to 42nd Street. The four-block stretch of 42nd Street to 44th Streets from Eighth Avenue to Sixth Avenue has something for everyone. Kids love the flagship Toys Я Us store (with its famous indoor Ferris wheel), Madame Tussaud's Wax Museum, a Disney store, as well as the ESPN restaurant and arcade and even a nearby Laser Park. Teens throng to the MTV studio and store, as well as the WWF store and the Virgin Megastore, where celebrities are often on hand to sign CDs. Parents can still be found after-hours at the legendary B.B. King's. There are also some great family restaurants from Carmine's (family-style Italian food) to Ruby Foo's (fun pan-Asian) to nearby Mars 2112 (a one-of-a-kind sci-fi themed restaurant), as well as two multiplex theaters for a total of sixteen movie screens.

Ground Zero

In the aftermath of the terrorist attacks of September 11, many visitors to New York City feel compelled to visit the site of the tragedy. Five buildings were destroyed, including the twin towers of the World Trade Center, and 3,000 lives were taken as hijackers flew two jet planes into the 110-story buildings.

Although there is not much to see now that the fenced-in, sixteen-acre site has been cleared, the huge absence of a building on such a large parcel of land in Lower Manhattan is, in itself, an amazing spectacle.

 **TRAVEL TIP**

Plan your itinerary based on approximately a ten-block radius of sights. Leave yourself time for tours—they can often take an hour or two—and don't forget to give yourself enough time to grab lunch along the way.

In January 2004, the Lower Manhattan Development Corporation announced the winners of an international competition (more than 5000 entrants from sixty-three countries) and the design for the World Trade Center Memorial was revealed. *Reflecting Absence,* designed by Michael Arad and Peter Walker, is composed of two large reflecting pools amid a large open space of trees. The names of the deceased are to be distributed, in no particular order, around one of the reflecting pools. There will be a passageway between the two pools where visitors can light candles. On a lower level, there will be an underground space for exhibits, a research library, and lecture halls. The unidentified remains of those killed will be housed in a room at this level as well.

Check the Lower Manhattan Development Corporation Web site, ✍ *www.renewnyc.com* or ✍ *www.wtcsitememorial.org* for development of this site. Ground Zero is located at West Street between Liberty and Vesey. To visit the site, take the E train to the World Trade Center subway station.

CHAPTER 7

New York City Landmarks

WHEN YOU CLOSE YOUR EYES and think of New York, certain places and experiences will always pop into your head. The Chrysler Building (from the opening credits of *Sex and the City*), the Metropolitan Museum of Art's Temple of Dendur (from all those swanky art openings in such movies like *Maid in Manhattan*), and those two lovable lions, Patience and Fortitude, that stand guard outside the New York Public Library—these are images that will always say "New York City." When you drive down the West Side Highway, the *Intrepid* Sea, Air & Space Museum watches over your progress in traffic like no other museum on the planet.

New York is a city of many wonderful places that are like nothing else. You probably won't be able to get them all in during one trip, unless you sign up for a half-day bus tour, but they may inspire you to come back for more.

Apollo Theater

✉ 253 West 125th Street

✆ 212-513-5300

✆ 212-513-5337 (performance tickets)

✍ *www.apollotheater.com*

The Apollo Theater, one of the best-known theaters in Harlem, is currently undergoing a renovation to bring this legendary perform-ance space up to contemporary Broadway standards. The Apollo was built in 1913 and opened (to white audiences only) as a bur-lesque house. By the mid-1930s, it had emerged as the premier show-case for black talent and black audiences. For three decades, the Apollo was a first-rate show palace, with performers running the gamut from Ella Fitzgerald, Duke Ellington, Nat "King" Cole, and Billie Holiday to James Brown, the Jackson Five, Stevie Wonder, Aretha Franklin, Stephanie Mills, and numerous others. Comics such as Bill Cosby and Richard Pryor took to the famous stage as well. The pop-ular amateur comedy hour began in 1935 and became an instant hit.

In the mid-1960s, Harlem and the theater met with tough times. It remained closed through most of the 1970s, opening for a short time as a movie theater. However, by the end of the decade, it was given landmark status and, by 1992, not-for-profit status as well. By the mid-1990s, a refurbished Apollo reopened, and today it is once again a hotbed of entertainment in Harlem.

The Apollo Today

While comedian Chris Rock and rap and rhythm and blues artists play to sold-out audiences, the Amateur Hour, on Wednesday nights at 7:30, is taped for television as part of the *Evening at the Apollo* television show, hosted by comic Steve Harvey. Tickets are hard to get.

The Apollo also offers an hour-long backstage tour that gives you the lowdown on numerous performers who've played the great hall, as well as a look at the theater, including the Walk of Fame and Tree of Hope. The gift shop sells books and other items relating to the Apollo.

Location and Hours

You'll find the Apollo at 253 West 125th Street. The Apollo is accessible by subway via the A or D train. Tours cost $11 to $13 per person, depending upon the day of the week. One-hour tours are available on Mondays, Tuesdays, and Thursdays at 11:00 A.M., 1:00 P.M., and 3:00 P.M.; at 11:00 A.M. only on Wednesdays; and at 11:00 A.M. and 1:00 P.M. on Saturdays and Sundays.

Chrysler Building

✉42nd and Lexington Avenue

Before the Empire State Building was constructed, the Chrysler Building was the tallest in New York City. With seventy-seven floors, standing 1048 feet high, the Chrysler Building is an art deco masterpiece that continues to inspire New Yorkers every night with its lit-up crown of steel. Noted for its creative and clever use of automotive ornamental detail, such as the radiator-cap gargoyles and hood-ornament eagles on the eight corners of the sixty-first floor, the building has been a favorite of architecture buffs for over seventy years.

═FAST FACT

In the 1930s, during Prohibition, the Chrysler Building housed a swanky speakeasy known as the Cloud Club on its sixty-sixth through sixty-eighth floors. It was said to have lavish pink-marble bathrooms and a bar featuring Bavarian wood, and members had their own private lockers. There was also an observation deck on the seventy-first floor.

The building is known for its elegant lobby, which features African red marble and a majestic mural depicting the construction of the building itself, with portraits of some of the actual workers. The lobby was once a showroom for Chrysler Plymouth cars. Each of the twenty-one elevators has a different design; one of them is perfectly restored and on display in the Brooklyn Museum.

Location and Hours

The Chrysler Building is located between 42nd and Lexington Avenue. It is accessible via subway on the D, F, V, N, R, 4, 5, or 6 train (42nd Street).

New York Public Library

✉ Fifth Avenue and 42nd Street

✆ 212-930-0830

✎ *www.nypl.org*

The Humanities and Social Sciences branch of the New York Public Library is a historic landmark, featuring Beaux Arts architecture. Built in 1911, it is a two-block literary oasis, housing some 6 million books plus millions of other documents. The library is a research facility, which means that you can't check the books out, but anyone can use it to do research in one of the eleven reading rooms. A well-trained staff can locate a book for you in anything from a few minutes to nearly an hour (depending on how busy the library is and how far they need to travel to find the book). The stacks extend underground from Fifth to Sixth Avenues. Cardholders can borrow books from any of the city's more traditional libraries, including the Mid-Manhattan Library, on 40th Street and Fifth Avenue, across the street.

This structure, however, is indeed worth visiting, even if it's just for a brief look around. Built for some $2 million—a sum originally raised to fund *two* libraries—this magnificent structure is guarded in the front by the two stone lions, Patience and Fortitude. Replicas are for sale in the library gift shop, book-end sized. The interior is brilliantly decorated with marble hallways and staircases leading to the recently renovated, grand main reading room, with its original chandeliers and oak tables. The library also houses a magnificent art collection.

There are numerous divisions within the building, including the Arts and Architecture Division, the Map Division, the Jewish Division, the Oriental Division, the Current Periodical Division, and so on. Special collections include rare books, photography, and prints. Free tours are offered and advised; they will provide you with a frame of reference. The enormity and grandeur of the building can be intimidating!

Lectures, special exhibits, and presentations are offered in the library. You may also stroll behind the building and visit Bryant Park, which is home to fashion shows and other events, and where you can relax with a cappuccino or pastry.

RAINY DAY FUN

Even most New Yorkers don't know that the original stuffed bear that A. A. Milne immortalized in *Winnie the Pooh*—which belonged to his son, Christopher Robin—can be seen "in the fluff" in the children's section of the Donnell Library, at ⊠53rd Street between Fifth and Sixth Avenues. This is really a wonderful children's artifact and worth a quick pop inside.

Location and Hours

The library can be found on Fifth Avenue between 40th and 42nd Streets. It is accessible by subway via the D, F, N, or R train (42nd Street and Sixth Avenue station). Tours are available Monday through Saturday at 11 A.M. and 2 P.M. Please call for hours of operation. The library is closed on most federal holidays.

Intrepid Sea, Air & Space Museum

⊠Pier 86 at 12th Avenue and 46th Street
✆ 212-245-0072
✎ *www.intrepidmuseum.com*
For an unusual museum experience, visit the USS *Intrepid*. The old aircraft carrier sits beside the Concorde, the submarine USS *Growler*, and the destroyer *Edson* on New York's Hudson River. Together, the air and sea craft provide an education in American flight and warfare technology from World War II to the present.

The *Intrepid*

The USS *Intrepid* was used by the U.S. Navy from 1942 until the early 1970s and saw action in World War II, Korea, and Vietnam. At its peak, the great ship housed more than 3,000 sailors and carried more than 100 airplanes and helicopters on the massive deck. The ship, weighing in at nearly 42,000 tons when loaded, is virtually a full military installation at sea, and fighter planes are still perched on the deck for viewing.

Most of the planes featured on the *Intrepid* were never actually carried by the ship, such as the A-12 Blackbird, one of the fastest, highest-flying planes ever built. The CIA had this titanium aircraft designed to photograph activities on the other side of the Berlin Wall during the Cold War. In contrast, a reproduction of a World War I biplane, complete with propeller, can be found on the lower deck.

Museum Features

The unique seaside museum also explores the undersea world, both on *Growler* and through special exhibitions about submarines and underwater study. Within the museum, you'll also find Pioneer's Hall, which looks back at the airplanes of the twentieth century, and the Technologies Hall, which highlights modern technology, including weaponry.

Onboard the ships of the *Intrepid* Sea, Air & Space Museum, you'll climb narrow staircases and squeeze through tight corridors. A tribute to the space program features a space capsule retrieved from sea, in the days before the space shuttle made a smooth landing on solid ground. You can also visit the Concorde, retired from British Airways, that once flew from London to Paris at supersonic speed.

There is a gift shop on the premises where you can buy the very popular *Intrepid* baseball cap. There is a "mess hall" inside, but the food is considerably better than that once offered to sailors, with a good selection of sandwiches and hot items.

☔ RAINY DAY FUN

The *Intrepid* Sea, Air & Space Museum is actually a good place to go during a rainy or cold day. There's a lot to do below deck, such as pilot a G-force flight simulator or explore the cockpit of a navy A-6 jet fighter. You can also watch a twenty-minute film on the museum and listen to real war stories from the volunteer crew members. There's also a station to send e-mail messages to the troops.

Location and Hours

The USS *Intrepid* is docked at Pier 86, at 12th Avenue and 46th Street, overlooking the Hudson River. It is accessible via the subway on the A train (the 42nd Street and Eighth Avenue) or the C or E train (50th Street and Eighth Avenue). Museum hours are 10:00 A.M. to 5:00 P.M. weekdays, open until 6:00 P.M. on weekends from April through September, but closed on Mondays October through March. Admission is $14 for adults; $10.50 for students over 12, seniors, and veterans; and $9.50 for children 5 through 11. Self-guided tours of the USS *Intrepid*, USS *Edson*, and USS *Growler* are free with admission.

Metropolitan Museum of Art

✉ 82nd Street and Fifth Avenue

✆ 212-535-7710

✍ *www.metmuseum.org*

The Metropolitan (known as the Met) is one of the top four in the world, right up there with the Louvre in Paris, the Prado in Madrid, and the Vatican Museum in Vatican City. Even if the kids insist they "hate art," you should bribe them by offering to buy them something in the kids' gift shop, where you'll find lots of good stuff for under $10. Besides, few boys have been known to be able to resist the lure of the incredible armor collection and the Egyptian mummies. And what young girl could turn down a tour of the costume institute?

There are more than 2 million pieces in the museum collection, and the Met is so large it will really take an entire day to see it all. Your best bet is to target the wings that interest you and your family the most. Check the special exhibits as you wait in line to make your suggested contribution. You can pick up a family guide at the information kiosk or download one online.

Let the Tour Begin

As you enter and head to the ticket area in the great hall, you will notice the marble stairway leading up to the famed European collection of nineteenth-century classics. To your left will be Greek and Roman art, and to your right is the Egyptian wing (where, if you go down the stairs, you will find the gift shop's sale merchandise, often at 50 percent off).

The Egyptian wing features some 35,000 objects, many of which are from the original installation of 1906. You can find ancient jewelry, mummies, sculpture, hieroglyphics, and the famed Temple of Dendur.

≡FAST FACT

The Temple of Dendur is an authentic Egyptian monument from the early Roman period. The Met accepted it as a gift from the Egyptian government in recognition of the American contribution to the international campaign to save the ancient Nubian monuments from flooding, after the construction of the Aswan High Dam.

The famous collection of armor includes armor, firearms, and swords from European as well as Japanese, Middle Eastern, and Asian collections, and it even features armor for horses.

The American Wing

The vast American wing provides a look at 14,000 paintings, sculptures, and decorative arts acquired by the museum since it was established in 1879. Here you'll find a restored Frank Lloyd

Wright living room from 1915 and Louis Comfort Tiffany's exquisite fountain, which adorns a beautiful scarf you can buy to take home with you. There's a terrific array of American furniture, as well as glass, textiles, quilts, and silver.

African, Oceanic, and American Art

The Met's first floor houses the arts of Africa, Oceania, and the Americas, featuring 16,000 objects spanning 3,000 years in the Michael C. Rockefeller Wing. Works from New Guinea, Melanesia, and Polynesia and stone objects from pre-Columbian cultures of Mexico and Central and South America highlight this vast and very rare collection.

European Art

The first floor is also home to the European sculpture and decorative arts, some medieval art (the Metropolitan's medieval branch, which includes the famed Unicorn Tapestries, can be found in a re-created European castle in Upper Manhattan, known as The Cloisters), and twentieth-century art (the famous Van Goghs, Monets, Cézannes, Jackson Pollocks, and Picassos).

 JUST FOR PARENTS

The Metropolitan's museum gift shop is superb. You'll find replicas of the jewelry from famous paintings as well as scarves, Christmas ornaments, mouse pads, tea sets, posters (framed and unframed), and signed limited editions of contemporary prints. This is a great place to pick up something for the folks back home, and there's always at least one item that screams "New York."

On the second floor, along with the European paintings (Renaissance through nineteenth century) and the American wing, you'll find musical instruments and Asian art, as well as the collection of drawings and prints and photographs.

Other Facilities

There is a completely redesigned cafeteria on the lower level where you can get hot meals, pasta, salads, soups, and so on. This is the best place to eat with children. There is also the Petrie Court Café on the ground floor, which serves sit-down meals. A second bar is located in the twentieth-century sculpture roof garden; it overlooks Central Park and is a delightful, even romantic, place to stroll during the summer.

Location and Hours

The Met is located at 82nd Street and Fifth Avenue. It is accessible via the subway on the 4, 5, or 6 train (86th Street). The museum is open Tuesday through Sunday from 9:30 A.M. until 5:15 P.M., and until 8:45 P.M. on Fridays and Saturdays. It is usually closed on Mondays. Suggested admission is $12 for adults and $7 for students and seniors. Children under 12 are free. Free tours are offered. Check the information desk for schedules. Audio tours of the collection are available for rent. There is validated fee parking, but it is limited. If you plan to visit Petrie Court Café, reservations are suggested; call ✆ 212-570-3964. Cocktails are served between 4:00 and 8:00 P.M. on the roof garden and in the balcony bar.

New York Stock Exchange

✉ 20 Broad Street at Wall Street
✆ 212-656-5165
🖉 www.nyse.com

Regardless of whether you play the market, it's certainly worth your while to pay a visit to the most significant stock exchange in the world. The New York Stock Exchange (NYSE) has seen active trading since 1792; it is now the largest stock exchange in the world, with traders wheeling and dealing a trillion shares of stock every day. Selling shares of stock is one manner in which businesses raise capital and build their companies. Thousands of these companies are listed on the New York Stock Exchange, many of which you are quite familiar with: McDonald's, General Electric, the Walt Disney Company, General Motors, and many more. Visiting the exchange will give you the opportunity to see how stocks are traded.

From the third-floor observatory, you can watch the madness as brokers buy and sell on the busy trading floor, using computer technology and a great deal of human energy and persistence. The sheer size and magnitude of the vast trading floor is exciting, particularly when you realize the dramatic implications the activities taking place down below have on economies worldwide.

A film explaining the hows and whys of stock trading and a presentation on how to read the ticker are part of the learning experience. Computer presentations and videos are available to learn more about the exchange.

≡FAST FACT

The Bowling Green is a small park located at the tip of Broadway in Lower Manhattan. It is considered to be a historic site, dating back to 1733. The subway station located at the site is one of the oldest, dating back to 1904.

Location and Hours

The New York Stock Exchange can be found at 20 Broad Street. It is accessible on the subway via the 2 or 3 train (Wall Street). You need to get tickets (which are free), so it's to your advantage to arrive by noon—this is a popular sight, and the market closes daily at 3:00 P.M. Guided tours run every half hour from 8:45 to 4:30 P.M., but it's more fun to be there before the trading floor closes.

Radio City Music Hall

✉ 1260 Sixth Avenue
✆ 212-247-4777
www.radiocity.com

Billed as the show palace of the nation, Radio City Music Hall opened in December of 1932 as the largest indoor theater in the world. Some 300 million people have now enjoyed entertainment at the famed 6,000-seat theater. The art deco elegance, twenty-four-karat gold-leaf grand foyer ceiling, and newly restored 4,178-pipe Wurlitzer organ create a unique ambiance. It's a mixture of warmth and excitement that makes the theater a special stop for both tourists and New Yorkers. A sixty-by-thirty-foot mural called *The Fountain of Youth* adorns the grand staircase in the main lobby, while the world-famous marquee wraps around the front of the building and spans a city block.

The multitiered theater has housed concerts, awards shows, television productions, family attractions, film premieres, and more. Although the acoustics and sight lines have always been excellent, a recently completed $122-million renovation to the landmark property has enhanced the theater with state-of-the-art video and audio technology.

RAINY DAY FUN

A highlight of the Radio City experience is the *Radio City Christmas Spectacular*. Usually running for nearly two months, from November into January, the Christmas Spectacular features the "Parade of the Wooden Soldiers" and "Living Nativity" shows. A staple of the hall for decades, the Christmas Spectacular is ideal family fare, but you must call and order tickets well in advance. Over a million people annually fill Radio City to see the show.

Radio City is also known for the Rockettes, who were first formed in 1925 as the Missouri Rockets in St. Louis. By 1933, the precision dance team had ended up in New York City on the stage of the brand-new Radio City Music Hall. Nearly seventy years later, they are still going strong. The troop of 150 dancers is famous for its high-kicking chorus line and is now seen both at Radio City and at other events and on television, including the *Late Show with David Letterman*, which is taped nearby.

If you can't see a show at Radio City Music Hall while you are in town, you might want to take a tour of the theater. Tours cover the premises from the grand stage to the backstage. The itinerary is subject to change because of rehearsals and preshow activities. A tour is, however, a good way to get a free glimpse of the evening's performance. You may even meet some Rockettes, though you should stand back if they're rehearsing—so they don't kick you.

Location and Hours

Radio City Music Hall is located at 1260 Avenue of the Americas (Sixth Avenue) between 50th and 51st Streets. It is accessible by subway via the D, B, F, V, N, or R train (Rockefeller Center station), as well as via the 1 or 9 train (50th Street). Radio City is accessible to people with disabilities; arrangements for wheelchairs can be made by calling ✆ 212-632-4039.

The one-hour tours of Radio City are offered Monday to Saturday, 10 A.M. to 5 P.M., and Sundays from 11 A.M. to 5 P.M. The cost is $17 for adults, $14 for seniors, and $10 for children under 12. To join the tour, simply show up at the box office or order online. Event tickets can be purchased at the Radio City box office, by telephone, or through Ticketmaster (✆ 212-307-7171; a surcharge applies).

St. Patrick's Cathedral

✉ 14 East 51st Street
✆ 212-753-2261
⌨ *www.ny-archdiocese.org*
Designed by renowned American architect James Renwick and completed in 1874, this magnificent church sits amid the busy Rockefeller Center area and remains the seat of the New York archdiocese. While holiday masses draw crowds and television cameras to cover the event at Christmas, numerous tourists visit the ornate

gothic-style cathedral daily. They stop and look around, awed by the majesty and magnificence of this grand cathedral, and are free to participate in daily masses and confessions, as well as the stations of the cross at 6:00 P.M.

The best-known cathedral in New York City, St. Patrick's is the largest Roman Catholic church in the United States, seating some 2,400 people. With its statues, the Rose Window, the Tiffany altar, the award-winning stations of the cross (from the 1893 Chicago World's Fair), its ornate white spires, as well as its sheer size and splendor, the cathedral is a very special stop for nearly 3 million tourists of all faiths who visit annually.

St. Patrick's Cathedral is but a few steps from Rockefeller Center and Radio City Music Hall, in the heart of midtown Manhattan. It is open to visitors from 7 A.M. to 8:30 P.M. It is a marvelous area to stroll through, enjoying the serenity and majesty of the sights and stores of the area, and the cathedral has a lovely crèche for the Christmas holidays. There is a gift shop on 50th Street between Madison and Park Avenues, which is open until 6:00 P.M. most evenings. It features religious Belleek china and Lladro porcelain sculptures, as well as rosaries and postcards.

Location and Hours

St. Patrick's is on Fifth Avenue between 49th and 50th Streets. It is accessible by subway via the D, B, F, V, N, or R train (Rockefeller Center) and via the 1 or 9 train (50th Street).

South Street Seaport

✉ 19 Fulton Street
✆ 212-732-8257
🖰 www.southstreetseaport.com

Spanning eleven blocks, the South Street Seaport is a combination historic site, shopping mall, and active fish market. Declared a historic landmark in 1967, the seaport was restored and remodeled over the next several years by the Rouse Corporation, the organization that also developed Quincy Market in Boston. The combination of historic ships and architecture, trendy stores, and spectacular views of the Brooklyn Bridge and the harbor make it a popular attraction.

The seaport's cobblestone streets are home to quaint shops, fine restaurants, mini-malls, a maritime museum, a fish market, piers, and, of course, sailing vessels. Ships docked along Pier 16 include several sailing vessels from the nineteenth century, some of which still offer rides. The *Pioneer,* a 102-foot schooner from 1885, sets sail several times daily, starting at 10 A.M. You can also set sail on a Seaport Music Cruise during the summer months, on a two-hour sunset cruise with a DJ or with live music. The *W. O. Decker* can hold up to six people for a unique tugboat ride along the river. Call ✆ 212-748-8590 for information.

 **TRAVEL TIP**

Some sights may have rules and regulations regarding strollers, cameras, and bringing food inside. Some may have restrictions; for example, pregnant women and young children are not allowed on the Skyride at the Empire State Building.

Other old sailing vessels sit docked along Piers 15 and 16. These include the tall sailing ship *Peking,* one of the largest sailing ships ever built; the *Wavertree,* the largest extant wrought-iron sailing ship; and the *Ambrose,* a lightship once used to guide ships into New York. Walking tours and special exhibits are also available.

Pier 17's fast-food eateries include Cindy's Cinnamon Rolls, Minter's Ice Cream, and the takeout franchise Wok and Roll. It is also home to numerous shops in a seaside mall. There are eateries of the sit-down kind all around the seaport, including Café Fledermaus for outdoor lunches.

The South Street Seaport Museum

✉ 207 Fulton Street, Pier 16

✆ 212-748-8600

🖱 *www.southseaport.org*

Just inland from the seaport, you will find the South Street Seaport Museum, founded in 1967. Inside this tribute to the vessels of the sea you can browse through paintings, prints, and drawings, as well as crafts, sailing gear, shipboard tools, handicrafts, and artifacts from the sailors and fishermen of a bygone era. The museum is also home to thousands of photographs and 2 million excavation items (some stored at other sites), many of which are also on display. There are three exhibit areas in all, plus a nearby gallery, children's center, and crafts center. There is also a huge maritime reference library and a working nineteenth-century press, Bowne & Co. Stationers.

≡FAST FACT

Quite the contrast to the skyscrapers that make up the New York skyline, Schermerhorn Row is a row of early nineteenth-century warehouses and courthouses along the south side of Fulton Street (at the South Street Seaport). The Row is home to shopping and restaurants. The stores themselves are from the modern era and include the Body Shop, Sharper Image, and other popular retailers.

Planning Ahead

To get the most out of a visit to the seaport, it's best to plan for a clear day to enjoy strolling and even going for a boat ride. Unless it's a particularly warm day, it's advisable to have a sweater, jacket, or sweatshirt along, as the East River breezes kick up while you are sailing. You might schedule walking around the seaport to coincide with breakfast or lunch. Remember to give yourself a couple of hours for the museum! The best thing about the seaport is that it provides a little of everything—history, shopping, activities, entertainment, photo opportunities, and food. It also provides a great place to stroll or sit and relax and watch the people. Give yourself several hours.

Location and Hours

The South Street Seaport is located between the East River and Water Street. It is accessible by subway via the 2, 3, 4, 5, E, J, M, or Z train (Fulton Street) or the A or C train (Broadway-Nassau).

The two-hour ride on the *Pioneer* costs $25 for adults, $15 for children 12 and under, and $20 for seniors or students with an ID. You can purchase tickets at the Pier 16 ticket booth. Call ✆ 212-748-8590 for information or to order tickets by phone from 9:30 A.M. to 5:30 P.M.

Seaport Music Cruises cost $20 with live music—$6 for children 12 and under, $10 for seniors, and $11 for college students. Call ✆ 212-630-8888 for sailing times.

The Seaport Museum costs $8 for adults, $6 for students, and $4 for children under 12. It's open daily from 10 A.M. to 6 P.M. Evening hours extend to 8 P.M. on Thursdays, from April through September. Hours are 10 A.M. to 5 P.M. from October through March. The museum is closed on Tuesdays during the fall/winter months.

United Nations

✉ First Avenue between 42nd and 49th Streets

✆ 212-963-8687 (tours)

✍ *www.un.org*

The United Nations was established in October of 1945, immediately after World War II. There were fifty-one countries in the initial formation, and their goal was to join together to maintain peace and provide humanitarian assistance around the world. Over the years, the United Nations has grown to include some 185 countries. Countries joining the United Nations agree to accept a charter that outlines the basic principles of international relations. While the U.N. has tried to help maintain world order and promote peace, it is not a lawmaking entity and has taken criticism for not being able to prevent international conflicts. Yet many conflicts have been averted with its help, and its policies and programs have helped to promote harmony between nations and respect for human rights.

The United Nations is affiliated with many other organizations that are involved in other activities, including international air travel, telecommunications, protecting the environment, and improving the quality of life for refugees and people living in poverty. UNICEF is one among many programs that the United Nations has established over the years to help the international community.

The United Nations is made up of six branches, five of which occupy an eighteen-acre tract of land in New York City. David Rockefeller originally donated the land, which is designated as international territory. The five components of the New York headquarters include the General Assembly, the Security Council, the Economic and Social Council, the Trusteeship Council, and the Secretariat. The sixth body is the International Court of Justice, which is headquartered at The Hague in the Netherlands.

Touring the U.N.

The vast riverside promenade overlooking the East River is spectacular, with a rose garden, carefully landscaped lawns, and sculptures from nations worldwide. There are three primary buildings on the site, including the General Assembly, the tall glass-enclosed Secretariat Building, and the Dag Hammarskjöld Library. Flags from all member nations flank the buildings and landscape.

The United Nations is best visited on a clear day so that you can stroll through the promenade and enjoy the scenery and the view. Guided tours are available every day except Thanksgiving, Christmas, New Year's Day, and weekends in January and February. The tours take you through all the main areas of the United Nations, including inside the General Assembly (unless it is in session) and Security Council Chamber. The numerous exhibits, artwork from around the world, and décor of the buildings are all explained.

The United Nations Bookshop on the premises features a vast assortment of books in many languages, plus marvelous children's books, posters, United Nations calendars, and more. At the gift center, you can purchase unique handcrafted items plus gifts from around the world, as well as flags and the more "typical" souvenirs.

The coffee shop in the public concourse offers light fare; the Delegates Dining Room is available for fine dining. Seating is for lunch only, between 11:30 A.M. and 2 P.M., and reservations are strongly suggested. Proper attire is a must—you may be sitting next to an important delegate from the other side of the world! Be on your best behavior.

There is also a post office on the premises, so you can get those postcards out immediately—with U.N. stamps.

RAINY DAY FUN

There is plenty of information available about the United Nations online. By logging on, you can learn all about the United Nations charter, its day-to-day activities, and the functions of the various branches and numerous associated agencies. Sites include the U.N. Home Page at *www.un.org*, a Web site locator at *www.unsystem.org*, and UNICEF at *www.unicef.org*. There is also a Web page devoted to humanitarian relief for victims of disasters at *www.reliefweb.int*.

Location and Hours

The United Nations is located at First Avenue between 42nd and 49th Streets. It is accessible by subway via the 4, 5, 6, E, or V train (Lexington Avenue and 51st Street). U.N. tours are given in some twenty languages and cost $10.50 for adults, $7 for students, and $8 for seniors. Each tour lasts forty-five minutes. They are available from 9:15 A.M. to 4:15 P.M., leaving the lobby of the General Assembly every thirty minutes. Children must be 5 or older.

The United Nations Bookshop is open Monday through Friday, 9 A.M. to 5 P.M., and opens a half hour later on weekends. Call ☎ 1-800-553-3210 for more information. The gift center is open from 9:00 A.M. to 5:15 P.M. (closed weekends in January and February).

CHAPTER 8

Central Park

CENTRAL PARK is an 843-acre oasis in the middle of the busiest city in the world. New Yorkers consider it a kind of communal backyard, where they bike, jog, walk their dogs, picnic, play Frisbee, and generally chill out.

You can go online to find out everything you need to know about the park, from its history to maps of its features, to a complete list of all the activities there; visit ✍ *www.centralpark.org*. Another good Internet resource is ✍ *www.cityparkfoundation.org*. For any information on the park, call the city information hotline, ✆ 311, or ✆ 212-NEW-YORK if you're calling from out of town.

💼 TRAVEL TIP

The Dairy, Belvedere Castle, and the Charles A. Dana Discovery Center at the Harlem Meer are the places to catch the free guided tours that will familiarize you with the park today and yesterday. Experienced tour guides will lead the way and fill you in on the nitty-gritty about the world's premier park. Most tours are given on the weekend, but there are some weekday tours as well. For tour information, call the tour hotline at ✆ 212-360-2727.

How It All Began

The idea to set aside space for a public park in Manhattan came to William Cullen Bryant as early as 1884. Bryant was inspired by the city parks of Paris and London. Over a decade later, Frederick Law Olmsted and Calvert Vaux began designing the rolling lawns and picturesque vistas that would make up Central Park, the first landscaped park in the country.

The vast acreage was improved over the twenty-year period from 1857 to 1877. Building the park was not an easy task; the land was primarily swamps, bluffs, and rocky outcroppings. Thousands of workers moved soil and blasted through rock, then planted trees and grass in its place. Some six bodies of water, three dozen bridges, and miles of irrigation pipes were part of the undertaking. Workers planted more than 400 varieties of trees and nearly 1,000 types of shrubs. A significant number of residents living on the site were displaced.

RAINY DAY FUN

Central Park has been a prominent feature in a number of movies, including *Ghostbusters,* where Tavern on the Green is the sight of a gargoyle run amok, to *When Harry Met Sally,* where Harry and Sally have lunch at the Boathouse Cafe. Of course, you can always rent the children's classic, *A Troll in Central Park* and watch it before or after you go. Other films shot in or around Central Park include *An Affair to Remember, Annie Hall, Barefoot in the Park, The Fisher King, Hannah and her Sisters, Kramer vs. Kramer, Love Story, Tootsie, Wall Street,* and *Zelig.*

Slowly the park emerged, stretching from 59th Street on the south end up to 110th Street on the north. From Fifth Avenue across to Central Park West, the equivalent of Eighth Avenue, the marvelous park became the crown jewel of the city, with fancy carriages and well-dressed New Yorkers parading along the paths. Since its completion, the park has been a refuge for New Yorkers and visitors looking for a respite from the busy city streets for a little while.

Central Park Today

Today, Central Park is a haven for bicycling, rollerblading, jogging, boating, ice skating, strolling, or taking a ride in a horse-drawn carriage. You'll find people playing Frisbee, softball, football, tennis, chess, and checkers, as well as people flying kites. There are great rocks for climbing, horses for riding, and places to sit and listen to concerts under the stars. From sunbathing to folk dancing, Central Park is the ultimate resort, and except for a few sites and activities that charge an admission, it's all free.

≡FAST FACT

Nearly 20 million visitors enjoy the riches of the park annually; more than fifty groups or organizations, including running clubs and bird watching groups, hold their gatherings in the park.

On a spring, summer, or warm fall or winter day, the park gives you the opportunity to step into another world within the city. The view of the high-rise buildings flanks the outskirts of the great park. As you venture further into the park, the sounds of traffic and the fast pace that is New York City will fade away. Everything in Central Park moves at a slower pace, except perhaps the rollerbladers. Strolling through, you'll find yourself stopping to enjoy street performers, including musicians, jugglers, mimes, dancers, and clowns. Buy a pretzel, climb the side of a giant rock formation, or simply toss down a blanket and lie on the grass. Designated "quiet areas" prohibit loud radios from disturbing your escape from the world.

Completely manmade, Central Park is full of sights, statues, lakes, ponds, bridges, and the second-most popular zoo in the city. Many of the best-known sights and landmarks within the park have been there since the nineteenth or early twentieth century.

The Central Park Wildlife Center

Commonly known as the Central Park Zoo, the wildlife center is one of the best bargains you'll find in the city. The zoo is small, but it's the source of many a smile from the millions of children who visit every year. The country's oldest public zoo, it was remodeled in the early 1990s; the neighboring children's zoo reopened in 1997.

The main zoo does not have "large" animals, such as lions and tigers, but it does have a large sea-lion pool as the centerpiece. (Feeding time is fun to watch.) To cool off, you might want to stop in the Polar Circle, an indoor enclosed exhibit featuring more penguins than you can count. The tuxedoed waddlers frolic in a re-created wintry arctic setting, complete with mini-glaciers and icy waters. Arctic foxes and tufted puffins also live in the Polar Circle.

⟆FAST FACT

The famous Delacorte clock is located just outside the zoo. It was constructed on top of an archway in 1965. It consists of six bronze animals on a small carousel that rotates on the hour, with the animals moving as the chimes are heard.

Venturing through the zoo, you will find a large land and water home for New York City's popular polar bear, who, after several weeks of sulking, at one point actually inspired the city to hire an animal psychologist to visit. There are actually three bears. They have plenty of room to play and are fun to watch, when they're not taking an extended nap. Nearby, you'll find Monkey Island, home to numerous Japanese snow monkeys and other simian species.

A large, indoor (and hot) tropical rain forest exhibit comes complete with tall trees, waterfalls, and other vegetation; it is home to numerous birds, Colobus monkeys, insects, and other living things. Following along the trail, you'll find yourself smack in the middle of the Amazon, right in the middle of New York City!

All in all, the beautifully landscaped zoo takes about an hour to visit at a leisurely pace. There is a café that serves primarily snack foods, hot dogs, and sandwiches. There's also a gift shop with all kinds of "zoovineers."

Location and Hours

The zoo, located at 64th Street and Fifth Avenue, is open year-round from 10 A.M. to 4:30 or 5:30 P.M., depending on the time of year. The winter months may be a bit brisk for strolling. Admission is $6 for adults, $1.25 for seniors, $1 for children ages 3 through 12, and free for children under 3. The zoo is accessible to people with disabilities.

Buying a ticket also entitles you to visit the neighboring Tisch Children's Zoo, where children can visit and pet goats, pigs, sheep, and other child-friendly animals. The small well-planned zoo is fun for the little ones. Summer days can make for long lines on weekends, but the lines generally move along quickly.

Central Park Playgrounds

Playgrounds can be found all throughout the park in different configurations. Some twenty-one playgrounds offer different themes and styles centered on fun activities, including the largest sliding board in Manhattan at East 67th Street's Billy Johnson Playground. Other playgrounds include the timber-style Diana Ross Playground at West 81st Street, donated by the singer, who played a concert in the park in 1983, and the Wild West Playground, sporting a Western theme with a small stream running through it.

Playgrounds also can be found off the Great Lawn at East 72nd Street, East 77th, 79th, 84th, 85th, and 86th Streets. Playgrounds around the reservoir are at East 96th Street, West 91st, 93rd, and 96th Streets. North end playgrounds are at East 100th and 108th Streets, 110th and Lenox Avenue, and on the west side at 100th and 110th Streets.

The park's playgrounds are well maintained and fenced in. Remember to be attentive to your children and to keep the playgrounds (and the park for that matter) clean.

The Carousel

The carousel in Central Park is over ninety years old, but it is not the park's original. The original carousel in the park was built in 1871 and turned by horsepower—and not the horsepower that runs your car! It was later destroyed in a fire and rebuilt, only to be destroyed by fire for a second time. In 1951 the park acquired a fifty-year-old carousel from Coney Island and refurbished it; this is the carousel in the park today. Adults and children can sit atop one of the many hand-carved horses and go for a spin on this antique treasure. The carousel is located mid-park by 64th Street. It costs $1 per ride.

Sports and Activities

Central Park has a wealth of sports and outdoor activities all year round, from ice skating in the winter to boating in the summer.

Wollman Memorial Rink

✆ 212-439-6900

✎ *www.wollmanskatingrink.com*

By winter, Wollman Rink is a mid-city paradise for ice skaters; in the summer months, the ice gives way to the Victorian Gardens Amusement Park. For those who enjoy watching, the terrace above offers a lovely view of the skaters. Ice skating prevails from November to March. Ice skating is $7 for adults and $3.50 for children under 17 and seniors. Skate rental is $3. It costs $4 to roller-skate for adults and $3.50 for children under 12 and seniors.

In the summer, you can rent inline skates for $6 (which includes safety gear), or just the safety gear for $3. Children under 14 must wear helmets (New York state law). If you want to skate around the park, skate rental is $15 plus a $100 deposit.

 TRAVEL TIP

You can also skate in the winter at Lasker Rink and Pool at 106th Street, mid-park; it is the only public swimming facility in the park during the summer months. For more information, call ✆212-534-7639.

The Charles A. Dana Discovery Center

✉Fifth Avenue and 110th Street
✆212-860-1370

The Dana Discovery Center (at the Harlem Meer) is one of the newest points of interest and education for children—and grownups too. The center, in a chateau at the northeast corner of the park, offers environmental studies on an 11-acre section of the recently restored Harlem Meer. Various exhibits and workshops focusing on ecology, orienteering, and nature, as well as walking tours and performances, are all found at the new center; during the week, it's a haven for class trips.

The Swedish Cottage Marionette Theater

✉79th Street Transverse
✆212-988-9093

This is a fun-filled place to find entertainment for the little ones. The cottage is originally from the nineteenth century and has since been renovated. The puppet shows are performed Tuesday through Friday at 10:30 A.M. and noon, and on Saturdays at 11:00 A.M., 1:00 P.M., and 3:00 P.M. Call to make reservations.

The Loeb Boathouse and the Lake

The boathouse and lake can be found on the west side of the park between 72nd and 77th Streets. The second biggest body of water in the park, the eighteen-acre lake is home to plenty of boating activity and makes for a scenic, romantic place to stroll. From April through September, you can rent a large rowboat for

$10 for the first hour, $2.50 for each additional quarter hour, but you must leave a $20 cash deposit. A gondola is also available for those who haven't been to Italy for a while.

Model Boat Rentals

Like the legendary Tuileries in Paris, you can rent miniature wooden boats and sail them along the Conservatory Waters, pushing them back and forth with wooden sticks. On spring and summer weekends, this is often a very crowded area. Boat rentals are on a first-come, first-serve basis and go for $10 per hour. This activity is seasonal, of course.

Tennis, Anyone?

Tennis players can enjoy swinging away on some thirty courts from April through November. If you'll be staying in the city for awhile or visiting often and you want to take advantage of Manhattan's few public courts, you can buy a season permit at the Arsenal, in the park at 64th Street and Fifth Avenue—for more information, call ✆ 212-255-8036. Permits cost $50 for adults, $20 for seniors, and $10 for children under 17. If you want to play once, you can purchase a single-day permit for $5 per person. These can be purchased at the courts on 96th Street toward the west side of the park, by the reservoir. Call ✆ 212-286-0205 for information. There's an on-site tennis store, where you can buy rackets and have old ones restrung.

And There's More

If you have a remote control or scale model sailboat, you can put your vehicle to the test in the Conservatory Waters just north of 72nd Street by Fifth Avenue.

Horseback riding is another one of the park's numerous activities. You can take a horse out from the Claremont Stables at 175 West 89th Street along one of several bridle paths through the park. Call ✆ 212-724-5100 for information. Riding costs $60 per half hour. The horses are tacked up in English saddles and bridles and are available to experienced riders only. Visa and MasterCard accepted.

Bicycle riding is also a very popular park activity. Bike paths designate where you can ride. You can rent a bike during the months of March through November from 10:00 A.M. to 6:00 P.M. The fee is $10 per hour plus a deposit, slightly more for bicycles for two.

If you'd prefer more sedentary activities, you can hit the Chess and Checker House near West 64th Street. There are numerous places throughout the park to sit and play these or other board games.

 JUST FOR PARENTS

Take a romantic carriage ride through Central Park. The horse-drawn carriages can be found lined up along Central Park South, between Fifth and Sixth Avenues, and 59th Street, at the southern end of Central Park across the street from the Plaza Hotel. Rides cost $34 for the first twenty minutes and $54 for a roughly fifty-minute tour. For more information call ☎ 212-246-0520. Like cab rides in New York, these are cash only, and please remember to tip the driver.

Sights and Landmarks

There is an awful lot to see and do in the park. You could spend an afternoon just looking for some of the famous landmarks, such as the statues and fountains.

Alice in Wonderland

The giant *Alice in Wonderland* statue, featuring huge bronze figures of Sir John Tenniel's classic illustrations of the Lewis Carroll tale, is one of the all-time kid favorites. It can be found north of the model boathouse on 75th Street. Most New Yorkers have at least one snapshot of themselves as kids crawling up the mushroom stalk. The philanthropist George Delacorte commissioned this statue from sculptor José de Creeft, in memory of his first wife, Margarita. It was dedicated in 1959.

The Arsenal

The Arsenal was built on the site in 1851, prior to the construction of the park. Today, the historic structure (on Fifth Avenue just inside the 64th Street entrance), serves mostly as office space for the Parks and Recreation Department. It housed Civil War troops back in 1864 and 1865, and in 1869, it served briefly as the first home of the American Museum of Natural History.

Balto the Alaskan Sled Dog

The famous Balto statue commemorates the Alaskan sled dog that saved a town by bringing medicine through the tundra to its sick inhabitants. The story is told in the classic animated children's movie, *Balto,* which you should rent before visiting Central Park. The statue is east of the Mall on 67th Street. This is a great place to take a picture. The dedication on the statue reads: "Dedicated to the indomitable spirit of the sled dogs that relayed antitoxins 660 miles across rough ice, across treacherous waters, through Arctic blizzards from Nenana to the relief of stricken Nome in the Winter of 1925."

Bethesda Terrace

Bethesda Terrace is home to the multilevel Bethesda Fountain, dedicated in 1873 and named for a pool in Jerusalem, with the *Angel of the Waters* sculpture sitting high atop and overlooking the European-style terrace. A stone staircase leads down to the three-tier fountain that sits near the Mall with a backdrop on the lake.

The view is spectacular from the top of the stairs, with rowboats in the background below lush trees with their branches and green leaves hanging over the waters. The boathouse can be seen to the right. The terrace surrounding the fountain is a busy stopping point for the numerous visitors who stroll by and stop to enjoy the beauty of the scene. Street performers, including jugglers, magicians, and musicians, delight the kids—and their parents, too, for that matter. Bethesda Terrace is by 72nd Street, toward the east side (or Fifth Avenue side) of the park.

≡FAST FACT

There are numerous statues throughout the great park, including a number of famed monuments to leaders from nations around the world. Among the many famous statues in the park are the *107th Regiment Civil War Statue* (commemorating Union soldiers) and *Still Hunt* (a panther perched on a ledge watching over one of the many trails).

Belvedere Castle

This is the only "castle" on park grounds. Located in the middle of the park at 79th Street, the massive stone structure was built in 1872 and has seen a few renovations since. The highest point in the park, the castle is the place to go to get a great view of the acreage around it, including the Great Lawn and the Delacorte Theater, home to Shakespeare in the Park, a free first-come, first-serve season of Shakespearean plays performed during the summer months. Inside the castle, you'll find the Henry Luce Nature Observatory (which looks at nature through microscopes and telescopes), various displays, programs for the kids, and workshops. The castle is also home to the instruments of the U.S. Weather Bureau. For over eighty years, meteorological instruments here have provided New Yorkers with the temperature in Central Park.

The Dairy

The Dairy was originally the Park's first fast-food restaurant. Today, the small Victorian building is a visitor center and gift shop, housing books and information about the park as well as souvenirs such as T-shirts, mugs, and framed photographs. Just north of the Wollman Rink, the Dairy is a place to get maps, buy books about the park, and find out about park events and park history. The Dairy is open Tuesday through Sunday from 10:00 A.M. to 4:00 P.M., and admission is free.

Hans Christian Andersen Statue

Another great photo op for the little ones, this larger-than-life statue of the children's author of such classics as *The Little Mermaid* and *The Ugly Duckling*, can be found just west of the model boathouse at 72nd Street. The statue depicts Andersen reading from *The Ugly Duckling*, as a bronze duck approaches.

The Harlem Meer

The Meer is an eleven-acre lake (or *meer*, in Dutch) that sits on the northeast corner of the park (by Fifth Avenue) at the foot of Harlem. It was restored and reopened in 1993 and features numerous plants, shrubs, trees, and winding paths through nature around the lake. There are walking tours offered for those who want to look more closely at and learn about the plant life. You can also find a newly created island.

The Harlem Meer is one of the few places in Manhattan where you can actually go fishing. Stocked with 50,000 minnows, large-mouth bass, catfish, golden shiners, and bluegills, the Meer is Central Park's fishing hole. Bamboo poles are available free of charge at the Charles A. Dana Discovery Center, adjacent to the Meer, and bait is free. Fish must be thrown back to maintain the careful ecological balance of life. Poles are available with a photo ID on a first-come basis Tuesday through Sunday from 11 A.M. to 4 P.M. Groups of up to twenty can reserve poles by calling ✆212-860-1370.

 TRAVEL TIP

Woodlands, meadows, and even battlegrounds from the War of 1812 can be found within a short walk from the Meer. Although many people still don't know about the Meer, in nice weather you can find some hundred people a day fishing there.

The Reservoir

The Reservoir is a 106-acre body of water, built in 1862 smack in the middle of the northern part of the park above 86th Street. It was renamed the Jacqueline Kennedy Onassis Reservoir in 1995. The path surrounding the reservoir, just more than 1.5 miles in length, is now the park's most popular jogging track, home to thousands of runners in training for races. Although the reservoir is no longer used for the city's drinking water, it still remains the largest body of water in the park. The view across the reservoir is stunning, and the trees, including cherry trees, and numerous birds make for great scenery. A reconstruction of the original fence is just being completed.

Lawns, Gardens, and Wide-Open Spaces

Many New Yorkers, particularly those in the city, live in modern apartments that are not as spacious as they would like. The park offers some elbow room—places to lie on the grass and enjoy the wide-open spaces. Of course, on a warm spring or summer day, those places can get crowded, but the serenity of the park can almost always be found if you look carefully. Off-the-beaten-path locations are often just down the road or over a large rock from the path you're on.

A truly awe-inspiring experience is lying in Central Park and looking up and out at the tall buildings standing high and flanking the peaceful setting. The city is so close, yet so far away; the park is a refuge unto itself. Two of the most notable wide-open spaces in the vast park are the Great Lawn and the Sheep Meadow.

The Great Lawn

A reservoir until the 1930s, this lawn was replanted, resodded, and redone in recent years to once again be one of the prime locations for outdoor fun in the park. Frisbees fly by, as do softballs and hardballs from countless games played all spring and summer on baseball diamonds, of which there are over two dozen in the park. The lawn has also seen massive crowds (with estimates of anywhere from 200,000 to nearly a million people) for concerts from Paul Simon, Elton John, and Diana Ross and others. Even the pope spoke to throngs of people on the Great Lawn. The lawn spans some fourteen acres of open air and has been the central gathering point for the largest crowds in the city.

≡FAST FACT

If you've got a dog and a Frisbee, you can play. Besides playing Frisbee catch with your favorite canine just for the fun of it, you can also enter the annual June tournament, which gives prizes for the most athletic mutt. This fun event takes place around 66th and 67th Streets on the west side of the park. For information, call ☎212-777-2297.

The Sheep Meadow

This really was a sheep meadow until the mid-1930s—it was a large flat piece of land, originally designed for military practice, but used as a pasture for the park's flock of sheep. Today, the sheep are long gone, and the fifteen-acre area on the west side of the park is a haven for sunbathers. There is less activity here than on the Great Lawn, with no ball playing or loud radios allowed. You may look up and see a kite overhead in the spring. Essentially, though, the Sheep Meadow is reserved for sedentary pleasures such as relaxing and picnicking. Just north of the Sheep Meadow is the Lawn Sports Center, which is home to croquet players and lawn bowlers.

Gardens Galore

Among the numerous gardens that highlight the park are the Shakespeare Garden, Strawberry Fields, and the Conservatory Garden. The Shakespeare Garden is tucked between the Swedish

Cottage and the Belvedere Castle. Dedicated to the great writer, the little-known garden was established in 1912 and restored in 1988. The nearby Delacorte Theater features free summer Shakespeare plays, produced by the Joseph Papp Public Theatre (call ✆212-539-8750 for more information). Plaques around the garden are inscribed with quotes from the works of Shakespeare, and the flowers within are those mentioned in his works, including thyme, sage, rosemary, and lavender and several varieties of seasonal flowers.

 JUST FOR PARENTS

Every summer since 1954, New Yorkers have been treated to free stellar performances of classic plays (usually Shakespeare) at the Delacorte Theater through Joseph Papp's Public Theatre. Recent actors include Natalie Portman, Meryl Streep, and Christopher Walken. Although tickets are free, you have to wait in line on the day of the show at 1:00 P.M., and you can only get two tickets per person. Performances are at 8:00 P.M. and the theater seats 2,000. Call ✆212-539-8750 for information.

Strawberry Fields, meanwhile, is dedicated to a writer, singer, and legend of a different era, John Lennon. The 2.5-acre west side garden is the result of a $1 million gift to the park by Yoko Ono. The couple visited the garden often when they lived across the street in the Dakota Apartments.

A serene setting, the romantic garden is home to tree clusters, outcroppings, and a marble mosaic with the word "Imagine" carved in it (a gift from the city of Naples, Italy); fans gather there each year on the anniversary of Lennon's tragic death. The garden is also home to gifts from countries around the world.

The Conservatory Garden is actually three gardens on three acres on Fifth Avenue near 105th Street, just south of the Harlem Meer. Originally opened in 1937, the outdoor gardens replaced greenhouses that occupied the site from 1899. A 1982 restoration and landscaping brought back these gardens that have been home to weddings and other festive occasions.

The North Garden is a French-style design surrounding a large bronze fountain known as *Three Dancing Maidens*. The flowerbeds around the centerpiece are lush with 20,000 tulips in the spring and 2,500 Korean chrysanthemums in the fall. The Central Garden features an Italian design with a big manicured lawn leading to a central fountain with huge surrounding hedges. Pink and white blossoms and trees surround the garden. The South Garden is English in style. A lily pond and large bronze fountain dedicated to the children's book *The Secret Garden* are surrounded by the trees, shrubs, and flowers that outline this third garden within the conservatory.

Free tours are given rain or shine on Saturday at 11:00 A.M.

═══FAST FACT

More than 200 species of birds have been spotted by bird enthusiasts in the park, primarily in an area known as "the Ramble," a thirty-seven-acre wooded area with wildly growing bushes, waterfalls, and even a brook. The area, near the East 79th Street entrance, can be somewhat deserted, so it may be best explored with others.

Fine Dining

Although for many fine dining in Central Park consists of whatever you pack for your picnic, there are several other options.

Tavern on the Green
☏ 212-873-3200
✍ *www.tavernonthegreen.com*

A glittering jewel, Tavern on the Green is a wonderful place to have a leisurely lunch, a romantic dinner, or even a terrific Sunday brunch. The structure, a classic example of mid-Victorian architecture, was originally built in the late nineteenth century (just off the entrance at West 67th Street) as a sheepfold to hold the park's resident flock. Today, thousands of tourists and New Yorkers flock to the upscale, sprawling, dazzling restaurant. From floor to ceiling and wall to wall, the restaurant's décor is stunning. Stained glass, exquisite chandeliers, ornate gold trim, flowers, statues, outdoor dining—it's all part of the experience.

With its expansive glass-enclosed Crystal Room looking out over the park, and sparkling lights lining the trees around the structure, Tavern on the Green provides a wonderful dining experience. During the holiday season, the lights and seasonal display are spectacular. Tavern on the Green offers jazz in the Chestnut Room and dining outdoors (in the warmer weather) in its outdoor garden. It is also the only place in the park to legally buy alcoholic beverages, and with that in mind, the restaurant offers an extensive wine list. There is dancing on weekend evenings, and the Easter Sunday meal at Tavern on the Green is legendary. There is also a delightful gift shop on the premises.

As for the food, the lobster bisque and crab cakes are favorites, as are the sirloin and shrimp brochette. Portions are large, so you could share with a child. There's an extensive children's menu, and the staff is very child-friendly. Dessert is always delicious, especially the chocolate banana mousse cake (which is surprisingly light). Reservations are a good idea, and they must be backed up by a credit card. An unclaimed reservation will be charged $25.

The Boathouse Café

☎ 212-517-2233

✐ www.thecentralparkboathouse.com

Located in the Loeb Boathouse, at East Drive between Terrace Drive and the 79th Street Transverse, the café serves light fare at reasonable prices. You can dine indoors or outside on the terrace overlooking the lake. If you can't find the Boathouse Café, a trolley will pick you up at 72nd Street and Fifth Avenue and take you there.

Other Options

While there are no other significant eateries in the park, there are other places to grab a bite, including the Ballplayers House, the Ice Cream Café, Mineral Springs Pavilion, and the Zoo Café. All are easily accessible and busy during the summer months.

≡FAST FACT

Just southeast of Bethesda Fountain, music fills the air throughout the summer as the sounds of jazz, blues, pop, country, Latin, African, and Calypso music emanate from the amphitheater. For a schedule and information, call ✆212-360-2777.

You can also stop at one of a wide range of vendors who are licensed to sell food in the park from carts. Or do as many New Yorkers do, and bring your own bag lunch or picnic lunch and settle down for a meal under the trees, surrounded by the skyline.

CHAPTER 9

Manhattan Museums

FEW CITIES OFFER as much cultural diversity as New York and very few, if any, can boast of such a vast array of museums. Nearly 150 museums grace the five boroughs, ranging from broad themes such as natural history or "art" to specific cultural, ethnic, or historical collections, including modern art, Jewish culture, and the city's own transit system.

From the maritime to the moving picture, the city's museums provide an eye-opening educational foray into the past, the present, and, in some cases, the future. Unlike those boring class museum trips of years ago, today's museum fuses the knowledge of well-trained guides with modern technology to best present everything from dinosaur bones to air force fighter jets. Tours, movies, computer educational centers, gift shops, restaurants, and even performances highlight the busy schedules that are the lifeblood of the city's museums.

The museums in this chapter are those found in Manhattan, but we have already covered the *Intrepid* Sea, Air & Space Museum, the American Museum of Natural History, and the Metropolitan Museum of Art (see Chapter 6). There are also several marvelous museums found in the other boroughs and on Long Island, which are covered in Chapter 11.

Visiting New York's Museums

Anyone visiting the city should plan on seeing at least a couple of these cultural institutions. They offer fun and education for the whole family, usually at a reasonable price. More importantly, they offer memories. Youngsters will remind you about the dinosaur that towered high above in the American Museum of Natural History, the sailing vessels at the Maritime Museum at the South Street Seaport, or the fire engines at the New York City Fire Museum. Adults will talk about the works of Picasso and Cézanne at the Museum of Modern Art, the Currier & Ives lithographs at the Museum of the City of New York, or the Temple of Dendur in the Egyptian Exhibit at the Met.

Museums are for the most part accessible to people with disabilities. Call ahead to find out where the accessible entrance is located and to get information on elevators (which are not always easily found).

Maps will help guide you through your museum of choice, and you'll see many people in the museum lobby planning out their course of action for the day. Remember, in the bigger museums, it's not likely that you'll be able to cover everything in one day, so enjoy what you see and leave the rest for another time.

Abigail Adams Smith House Museum

✉ 421 East 61st Street
✆ 212-838-6878

The museum has two parts, formally known as the Abigail Adams Smith House Museum and the Mount Vernon Hotel and Garden Museum. Surrounded by the high-rise apartment buildings that comprise much of the Upper East Side, this quaint house and garden was made into a museum for visitors coming to the 1939 World's Fair in Queens. Once part of a much larger property owned by Abigail Adams (daughter of John Adams) and her husband, Colonel William Smith, the museum you see today was originally a carriage house built in 1799. The neighboring mansion became a hotel in the early nineteenth century. However, when the hotel burned down, this carriage house then became a (much smaller) hotel. It later served as a private residence before becoming a museum.

The stone structure has been refurbished over the years and houses nine rooms of furnishings from the Federal period. The Colonial Dames of America are responsible for the restoration and upkeep of this city landmark. The gardens around the small museum, when in bloom, are quite beautiful.

 TRAVEL TIP

When the admission fee for a museum is a "suggested donation," remember that museums operate thanks to benefactors. The suggestion is a strong one, so consider it an admission price, unless you are on an extremely tight budget.

Friendly and informed tour guides will fill you in on the background and history of this delightful little museum. A gift shop sells books, posters, and other historic items representing the period.

The museum may not merit a separate trip, but if you are shopping at Bloomingdale's, or simply visiting the Upper East Side, it's a nice little place to drop by for an hour or so. There's a tranquility you'll feel as you walk through the gate and step into this little oasis away from the big city.

The museum is a bit of a secret, so it doesn't get too crowded. Don't even think about parking around here, unless you want to find a meter on First Avenue and feed it every hour until 4:00 P.M. (when you have to move your car or lose it to a tow truck).

Location and Hours

The museum is located on East 61st Street, between First and York Avenues. It is accessible by subway via the 4, 5, or 6 train (59th Street station).

The Abigail Adams House Museum is open Monday through Friday from noon to 4 P.M. and Sundays from 1 P.M. to 5 P.M., with later hours on Tuesdays in the summer. The museum is closed in August and on major holidays. Admission is $4 for adults, $3 for seniors and students, and free for children under 12. Call for information and to confirm hours (since they are limited).

Children's Museum of Manhattan

✉Tisch Building, 212 West 83rd Street

✆ 212-721-1234 (information)

✆ 212-721-1223 (staff)

✐ www.cmom.org

A marvelous place to spend an afternoon with the kids, the Children's Museum of Manhattan (CMOM) has hands-on exhibits providing fun for kids ages 2 to 10. Founded in 1973, the museum is designed to enhance learning in five key areas, including literacy, the arts, media and communication, the environment, and early childhood education.

A quarter of a million children visit annually to take part in the various interactive exhibits. The museum hosts a series of traveling children's exhibits on the main floor and in the basement, on such things as the human body, or how an artist develops an idea into artwork. An urban tree house (open May through September) teaches children about their environment.

On the higher floors, you'll find various activity rooms featuring arts and crafts, climbing, and a small theater where puppet shows, storytelling, and other performances are given. The Time Warner Center for the Media allows children to take part in their own television shows on CMOM-TV, with real cameras and a state-of-the-art production center. The museum also provides workshops, classes, and several outreach programs to children and families of the community.

One of the nicest aspects of the museum is that it avoids video and computer-generated activities, allowing children to see, hear, and discover the real sights and sounds around them as they play. This is a museum for children—not about them—designed to pique their interest. You will enjoy seeing it all through their eyes. Get a schedule when you enter, and you'll know what shows or workshops or story readings are taking place that day. When you're done, be sure to wash your children's hands, since hundreds of eager youngsters enjoy the hands-on museum every day.

There is a small gift shop with children's items, including toys and books that emphasize learning. There is no restaurant on the premises. Strollers and food are not allowed, so you'll have to check them when you come in.

Location and Hours

The Children's Museum of Manhattan is located in the Tisch Building on West 83rd Street. It is accessible by subway via the 1 or 9 train (79th or 86th Street station).

The museum is open Wednesday through Sunday and on public school holidays from 10 A.M. to 5 P.M. Admission is $7 for children and adults, $4 for seniors, and free for children under a year old.

The Cloisters

✉ 191st Street in Manhattan
✆ 212-923-3700
✍ www.metmuseum.org

Perched high above the Hudson River and tucked away in Fort Tryon Park is The Cloisters, a marvelous museum dedicated to medieval art and architecture. The Cloisters has one of the most extensive collections in the world of art and artifacts from the period between the twelfth and sixteenth centuries. Byzantine, early Christian, Romanesque, and Gothic works are all represented in this site, run by the Metropolitan Museum of Art.

Silver, enamels, stained glass, metalwork, ivories, jewelry, and fifteenth-century manuscripts are all on exhibit. Among the many highlights are the renowned fifteenth- and sixteenth-century Unicorn Tapestries. From the galleries, you can stroll out into the lavish gardens, with their rich and varied plant life. The building, which opened in 1938, is unusual in that it was built to represent cloisters (places devoted to religious seclusion, such as a monastery) of several different medieval styles, including French and Spanish.

The setting and exhibits complement one another, creating an atmosphere of medieval times; sometimes concerts are held with medieval music, to enhance the experience. Special programs, gallery talks, and other presentations are held on Saturdays.

After your journey to the past, you will want to explore the grounds surrounding the sprawling structure, Fort Tryon Park. Have a truly good lunch at the New Leaf Café or bring a picnic lunch and eat on the grounds of the park, visit the museum, and enjoy the marvelous views of the Hudson River below.

The Cloisters is Upper Manhattan's foremost sight and worth the trip. There is a wonderful gift shop on the premises that is always well stocked with knights and princess paraphernalia for kids, and it's all quite affordable.

≡FAST FACT

Every third weekend of September, the annual medieval festival is held in Fort Tryon Park. There are free jousts, as well as vendors selling medieval wear for kids (plastic lances, shields, and armor) and adults, as well as "medieval" food, such as turkey legs or fried dough. It is a great way to spend a fall afternoon.

Location and Hours

The Cloisters is located at Fort Tryon Park, on 191st Street in Manhattan. It is accessible by subway via the A train (190th Street station).

The museum is open Tuesday through Sunday from 9:30 A.M. to 5:15 P.M. from March through October and until 4:15 P.M. from

November through February. Tours are free. Suggested admission is $8 for adults, and $4 for students and seniors, and free for children. It's suggested you call to confirm in advance.

Cooper-Hewitt National Design Museum

✉ 2 East 91st Street

✆ 212-849-8420

🖰 http://ndm.si.edu

The former estate of Andrew Carnegie, the Cooper-Hewitt National Design Museum is now the last branch of the Smithsonian Institution remaining in New York, now that the Heye collection of Native American art has moved to the National Mall in Washington, D.C. Exhibits include an extensive collection of arts and crafts by designers of outstanding decorative objects in the form of textiles, jewelry, drawings, prints, woodwork, and even wallpaper. In short, if you can think of anything that has been "designed," you might find it here.

The museum initially housed the collections of industrialist Peter Cooper and his granddaughters, Amy, Sarah, and Eleanor Hewitt. Exhibits from the massive collection change every few months, as the Cooper-Hewitt facility is not as large as some of the city's other museums. Still, it does own the Beatles' psychedelic Rolls Royce and has an incredible collection of wallpaper.

A library houses numerous seventeenth- and eighteenth-century books on design and architecture. There is a gift shop on the premises that sells designed objects, books, and gift items. A recent multimillion-dollar renovation has given the Cooper-Hewitt National Design Museum a new look.

Location and Hours

Cooper-Hewitt is accessible by subway via the 4, 5, or 6 train (86th or 96th Street station). Parking in the area is not easy to find, making public transportation your best bet.

The design museum is open Sundays from noon to 5:00 P.M., Tuesdays from 10:00 A.M. to 9:00 P.M., and Wednesday through Saturday from 10:00 A.M. to 5:00 P.M. It is closed on Mondays. There is no restaurant on the premises. Admission is $10 for adults, $7 for seniors and students, and free for children.

☂ RAINY DAY FUN

To save money, you might take advantage of one of several "free" evenings offered by museums, usually for three hours at some point during the week. This is actually wonderful if you have kids who can't handle more than that and makes a different evening out. The Guggenheim has pay-what-you-wish Fridays from 6:00 to 8:00 P.M. and the Jewish Museum has the same policy on Thursday nights.

The Frick Collection

✉ 1 East 70th Street
✆ 212-288-0700
🖳 www.frick.org

You've seen them in numerous art history books; now you can see them in person. They're the paintings by the old masters, appropriately housed in a 1913 mansion that was transformed into a museum in 1935. Henry Clay Frick, former Pittsburgh steel giant, built the mansion as a Manhattan home to house his family and the art collection.

Upon entering the Frick, you'll feel as if you are entering an elegant private mansion. You will head straight for the prime attractions in the living room and foyer. There you'll find great works of art, including Rembrandt's *Self-Portrait* and *The Polish Rider,* along with works by El Greco, Piero della Francesca, Vermeer, Whistler, Goya, and other legendary painters of the fifteenth and sixteenth centuries. The Frick sells a guide to its paintings and offers prerecorded self-guided tours with lively, fascinating commentary about each work.

The collection is so vast that paintings hang by the staircase, in the east wing, which was added in 1977, and even in the garden, where you'll find Edouard Manet's *The Bullfight* (1864). The garden, meanwhile, designed by landscape architect Russell Page, is a marvelous glass-enclosed courtyard that provides a sanctuary from the rest of the city and the rest of the world.

The museum is not as enormous as some of the others along museum row (Fifth Avenue station), but what it lacks in size it more than makes up for in quality; it features a truly priceless collection of awe-inspiring artwork. Lectures and chamber music concerts are also given on occasion. The Frick Library, in an adjacent building, contains hundreds of thousands of photos of the artwork and a quarter of a million publications. The library is open to scholars, students, and artists.

A gift shop sells posters, books, and reproductions of the great works. There is no restaurant. Free lectures and chamber music concerts are occasionally held.

Location and Hours

The Frick is accessible by subway via the 6 train (68th Street station). Parking in the area is very difficult. Although the museum can be covered in a couple of hours, you may want to enjoy a leisurely stroll through the garden.

The Frick is open Tuesday through Saturday from 10:00 A.M. to 6:00 P.M. and Sundays from 1:00 P.M. to 6:00 P.M. and is closed on Mondays and major holidays. Admission is $12 for adults, $8 for seniors, and $5 for students; children under 10 are not admitted.

The Guggenheim Museum

✉ 1071 Fifth Avenue

✆ 212-423-3500

✆ 212-423-3878 (SoHo branch)

✐ *www.guggenheim.org*

The giant spiral shape of the Guggenheim is hard to miss. The distinctive architecture is the work of Frank Lloyd Wright, and the museum features both permanent and special exhibits.

Built in the late 1950s, the Guggenheim was designed to display the vast collection of modern works of Solomon R. Guggenheim. Frank Lloyd Wright died before the building was complete, making this his final masterpiece. Patrons wind their way down the six stories of the sprawling circular structure while viewing great works of art. An additional tower gallery was opened in 1992 with the intention of housing the growing collection of permanent features, but it's a particular favorite with kids who visit. If there is an exhibit of 1960s or 1970s pop art (such as the Claes Oldenburg, James Rosenquist, or Robert Rauschenberg or even the Harley-Davidson exhibits of the past), this is the perfect place to launch a child's love of art.

TRAVEL TIP

Although most museums are closed on Mondays, some New York museums are closed on different days. The Guggenheim is closed on Thursdays, the Museum of Modern Art (MoMA) is closed on Wednesdays, and the Jewish Museum is closed on Saturdays.

Inside the Guggenheim, visitors can enjoy the works of French impressionists, cubists, surrealists, and the Abstract Expressionists. Picasso, Chagall, Klee, Kandinsky, Degas, Manet, Toulouse-Lautrec, and van Gogh are all represented in a seemingly priceless collection. In 1990 the museum acquired more than 200 works of American minimalist art from the 1960s and 1970s, and in 1993, 200 photographs by Robert Mapplethorpe introduced photography into the permanent collection.

The museum has an entire program of special events for families. These often include a meeting with some of the most important artists in America, so go online before you come, and buy the tickets to these events ahead of time. It could be a once-in-a-lifetime event!

On the premises, you will find a museum store featuring books on contemporary and modern art, plus gifts, jewelry, toys, and various other unique items. The museum café is a casual place to grab a snack.

Location and Hours

The Guggenheim is located on Fifth Avenue between 88th and 89th Streets. It is accessible by subway via the 4, 5, or 6 train (86th Street station).

Admission to the Guggenheim is $15 for adults, $10 for students and senior citizens, and free for children under 12. The price includes admission to the downtown Guggenheim SoHo Branch, which opened in 1992; it's located at 575 Broadway by Prince Street and houses 30,000 square feet of exhibits in six additional galleries. Hours for the Guggenheim are Monday through Wednesday from 10:00 A.M. to 6:00 P.M. and Friday through Sunday from 10:00 A.M. to 8:00 P.M. On Fridays, from 6:00 to 8:00 P.M., the museum has a pay what you wish policy. The museum is closed on Thursdays.

≡FAST FACT

The Upper East Side along Fifth Avenue is known as Museum Mile, where several of the city's premier museums are located, including the Metropolitan Museum of Art, the Guggenheim (which also has a SoHo branch), and the Museum of the City of New York.

Jewish Museum

✉ 1109 Fifth Avenue at 92nd Street
☎ 212-423-3200
🖰 www.jewishmuseum.org

The Jewish Museum celebrated its 100th anniversary in 2004. It is housed in a mansion that was built at the start of the twentieth century. The history presented within these walls dates back thousands of years, recounting the story of the Jewish people. The lower two floors of the four-story structure are set up for ongoing special exhibitions; the top two floors house a permanent exhibit, "Culture and Continuity: The Jewish Journey."

In the permanent collection, you'll find artifacts (such as those from the ancient Dura Europos synagogue, built many centuries ago), along with photographs and texts. From the exodus out of Egypt to the festival of Hanukkah, the drama and significance of the stories are evident. There is also a section dedicated to rituals and Jewish tradition, featuring ancient prayer shawls, menorahs, wedding cups, and other items, plus a film explaining some of the longtime traditions.

Another section is devoted to the Holocaust. Although this is not the focus of the museum as a whole, it is included as part of a much larger history. There is also a section of the museum dedicated to the history of anti-Semitism. Representative work by Jewish artists is included in the various sections. A film and artwork reflecting Jewish culture in the contemporary world, plus a children's gallery, round out the substantial museum. In fact, with the expansion in the early 1990s, this is now the largest Jewish museum devoted to culture and history outside of Israel.

The exhibitions, the films, and computers (providing information and even asking philosophical questions from the Talmud) can take several hours to experience fully. There is often a wait to get in, so plan early and, as with most of the city's museums, try for a weekday. A gift shop offers books and other items relating to Jewish culture. You'll also find a café on the premises.

Location and Hours

The Jewish Museum is located on Fifth Avenue at 92nd Street. It is accessible by subway via the 4, 5, or 6 train (96th Street station).

The museum is open Sundays, Mondays, Wednesdays, and Thursdays from 11:00 A.M. to 5:45 P.M. and on Tuesdays from 11:00 A.M. to 8:00 P.M. It is closed on Saturdays. Admission is $10 for adults, $7 for seniors, and free for children under 12. On Thursday evenings from 5:00 to 8:00 P.M., the museum has a pay-what-you-wish program—and it's very busy.

 TRAVEL TIP

Museums, in general, are not always known for fine dining. The food in the museums runs the gamut from sit-down restaurants, such as the marvelous Sunday brunch at the New Leaf Café (partially brought to us by the good graces of Bette Midler), to cafeteria-style food and basics like hot dogs, sandwiches, and snack foods.

Lower East Side Tenement Museum

✉ 90 Orchard Street

✆ 212-431-0233

✎ *www.tenement.org*

Housed in an actual tenement that was home to a total of more than 7,000 immigrants in the years from 1863 to 1935, the museum offers several guided tours through furnished rooms stocked with photos and artifacts. Together, these tell the story of the immigrants who lived not only here but throughout the part of Manhattan known as the Lower East Side.

The museum, chartered in 1988, is small (compared to the massive museums of Upper Manhattan), and exemplifies urban dwelling and the immigrant experience. Several first-rate tour guides recount the stories of different families who lived in the tenement and describe the possessions that were donated to the museum.

Across the street at the visitors' center, visitors can view a film featuring interviews with historians and former residents of the old tenement. A slide show called *Urban Pioneers* describes the history of the tenement. Free outdoor exhibits are also featured. A gift shop sells books and other materials relating to the Lower East Side. Walking tours and other special tours highlight aspects of the surrounding neighborhood.

This museum should appeal to anyone whose family first settled in the Lower East Side after stepping off a ship onto Ellis Island. It's truly inspiring to learn how so many people managed to survive and even prosper in this neighborhood of poor immigrants.

Location and Hours

The Tenement Museum is located on Orchard Street. It is accessible by subway via the B or D train (Grand or Delancey Street station). You can also find free parking in the lot on Broome Street, between Norfolk and Suffolk, for up to four hours.

The museum is accessible by guided tours only, which take about an hour. The cost is $10 for adults and $8 for students and seniors. Tours begin in the visitor center Tuesday through Friday on the hour from 1 to 4 P.M. and on Saturdays and Sundays from 11 A.M. to 4:30 P.M. It is strongly recommended that you make a reservation or buy tickets ahead of time over the Internet.

Museum of Modern Art

✉ 11 East 53rd Street

✆ 202-708-9400

✐ *www.moma.org*

The Museum of Modern Art has just undergone an $858-million renovation that doubled the size of this important museum. It is set to reopen in November 2004, when the museum will celebrate its seventy-fifth anniversary. Between May 2002 and November 2004, items from the museum's permanent collection have been relocated to a site in Long Island City in Queens. Though you won't be able to see all the classic works from the museum's permanent collection at the temporary Queens location, you can still see Rousseau's *Sleeping Gypsy* and scores of works by Matisse, Picasso, Cézanne, Miró, Mondrian, Brancusi, and Pollock.

The new museum will be 63,000 feet and will incorporate some of the original design elements of Philip Johnson's 1953 design, such as the sculpture garden, in the new concept designed by Yoshio Taniguchi.

The Museum's Design Shop is still open during the renovation. It is located across the street at 44 West 53rd Street (call for info at ☎ 212-767-1050). A second shop at 81st Spring Street (information at ☎ 212-613-1367) is also open.

See Chapter 11 for information about the temporary MOMA museum, including location and directions.

Location and Hours

The Museum of Modern Art is located on East 53rd Street, between Fifth and Sixth Avenues. It is accessible by subway via the E and V train (53rd Street/Fifth Avenue station).

RAINY DAY FUN

Raining in New York? Head to the Museum of Television & Radio, where you and your kids can watch just about anything you want. It's a great way to introduce your kids to memories from your childhood. Favorites include old *Twilight Zone* and *Batman* episodes, as well as the video of the moon landing.

Museum of Television & Radio

✉ 25 West 52nd Street

☎ 212-661-6600

🖰 *www.mtr.org*

There is not a child in America who does not love this museum. Established in 1965 by William Paley and later moved to this sleek Midtown location, the Museum of Television & Radio is essentially a place to watch old television programs or listen to radio programs. Special tributes and galleries highlight the early years of television. Old television shows on display include Edward R. Murrow broadcasts and the Beatles' first appearance on *The Ed Sullivan*

Show (the most watched program at the museum). Vintage commercials provide a fascinating, whimsical glimpse of the past five decades and illustrate how society has changed.

Two theaters and a screening room, however, are used for interesting seminars and special evenings dedicated to television luminaries. The schedule for these gatherings is worth checking out. There's a small gift shop in the lobby.

Location and Hours

The Museum of Television & Radio is located on West 52nd Street between Fifth and Sixth Avenues. It is accessible by subway via the E and V train (53rd Street/Fifth Avenue station).

The museum has free tours on Tuesdays and is open Tuesday through Sunday from noon to 6 P.M., except Thursdays when the museum is open until 8 P.M. Admission is $10 for adults, $8 for students and seniors, and $5 for children under 14.

RAINY DAY FUN

Every Saturday from 10:00 A.M. until noon, the Museum of Television & Radio offers a special radio re-enactment where up to twenty kids (over the age of 9) get to re-enact an old radio play from the original script with sound effects. It's $7 per person, and you have to make a reservation, but you can take home a tape!

Museum of the City of New York

✉ 1220 Fifth Avenue

✆ 212-534-1672

🖳 *www.mcny.org*

If you're visiting New York City, why not learn firsthand about its history? This is one of two museums (along with the museum of the New-York Historical Society) devoted to the history of the city it calls home. With an enormous wealth of materials of all types, this is, perhaps, the more "fun" of the two galleries paying homage to New York City.

Set in a massive mansion looking out on the northern portion of Central Park, the Museum of the City of New York offers provocative special exhibitions along with a wide range of permanent exhibits celebrating different aspects of the city. It's a good idea to choose your favorites, as you'll never get to all of it in one day.

Major exhibits found in the vast museum include the prints and photography collection. This group includes thousands of photographs to trace the history of New York City, along with the largest known collection of Currier & Ives lithographs.

You don't have to be a theater aficionado to appreciate the stunning theater collection celebrating the Great White Way, Broadway, and American theater. Costumes and memorabilia, set designs, posters, paintings, and photographs recount the legends of the Broadway stage as well as Yiddish theater, which thrived in New York in the early twentieth century.

A decorative arts collection includes precious metals and other rare items. The highlight is a look at New York's furniture from 1790 through 1890, some of which is built better than furniture made in 1990.

The exhibit "New York Toy Stories" is a tribute to toys of the children of the city, dating back to the 1800s. Cast-iron toys, wooden soldiers, mechanical toys, rare dolls, boats, and renowned dollhouses are on display in this unique exhibit that all ages can enjoy.

The museum shop sells items relating to the exhibits and to the city of New York, including books, videos, and toys (not the ones on display, but some good reproductions). You can buy New York City photo reproductions or reproductions of Currier & Ives prints that provide a nice reminder of your trip (even better than postcards).

There is no restaurant in the museum and few choices in the surrounding blocks, so eat before or after your visit.

Location and Hours

The Museum of the City of New York is located on Fifth Avenue at 103rd Street. It is accessible by subway via the 4, 5, or 6 train (103rd Street station). The museum does not have parking, and it's not easy to find a space in this area, so take public transportation.

The museum is open Wednesday through Saturday from 10:00 A.M. to 5:00 P.M. Tuesdays are for tour groups only. On Mondays and all legal holidays, the museum is closed. Fees vary depending on the length of the tour and the program. Suggested admission to the museum is $7 for adults; $5 for seniors, students, and children; and $12 for families.

Neue Galerie New York

✉ 1048 Fifth Avenue
✆ 212-628-6200
✐ *www.neuegalerie.org*

This recently opened gem of a museum, dedicated to modern German and Austrian art, is housed in a beautifully restored 1914 mansion designed by architects Carrère and Hastings, designers of the New York Public Library building. It has impressive collections of works on Vienna at the turn of the nineteenth century, including many works by Gustav Klimt, Oskar Kokoschka, and their contemporaries. There are many examples of the German decorative arts, as well as architecture. Two close friends started the museum, an art collector and a museum exhibitor who shared a passion for this period in art.

Location and Hours

Neue Galerie New York is located on Fifth Avenue and 86th Street. It is accessible by subway via the 4, 5, or 6 train (86th Street station).

This private museum really is very private. It is closed Tuesday through Thursday. Children under 12 are not allowed, and parents must accompany children under 16. Admission is $10 for adults and $7 for seniors and students. The Neue Galerie is open 11:00 A.M. to 6:00 P.M. Saturdays, Sundays, and Mondays and 11:00 A.M. until 9:00 P.M. on Fridays.

≡FAST FACT

The Dakota Apartments on Central Park West and 72nd Street was the site of John Lennon's assassination. It had been used as the model for the Bram in Ira Levin's *Rosemary's Baby*. Recently steam-cleaned, it is now a tan color, but many New Yorkers prefer this pricey co-op's darker look. The home of Roberta Flack, Lauren Bacall, and Rex Reed, it was built in 1884 and was designed by the architect who designed the Plaza Hotel.

The New York City Fire Museum

✉ 278 Spring Street
✆ 212-691-1303
⌨ *www.nycfiremusem.org*

No, it's not the Metropolitan Museum of Art, but to a five-year-old, it's probably a lot more fun. Set in a 1904 firehouse, with tours by real firemen, the museum provides a walk through the history of firefighting, from horse-drawn carriages to modern "jaws of life" rescue equipment.

But the museum is more than a display of firefighting equipment. For those who want to learn a bit more about "New York's Bravest," especially in the wake of September 11, there is information about aspects of firefighting skills and equipment, including the hose, hydrant, ladders, and so on. You'll even learn about animals that have helped fight fires, including the Dalmatian, which has become the mascot of firefighters everywhere.

Exhibits range from toy fire trucks to very real shields, uniforms, and fireboat equipment. In contrast to other museums, you might find this one less crowded on the weekends, when the class trips aren't visiting. Although they probably won't appreciate the historical aspects, it's a great place to stop by with the kids for a couple of hours, particularly if you are planning a day at other Lower Manhattan sights, such as the Stock Exchange, which may be less interesting to a six-year-old.

The museum gift shop sells toys, books, and T-shirts. The museum has no restaurant, but there are plenty of places to eat in the area.

 JUST FOR PARENTS

While the kids are looking at the uniforms and old firefighting tools, you might want to look at the memorial exhibit featuring photos, paintings, children's artwork, and found objects from the site of the September 11 terrorist attacks, where 343 firefighters lost their lives.

Location and Hours

The New York City Fire Museum is located on Spring Street, between Hudson and Varick. It's accessible by subway via the C or E train (Spring Street station). Some parking is available in front, but as usual it's probably best to take public transportation.

The museum is open Tuesday through Sunday from 10 A.M. to 4 P.M. Suggested admission is $5 for adults, $2 for students or seniors, and $1 for children under 12.

The New York City Police Museum

✉ 100 Old Slip
✆ 212-480-3100
🖱 *www.nycpolicemuseum.org*

This 158-year-old museum highlights the history of the police in New York City. It features some wonderful exhibits on tracking down criminals, fingerprinting, and forensics, topics that are all quite "hot" at the moment with kids. There is a Hall of Heroes for the officers who were killed in the line of duty. There is also a special memorial to commemorate the police and port authority officers killed in the terrorist attacks of September 11.

Location and Hours

The New York City Police Museum is located on Old Slip near South Street. It is accessible by subway via the R or W train (White Hall station) or the 4 or 5 train (Bowling Green station). Open Tuesdays through Sundays, 10:00 A.M. to 5:00 P.M. Suggested admission is $5 per person.

The New-York Historical Society

✉ 2 West 77th Street

✆ 212-873-3400

🖥 *www.nyhistory.org*

Founded in 1804, when "New-York" was still hyphenated, the museum houses literally millions of examples of Americana, including books, newspapers, maps, manuscripts, photographs, silverware, antique toys, posters, political cartoons, architectural drawings, carriages, furniture, and much, much more. The second oldest historical society in the country, the society's goal is to preserve all kinds of materials related to the city of New York. From George Washington's inaugural chair to the world's largest collection of Tiffany lamps, a wealth of cultural history is represented here. Furniture is displayed chronologically so that you can take notice of the changes in design and style through the centuries. Two artistic highlights of this museum that you should not miss are the gallery of 1830s paintings from the collection of Luman Reed and the watercolors by John James Audubon—432 of them!—for his book *Birds of America*. There are also changing exhibits featuring items from the collection.

The historical society has a gift shop but no restaurant on the premises. Also found here is one of the most extensive American history research libraries you'll ever encounter.

Location and Hours

The New-York Historical Society is located at 2 West 77th Street at Central Park West. It is accessible by subway via the 1, 2, 3, or 9 train (72nd Street station). Parking is difficult, so unless you want to pay for a neighborhood garage (if they have room), take public transportation.

The museum is open Tuesday through Saturday from 11:00 A.M. to 6:00 P.M. The library closes at 5:00 P.M. An adult must accompany any children. You can probably cover the museum in half a day at a leisurely pace. Admission is $8 for adults and $5 for students, seniors, and children. Guided tours are at 1:00 and 3:00 P.M. They generally focus on certain sections of the museum, so ask if they cover the area(s) of interest to you.

 TRAVEL TIP

CityPass is a wonderful way to save money. For $45 for adults, and $39 for children, you can visit seven of the city's most popular attractions: the Empire State Building Observatory and Skyride; the American Museum of Natural History; the Metropolitan Museum of Art; the Guggenheim Museum; the Museum of Modern Art; and the *Intrepid* Sea, Air & Space Museum. You can buy the CityPass at any of the sites or online at ✎ *www.citypass.com.*

The Studio Museum in Harlem

✉ 144 West 125th Street
✆ 212-864-4500
✎ *www.studiomuseum.org*

The Studio Museum opened in 1968 as an exhibition space. It has grown over the past thirty-two years into a full-fledged museum, with galleries, workshops, and even a sculpture garden.

Recently, new permanent galleries have opened that add another 72,000 square feet of exhibit space to the current galleries. The collection includes nineteenth- and twentieth-century African-American paintings, sculptures, twentieth-century Caribbean art, and traditional and contemporary art and artifacts from Africa.

Some 100,000 visitors yearly browse the galleries that make up Harlem's premier museum. The museum should not disappoint anyone, especially those interested in African-American art.

Location and Hours

The Studio Museum in Harlem is located on West 125th Street. It is accessible by subway via the A, B, C, or D train (125th Street station). Public transportation is the best way to get there, but there is parking in a municipal lot on 125th Street and Lenox Avenue.

The museum is open Wednesday through Friday and Sundays from noon to 5:00 P.M. and on Saturdays from noon to 6:00 P.M. It is closed Mondays and Tuesdays. A museum shop in the lobby sells books and gift items relating to the exhibits of the museum. Admission is $7 for adults and $5 for students and seniors.

Whitney Museum of American Art

✉ 945 Madison Avenue and 120 Park Avenue (two locations)
✆ 1-877-WHITNEY
✎ www.whitney.org

Founded in 1930, the Whitney now houses more then 12,000 works of art by nearly 2,000 artists. The museum features twentieth-century and contemporary American art including paintings, sculpture, photography, and more. Most famous for its awesome collection of New York impressionist painters of the Ash Can school, it has an extensive collection of works from the estate of Edward Hopper. Also included in the Whitney's collection are examples of Alexander Calder's circus figures as well as his mobiles. People are also fond of the works of Beckman, Marsh, Gorky, Hartley, and others that are part of the permanent exhibits viewed by nearly half a million visitors each year.

The current 1966 building, designed by German Bauhaus architect Marcel Breuer (of Breuer chair fame) was recently expanded by 7,600 square feet. It is actually the third structure to house this famous collection started by Gertrude Vanderbilt Whitney. The oddly shaped building is a work of art itself, surrounded by a sculpture garden and walls.

≡FAST FACT

For more than half a century, the Whitney Biennial has been the place where emerging artists launch their careers. It is also the place where New Yorkers see the rest of the art world, and you would be surprised how many kids are in attendance. If you are lucky enough to be visiting during a biennial year, try to make this event. Any material that is inappropriate for children will be marked as such outside the room.

Sarabeth's Restaurant is open for lunch and brunch within the Whitney. The Whitney Museum Store and Museum Bookstore offer gift ideas and books primarily about American art.

The museum has an extensive program of family and children's art activities. Go online before exploring and see if there is a half-day program when you are visiting. It will be worth it!

Location and Hours

The Whitney Museum of American Art is located on Madison Avenue at 75th Street. It is accessible by subway via the 4, 5, or 6 train (77th Street station). There is also a branch at 120 Park Avenue at 42nd Street across the street from Grand Central Station. Take public transportation; this is a very busy area, not known for its street parking.

The museum is open Tuesday through Sunday from 11:00 A.M. to 6:00 P.M., except Thursday, when hours shift to 1:00 to 8:00 P.M. The Whitney is closed on Monday. Admission is $12 for adults, $9.50 for seniors and students with a valid ID, and free for children under 12. Admission is also free for New York City high school students with a valid ID.

CHAPTER 10

The Boroughs

FOR MANY, "THE CITY" refers to Manhattan only. Even residents of the Bronx, Queens, Staten Island, or Brooklyn will say, "We're going to the city for the evening," without considering that they are already in the city. But more than 80 percent of New York's population lives outside of Manhattan—in Queens, Brooklyn, the Bronx, and Staten Island—and they have developed exciting, different communities full of great restaurants and shopping that are worth visiting on their own. You can get almost anywhere in the boroughs from midtown Manhattan in about forty-five minutes by train.

With the Museum of Modern Art's temporary relocation Long Island City and the terrific Isamu Noguchi Museum, Queens is one of the great day trips for art. Any baseball lover will have to visit Yankee Stadium in the Bronx or Shea Stadium in Queens, and Brooklyn has its Dodger history as well. The Bronx Zoo is a world-class attraction, as is the Brooklyn Aquarium. The view of the Manhattan skyline and the Statue of Liberty are just incredible from that twenty-minute ride on the Staten Island Ferry, so venture beyond the shores of Manhattan. You'll be amazed and amused.

The History of the Boroughs

New York City's five boroughs, along with the New Amsterdam Settlement of Lower Manhattan, grew in population through the eighteenth and nineteenth centuries and established themselves as independent communities of their own. Although the boroughs were officially united as a city in 1898, it was the subway system of the early 1900s that made commuting between four of the five boroughs much easier. This allowed the diverse populations of the city to expand into the Bronx, Brooklyn, and Queens. Subway connections made the boroughs outside of Manhattan far more easily accessible.

RAINY DAY FUN

After a few hours in New York, you'll realize that New Yorkers have a real passion for the borough they live in. Street vendors have finally caught on to this, and now you can buy T-shirts, baseball caps, and sweatshirts with "Brooklyn" or "The Bronx" emblazoned on them. Queens and Staten Island just don't seem as popular.

Much of the land in the boroughs was once farmland, but today you'd be hard pressed to find many farms. All four of the "other" boroughs are vibrant centers of activity, with private homes and apartments complemented by numerous small businesses, office buildings, parks, and even beaches. Millions of New Yorkers commute into Manhattan every day for work; many others work within the boroughs.

Venturing Outside Manhattan

Most vacationers to New York City will likely spend the bulk of their trip in Manhattan, unless they have a particular reason (such as visiting family or friends) to spend much time in the other four boroughs. There is, however, a lot to see and do in the other boroughs. From seafood at Sheepshead Bay in Brooklyn to the hot dogs at Yankee Stadium in the Bronx, there are a host of flavors that characterize each borough and a large multicultural population to match. Brooklyn, home to more than 4 million New Yorkers, is large enough to qualify as the fourth largest city in America. Staten Island, on the other hand, is the least populated of the boroughs, with only 400,000 residents.

 **TRAVEL TIP**

There are municipal parking lots in every borough (even Manhattan) that charge $2 an hour in quarters. Go to the New York City Web site, ✑ *www.nyc.gov*, and search for municipal lots. If you plan on parking on the metered streets of New York or in municipal lots, go to the bank and get a roll of quarters to keep in the glove compartment. Store owners will not change your dollar bills into quarters for free, and they won't give you more than a dollar's worth with a purchase.

Runners in the New York City Marathon (which takes place in November) actually manage to make their way through all five boroughs, beginning in the morning in Staten Island and ending in the afternoon in Manhattan, at the finish line in Central Park. For most of us, however, it's more enjoyable to explore the boroughs on separate trips.

Getting There and Getting Around

You can get to any of the boroughs by public transportation, but some sections are hard to reach by train and will require an additional trip by bus. There are also a number of express buses that service the various neighborhoods in the boroughs, as well as stops on MetroNorth and the Long Island Railroad in Queens.

Most people drive in the boroughs. Traffic can be difficult on major roadways at peak hours, but in general driving is a preferred way of getting around in the four "other" boroughs, especially if you have an itinerary of several sights planned. Bus service is not as frequent as in Manhattan; subways only go to certain destinations in each borough; and taxis are not easily found, unless you call for one.

Parking is easier than in Manhattan in many areas, although in some highly residential neighborhoods, such as Forest Hills in Queens, it can still be very tough. Ask about the parking and traffic and whether or not a subway or express bus goes to your destination. (The city has privately run express bus service to and from many prime locations in the boroughs.) You can call the city's information line, at ✆ 311 (or ✆ 212-NEW-YORK from outside the city), and they will tell you which express buses service your desired destination.

 TRAVEL TIP

Manhattan is the only borough that uses the 212 area code. The Bronx, Brooklyn, Queens, and Staten Island all require you to dial 718. In the last year, a 646 area code has been added to the Manhattan calling area that can also be used for a cell phone. However, 917 is the most frequently used area code for New York City cell phones.

Bridges will get you from one borough to the other. For example, the Verrazano Bridge connects Staten Island and Brooklyn, the Whitestone Bridge and Throggs Neck Bridge connect Queens and the Bronx, and so on. Local streets such as Atlantic Avenue as well as major roadways like the Jackie Robinson Parkway and the Brooklyn Queens Expressway will take you from Brooklyn to Queens or vice versa.

Visiting Brooklyn

Ebbets Field and the Brooklyn Dodgers, the Cyclone at Coney Island, Jackie Gleason, and *The Honeymooners* are all part of the rich culture that characterizes New York City's second-most visited borough.

The onetime home of Woody Allen, Mae West, Neil Diamond, Mel Brooks, Barbra Streisand, and numerous other celebrities, Brooklyn is the composite of numerous distinctively ethnic neighborhoods including Brighton Beach, with its large Ukrainian and Russian population, the Italian community of Bensonhurst, and the numerous Orthodox Jews that make up Borough Park.

There's no doubt as you drive or walk through different sections of Brooklyn that the neighborhoods take on their own identities. Park Slope, for example, is a trendy outgrowth of Manhattan, with fashionable shops and cafés. Sheepshead Bay is home to seafood fresh from the fishing boats that dock at the marina. Brooklyn Heights, sitting high on a hill overlooking Manhattan, is still a posh neighborhood, founded in the early nineteenth century as a suburban alternative to "city life." Bensonhurst is an older Italian-American neighborhood, rich with tradition. Row houses and red brick buildings characterize the various residential neighborhoods, stores line the busy streets, and municipal buildings make up the downtown section of the busy borough.

There is plenty to enjoy while visiting Brooklyn, including Manhattan Beach and Coney Island, a wealth of activities in Prospect Park (which houses the borough's only zoo), the Brooklyn Aquarium, the children's museum, and various historical sights. You can stroll through the galleries of Williamsburg or along the Brooklyn Heights Promenade, or you can stop at a bistro in Park Slope. A seafood dinner in Sheepshead Bay can be topped off with an evening at New York's oldest comedy club, Pips, or you might drop by a hot club in emerging Fort Greene or Prospect Park. A ride along the Belt Parkway will take you along the shoreline around the borough.

While Brooklyn is home to a lot of small, tight-knit neighborhoods, the overall borough is one in which residents take great pride. It truly is a city within a city.

≡FAST FACT

DUMBO (Down Under the Brooklyn Bridge Overpass) is Brooklyn's answer to Manhattan's SoHo. It has become the location for a number of art galleries, as well as some very nice cafés and restaurants.

Destination Queens

The largest of the five boroughs, Queens has been the home of two World's Fairs, the city's two major airports, the Mets, Queens College (its heralded alumni include Jerry Seinfeld, Paul Simon, and Marvin Hamlisch), and more. Queens is a far-reaching borough in the center of it all. It connects to Manhattan and the Bronx by bridge and to Brooklyn and Long Island by land.

Named for Queen Catherine, the wife of King Charles II of England, and colonized in 1683, the sprawling borough of Queens combines a taste of the suburbs with an urban flavor. There are a host of major highways zigzagging their way through the borough, connecting with Long Island and New York's two major international airports. The maze of roads was developed because of the two World's Fairs that were held here in the twentieth century.

Numerous architectural styles typify the various neighborhoods, including old red brick buildings, row houses, and attached houses of the 1950s and 1960s. There are large estates in the aptly named area of Jamaica Estates, and a quaint old-fashioned, wall-enclosed residential community called Forest Hills Gardens. You will also find some modern office buildings springing up—along with movie studios—in Long Island City.

Not unlike Brooklyn, Queens has its share of ethnically diverse neighborhoods. The borough is most famous for its wonderful

Greek restaurants in Astoria and its own Chinatown in Flushing. In fact, a total of more than 120 languages are spoken by Queens residents. In the middle of this multilingual borough is the Unisphere, a giant metal sculpture of the globe, in Flushing Meadow Park. Once a garbage dump, the park was transformed into the fairgrounds to host the 1939 and later the 1964 World's Fairs.

Queens is often the first part of New York that visitors will see if flying into the city. Once out of baggage claim, you are likely to be on either the Van Wyck or Grand Central Expressways en route to Manhattan. A return trip for a visit, however, can take you to one of a few historical sights, a ballgame at Shea Stadium, tennis at the U.S. Open, or a film or science museum.

 TRAVEL TIP

Driving in Queens can take some getting used to. Avenues and streets can have the same name, because they are numbered, so you might find yourself on a crossroad between 20th Drive and 20th Avenue.

The borough is home to the Kaufman Astoria and Silvercup film studios, just a stone's throw from Manhattan. The studios are once again thriving. In fact, Queens was host to a great number of classic films made by screen stars of the 1920s and 1930s, including Edward G. Robinson, Marlene Dietrich, the Marx Brothers, and many others. It is hoped that at least one of the studios will add guided tours and provide another fun stop for tourists and New Yorkers to visit.

The Bronx

The Yankees (or "Bronx Bombers," as they're also known), the famed Bronx Zoo, a spectacular botanical garden, Edgar Allan Poe's house, one of the oldest golf courses in the country, and a small island of fishermen and fabulous seafood restaurants are all found in the Bronx.

The borough was named after Jonas Bronck, a Swedish sailor who built a farm on the land in the seventeenth century. By the nineteenth century, fashionable estates, parks, the Botanical Gardens, and other marvelously landscaped areas set the tone. Homes were spread out, and life was grand along the Grand Concourse, the major thoroughfare of the borough. It wasn't until the twentieth century, and after World War II in particular, that the Bronx started to reflect the poverty and despair that has plagued much of the borough over the past twenty-five years.

 JUST FOR PARENTS

Who would believe that one of the most romantic sites in all of New York is in the Bronx? In the middle of City Island, there is a tiny inn and restaurant called the Refuge Inn (at ✆718-885-1519). Run by two French immigrants, it is the perfect spot for a city getaway or just a very romantic dinner for two.

While areas like the South Bronx epitomize urban decay with their tenements, burned out buildings, and boarded up storefronts, parts of the Bronx have survived and others have seen growth. Apartment complexes like the massive Co-op City brought afford-able housing to many in the housing crunch of the 1960s and 1970s. Fordham University, meanwhile, continued to be a leading educational institution, and the borough's longtime landmark sights remained popular, keeping the Bronx a viable location for visitors. Parks like Van Cortlandt, spanning 1,146 acres, with numerous attractions including the oldest municipal golf course in the country and horseback riding, and mansions like Wave Hill in the fashion-able section of Riverdale, epitomize the history of the only borough attached to the mainland.

Like most of the city, the Bronx has a wonderful diversity of ethnic neighborhoods, including the Caribbean section of Williamsbridge and Woodlawn and the Italian-based Belmont, with its local shops, bakeries, and old-time New York flavor.

Staten Island

The Rodney Dangerfield of the boroughs, Staten Island gets no respect. It's the only borough that has never had a major league baseball team, and it still remains separated from the subways that connect the other four boroughs. Until 1964, the year that saw the opening of the Verrazano Bridge, Staten Island was even more separated from the rest of the city. To many New Yorkers, Staten Island is still an enigma. Ask a resident of the other four boroughs to name a neighborhood in Staten Island, and most won't be able to do so.

The History

Staten Island's inclusion as part of the city came as a prize in a sailing contest in 1687, when the Duke of York gave the island to Manhattan. Residents of the borough today, in response to being the "fifth wheel," sometimes talk of separating from the rest of New York City. In fact, in 1993 they voted to do so, but it never happened. In time, the borough may well become a separate city.

RAINY DAY FUN

Even native New Yorkers don't know that Staten Island has a zoo. It's small but that's what makes it so charming. You'll find a South American rain forest, a reptile house, an aquarium, a children's center, and an "African Savannah at Twilight." For more information, call them at ☎ 718-442-3100 or visit their Web site at ✉ www.statenislandzoo.org.

While it remains part of New York City, Staten Island is a suburban, sprawling setting, rich with its own ethnic and cultural diversity. The island is an enjoyable twenty-five-minute ferry ride from Manhattan. Less densely settled than the other boroughs, it has several large open spaces, including the Greenbelt, La Tourette Park, Willowbrook Park, William T. Davis Wildlife Refuge, and various significant attractions, including Historic Richmond Town and the Snug Harbor Cultural Center.

Other cultural attractions include the Garibaldi-Meucci Museum, housed in a converted farmhouse, and the Jacques Marchais Museum of Tibetan Art, housed in a building designed to look like a Tibetan temple. It even has a small zoo. A day trip to Staten Island can cover the sights and sounds of this often-overlooked but very pleasant borough. And you'll be able to tell friends (and many New Yorkers) about an area they haven't yet taken the time to visit.

CHAPTER 11

Borough Museums and Other Attractions

ONCE YOU MAKE UP YOUR MIND to explore the city outside the confines of Manhattan, there's just no going back. When you realize how much there is to see outside that crowded twenty-mile island, and how easy it is to get there, you feel like you've been offered a whole other look at New York City.

And you have. Outside of midtown Manhattan, there is a whole "secret" New York that only native New Yorkers, passionate sports fans, inquiring gourmets, and the truly adventurous have ever really explored. In its own way, the boroughs are fairly uncharted territory and absolutely wonderful.

Brooklyn Museums and Attractions

You'd be surprised at what a delightful day you can have in Brooklyn visiting museums, gardens, and fun restaurants. In size and population, Brooklyn is as big as many of our country's larger cities.

The New York City Transit Museum
✉ Boerum Place and Schermerhorn Street
✆ 718-330-3060
✍ *www.mta.nyc.ny.us/mta/museum*

What better place to house a transit museum than in an old subway station from the 1930s. Yes, the subways of New York can be crowded, and the stations can be roasting hot during the summer months, but there is a rich history to the subways that lurk below the city streets. The museum, which opened in 1976 in a station that had been closed some thirty years earlier, houses some 4,000 artifacts, including scale models of historic trains, mosaics, a bus and trolley exhibit, an assortment of turnstiles, tools, artwork, a working signal, and more. Drawings, posters, and photographs show the transition of the city through its subways, but the most representative examples are eighteen restored subway cars.

RAINY DAY FUN

Brooklyn also has a great interactive children's museum, the Brooklyn Children's Museum at ✉145 Brooklyn Avenue in Crown Heights (on the Web at ✑ *www.brooklynkids.org*). Here, kids can crawl through tunnels and pet animals. There's a free trolley service to the Brooklyn Children's Museum from the Brooklyn Museum of Art.

Some 150,000 visitors come to the Transit Museum annually to get a glimpse of what New York's underground has looked like over the past century. Lectures, excursions, walking tours, and other programs explore the transportation facilities and their impact on the city. Special events include art exhibition openings, demonstrations of emergency rescues, an annual bus festival with vintage city buses, and more. The Transit Museum store and annex opened in 1999 in Grand Central Station (in Manhattan), selling and displaying other items relating to the transit system, including "token" watches, strap-hanger ties, and more.

Location and Hours
The New York City Transit Museum is located on Boerum Place and Schermerhorn Street. It is accessible by subway via the 2, 3,

4, or 5 train (Borough Hall station). It is open Tuesday through Friday from 10:00 A.M. to 4:00 P.M. Admission is $5 for adults and $3 for children.

Coney Island

Coney is the English spelling for the Dutch word *konijn,* meaning rabbit. Coney Island was named for the many rabbits that were once found in the area, but it is not actually an island. The neighborhood is located along Surf Avenue between 37th Street and Ocean Parkway in Brooklyn. Coney Island is accessible by subway via the D, F, and Q trains.

Coney Island was once the hotspot of the borough, billed as the World's Largest Playground. It its heyday, the early 1900s, attractions like an elephant-shaped hotel, a replica of Baghdad called Luna Park, and a popular nightspot called Dreamland drew large crowds, along with the always popular beach, amusement park, and 2.5-mile boardwalk.

Today, a stroll on the boardwalk is the perfect way to take in the sea air, and the beach is the place for sun and relaxation in the summer heat. Nathan's has been serving their world-famous hot dogs since 1916, and you can still relish the experience. The amusement park, Astroland, has seen its share of wear and tear, but it is still home to the breathtaking (literally) Cyclone roller coaster. The screams of the other thrill rides still echo through the park all summer long. Dante's Inferno, the haunted house, is scary even from the outside, and the Ferris wheel will give you a view of all of Coney Island and much of Brooklyn. New and old rides for all ages are part of the Astroland experience, which, along with Rye Playland, just north of the Bronx in Westchester, and Adventureland, on Long Island, are among the few amusement parks around New York City.

Many people are nostalgic about Coney Island; you can experience that feeling yourself just by looking at the old parachute jump ride, now simply "the tower," which hasn't been operative for over thirty years. You can also see the history of Coney Island at a small

Coney Island museum. The Sideshows by the Seashore and Museum (at ✉ West 12th Street and Surf Avenue; call ✆ 718-372-5159 for information) are home to an old-fashioned circus sideshow with a fire-eater, sword-swallower, and other entertainers, as well as a museum with memorabilia from the neighborhood's illustrious past. The boardwalk also leads to the New York Aquarium.

≡FAST FACT

In the movie *Annie Hall,* Woody Allen claimed he grew up in a house under the roller coaster in Coney Island. The house, once a residence and now an office, is real. It is under the old Thunderbolt roller coaster, which closed many years ago when the famed Cyclone took the neighborhood by storm.

In the off-season, October through April, the neighborhood is relatively deserted, except for a visit by the Polar Bear Club. This bunch of "zanies" make the news every January by putting on their bathing suits and heading into the ocean for a really chilling experience.

If you're heading to Coney Island, prepare to spend the day— a warm late spring or summer day. Bring your blanket, sunscreen, and some patience—parking is not easy. You can take the subway (D, F, or Q train), but it's a long ride from Manhattan. Coney Island can still provide, after all these years, some good outdoor family fun in an old-time landmark neighborhood that is a staple of Brooklyn's historic past.

🧳 TRAVEL TIP

The Coney Island season kicks off in May with the Mermaid Parade, a nearly twenty-year tradition in which a parade of women, and some men, dress up in their mermaid best to parade along the boardwalk.

The New York Aquarium

✉ Surf Avenue and 8th Street

✎ *www.nyaquarium.com*

The city's only full-scale aquarium has been in Coney Island since the mid-1950s, and it attracts thousands of visitors annually. On fourteen acres off the boardwalk, the New York Aquarium has operated longer than any other similar facility in the country. There are temporary exhibits and special events on occasion, but the permanent attractions are the major crowd pleasers. Such popular exhibits include the "Sea Cliffs" exhibit, with walruses, penguins, and seals in a re-creation of their native habitat, and the Aquatheater, where the dolphins perform (from May to October) much as they do at SeaWorld.

From Beluga whales to thousands of varieties of fish in a host of massive tanks, the aquarium is packed with delights of the underwater world. A 90,000-gallon shark tank will put you eye-to-eye with 400-pound sand tiger sharks while sting rays whiz by. Computer-enhanced over the years, the aquarium also offers a wealth of information for learning more about the creatures of the sea.

The aquarium is fun for both children and their parents. It's an enjoyable place to spend a few hours after a stroll on the boardwalk. It can, on summer weekends, get overly crowded, with long lines to see everything, so it's best to arrive early on a weekday if possible.

The aquarium offers dining at an indoor cafeteria and an outdoor snack bar with tables on the deck overlooking the boardwalk.

Location and Hours

The New York Aquarium is located on Surf Avenue and 8th Street in Coney Island. It is accessible by subway via the D train (Coney Island/Stillwell Avenue station). Parking is available for $7, but lots fill up quickly on weekends, so get there early.

The aquarium is open every day and can be visited Monday through Friday from 10:00 A.M. to 5:00 P.M. and on weekends and holidays (during the summer months) from 10:00 A.M. to 5:30 P.M.

Admission is $11 for adults, $7 for seniors and children ages 2 through 12, and free for children under 2. Children under 16 must be accompanied by an adult.

The Brooklyn Botanic Garden

✉ 1000 Washington Avenue

✆ 718-623-7263

⌨ *www.bbg.org*

Smack in the middle of Brooklyn are fifty-two of the most lavishly beautiful acres New York City has to offer. More than 750,000 people visit this spectacular tribute to Mother Nature annually. The Brooklyn Botanic Garden is located among the red brick buildings, row houses, storefronts, and municipal buildings that characterize much of the borough.

Consisting of several gardens, greenhouses, and exhibits, all in one sprawling location, the garden offers a visual mirage of colors and a host of pleasing fragrances. Included on the grounds are the following:

- Shakespeare Garden
- Cranford Rose Garden
- Japanese Hill-and-Pond Garden
- Fragrance Garden
- Children's Garden
- Osbourne Garden
- Steinhardt Conservatory

- C.V. Bonsai Museum
- Celebrity Path
- Visitors' Center
- Garden Gift Shop
- Terrace Café
- Palm House
- Three large pavilions

The Cranford Rose Garden features tens of thousands of rose bushes, in numerous varieties. They grow in formal beds, up over arches, and onto the accompanying pavilion. The Rose Garden opened in 1928 and comprises just one of the acres of this massive outdoor flower gallery.

The Children's Garden, first opened in 1914, is a place where children can learn about plants by enjoying the hands-on experience of planting and gardening. Instructors teach children of all ages about the plants, insects, and animals. It's both fun and educational. A thirty-minute tour covers activities and displays and gives children a chance to care for and harvest flowers and vegetables. Some 25,000 youngsters have tended this garden over the years.

The Japanese Hill-and-Pond Garden is brilliantly landscaped and features bridges, waterfalls, a pond, a viewing pavilion, a waiting house, and shrubs carefully designed and shaped.

≡FAST FACT

The Brooklyn Botanic Garden features its own Celebrity Path in homage to the many famous Brooklynites who have presumably visited there. Among those included are Mel Brooks, Mary Tyler Moore, and Maurice Sendak; their names are inscribed on stepping stones.

The Fragrance Garden, built in the 1950s, is designed for people who are visually impaired. It features flowers in raised beds, various aromas, and textured foliage. Enjoyed by the sighted as well, it is the only major garden of its kind.

The Shakespeare Garden, like its Central Park counterpart, features flowers mentioned in the works of William Shakespeare in a setting modeled after an English cottage garden.

Osbourne Garden is a formal setting, complete with fountain, seating, and columns found in traditional Italian gardens. Within the three-acre garden is a 30,000-square-foot center lawn surrounded by flowering trees and shrubs.

The Steinhart Conservatory, built in the late 1980s, is a modern $25-million complex. Its greenhouses display the thousands of indoor plants that are part of the Botanic Garden.

The Terrace Café offers gourmet lunches and beverages with outdoor dining in the warmer months; the Palm House, a catering facility, offers luncheons and parties.

Location and Hours

The Brooklyn Botanic Garden is located on Washington Avenue, on the south side of the Brooklyn Museum. It is accessible by subway via the 2 or 3 train (Eastern Parkway/Brooklyn Museum station). Parking is available for a fee.

From April through September, the garden is open Tuesday through Friday from 8:00 A.M. to 6:00 P.M. (weekends, 10:00 A.M. to 6:00 P.M.). From October through March, hours are reduced, and the garden closes at 4:30 P.M. The garden is closed on Thanksgiving, Christmas, and New Year's Day. Admission is free to the public all day Tuesdays (except holidays) and Saturday mornings until noon; otherwise, it is $5 for adults over 16, $3 for seniors and students with IDs, and free for teens and children 16 and under.

Guided tours are free and feature seasonal highlights. They are offered at 1:00 P.M. on weekends, except major holiday weekends. Thirty-minute Children's Garden family tours (free with your admission) are offered on Tuesday afternoons at 2:00 P.M. in June, July, and August. Group tours and lunch tours can also be set up (for a fee) by calling ✆ 718-623-7220. The visitors' center is staffed by volunteers who will fill you in on programs, courses, seminars, and events.

Brooklyn Museum of Art

✉ 200 Eastern Parkway
✆ 718-638-5000
✍ *www.brooklynmuseum.org*

Of museums in New York City, the Brooklyn Museum is second in size only to the Met. This is a substantial museum with numerous exhibits featuring historic works from around the world as well as classic American art. Founded in 1823 as the Brooklyn Apprentices Library Association (with Walt Whitman as one of its first librarians), the museum now resides inside a massive 1893 structure designed by McKim, Mead, and White. It houses more than 1.5 million paintings, artifacts, drawings, photographs, and more and has just completed a massive renovation that will make it look like the first-class museum it truly is.

≡FAST FACT

As you enter the Brooklyn Museum of Art, look for the allegorical figures of Brooklyn and Manhattan. These were originally designed for the Manhattan bridge by Daniel Chester French, who designed the Lincoln Memorial in Washington, D.C.

One of the world's most renowned collections of Egyptian art—Brooklyn Museum curators go to Egypt every year for digs—covers the third floor, with a chronological display dating back to 1350 B.C. Jewelry, ivory, gold, and other invaluable objects can be found. A separate exhibit entitled "Temples, Tombs, and the Egyptian Universe" houses nearly 200 more Egyptian artifacts.

Carved ivory and numerous items including masks and shields from Central Africa and arts of the Pacific from Polynesia, Malaysia, and Indonesia are also found in the huge building. There is a large collection of pan-American art including a fifteenth-century Aztec stone jaguar, textiles, ceramics, and gold objects. You'll even find portraits of the kings of the Inca Empire, painted in Peru. An extensive collection of Asian art includes works from Cambodia, China, India, Iran, Japan, Thailand, Tibet, and Turkey, as well as Korea.

Some twenty-eight period rooms are also displayed, ranging from a seventeenth-century Brooklyn Dutch farmhouse to a twentieth-century art deco library. A walk through the rooms offers a look at a chronology of styles of décor in America spanning more than two centuries. Paintings and sculptures from American and European artists also span some five centuries. You'll note there are classic painters represented, including Monet and Degas, in this large, often-overlooked museum.

While the museum may not dazzle the younger set, it does provide a great cultural history for visitors from around the world. A sculpture garden is ideal for a pleasant stroll outdoors; inside the museum you'll find shops and a café.

☂ RAINY DAY FUN

For the past five years, the Brooklyn Museum of Art has hosted an all-day long series of programs with art, music, and dancing called "First Saturdays," where the museum and its events are free. It is one of the museum's most successful programs and is widely attended, especially in the summer. Guaranteed, it's fun for all!

Location and Hours

The Brooklyn Museum of Art is located at 200 Eastern Parkway. It is accessible by subway via the 2 or 3 train (Eastern Parkway/Brooklyn Museum station).

The museum is open Wednesday through Friday from 10:00 A.M. to 5:00 P.M.; Saturdays from 11:00 A.M. to 6:00 P.M.; the first Saturday of the month from 11:00 A.M. to 11:00 P.M.; and Sundays from 11:00 A.M. to 6:00 P.M. Suggested admission is $6 for adults, $3 for students with a valid ID, and free for children under 12.

Places to Visit in Queens

Queens was once the center of the New York film scene. The borough has become a bit of an art center at present, so you can have an unusual day touring its one-of-a-kind sights.

American Museum of the Moving Image

✉ Thirty-fifth Avenue at 36th Street

✆ 718-784-0077

✆ 718-784-4520

✍ www.ammi.org

Although you can't tour the studios, you can get a great glimpse at movie making history at the American Museum of the Moving Image (also known as AMMI). Just over the bridge from Manhattan, and within close proximity to the Silvercup and the old, still very busy Kaufman Astoria Studios, this special museum pays tribute to the powerful and influential media that are motion pictures and television. From the early days of film in Queens to the digital media, there is a lot represented in these archives.

The 50,000-square-foot museum, opened in 1988, is housed in part of the historic old studio built by Paramount in 1920. Three floors of exhibit space feature attractions such as "Behind the Screen," a look at the history of the cinema, complete with movie memorabilia and photos from studios local and worldwide. Television is not neglected either; memorabilia include the diner set from *Seinfeld*.

Also featured in the museum are fourteen interactive exhibits. Visitors learn sound and music editing, and they can make their own animated cartoon or a video flip book. You can even dub your own voice over a movie scene. The charming, whimsical Tut Fever Movie Palace is a mini-theater built like the movie palaces of the 1930s, showing classic images and serials like *Flash Gordon, Buck Rogers,* and *The Lone Ranger.* Ongoing film programs are featured on weekends at 2:00 and 4:00 P.M. A computer space exhibit of classic video arcade games and new home-computer games brings the museum into the twenty-first century.

A store sells movie books, toys, posters, postcards, and other objects with movie and television themes. There is also a café for light dining and snacks. More of an actual "museum" than its "video library" counterpart (the Radio and Television Museum in Manhattan), AMMI is off the beaten path but worth the short ride.

Location and Hours

The American Museum of the Moving Image is located on Thirty-fifth Avenue in Astoria, one mile from the Queensboro Bridge. It is accessible by subway via the R train (Steinway Avenue station). Or you can drive and park without much trouble on the weekend.

AMMI is open Tuesday through Friday from noon to 8:00 P.M. and Saturdays and Sundays from 11:00 A.M. to 6:00 P.M. It is free every Friday from 4:00 to 8:00 P.M. Admission is $11 for adults, $7.50 for seniors and college students with a valid ID, and $5 for children.

Hall of Science

✉ 47-01 111th Street

☎ 718-699-0005

🖊 www.nyhallsci.org

Part of the 1964 World's Fair, this museum closed in the 1970s and reopened in the late 1980s. An interactive hands-on museum, the Hall of Science features more than 200 exhibits for youngsters and parents to explore, play with, and learn from, including a high-powered telescope. Microbiology, quantum physics, geology, audio technology, and other subjects are covered in a fun way; kids can learn while enjoying themselves.

≡FAST FACT

The minor league farm team for the Mets, the Brooklyn Cyclones, has a field in Coney Island and a fan base as devoted as any major league team's. If you don't feel like paying for stadium tickets for a ballgame, head to KeySpan Park.

A 30,000-square-foot outdoor science playground adjacent to the museum features an oversized seesaw, a giant pinball machine, and other activities to climb in, climb on, run through, and explore. Designed to show the principles of physics while providing a good time, the playground/science park is open for children 6 and over.

The museum has a gift shop with a wide range of science-related items, from inexpensive gadgets to toys, books, and even telescopes. There is no restaurant, but you can buy snacks and sandwiches from a vending machine or bring your own food for a bite in the dining area.

Location and Hours

The Hall of Science is located at 4701 111th Street in Flushing Meadow Park. It is accessible by subway via the 7 train (111th Street station). Parking isn't hard, with some 600 available spaces on the twenty-two-acre site.

The hall is open Monday through Wednesday from 9:30 A.M. to 2:00 P.M.; Thursdays, Saturdays, and Sundays from 9:30 A.M. to 5:00 P.M.; and Fridays—for free between September and June—from 2:00 P.M. to 5:00 P.M. Admission is $9 for adults, $6 for children and seniors, and $2.50 for toddlers. There is a $3 per-person charge for the science playground.

Queens Museum of Art

✉ Flushing Meadow Park

✆ 718-592-9700

🖉 www.queensmuseum.org

The third of three very distinctive museums in Queens features the history of the two major World's Fairs held in Flushing Meadow Park, complete with memorabilia. But that's not the exciting part of this 1939 building, which was known as the New York City exhibit in the 1939 and 1964 World's Fairs. The reason to visit the museum is the 9,000-square-foot miniature replica of New York City. It represents the entire city, block by block, house by house, with changes made from time to time as new buildings replace older ones. The scale is one inch per 100 feet, and the detail is awesome. Much safer than a helicopter ride over the city, you could stand and look at the buildings, the bridges, and the neighborhoods for hours (unless the place is too crowded). It's truly remarkable!

Also in the museum you'll find an extensive Tiffany lamp exhibition, plus an exhibit about the building itself. There is also an adjoining ice-skating rink, if you want to take a spin on the ice during the winter months.

A gift shop sells World's Fair mementos. There is no restaurant. Just outside the museum is the giant metal Unisphere, a throwback to the great World's Fair days.

Location and Hours

The Queens Museum of Art is located in Flushing Meadow Park. It is accessible by subway via the 7 train (Willets Point/Shea Stadium or 111th Street station).

The museum is open Wednesday through Friday from 10:00 A.M. to 5:00 P.M. and Saturdays and Sundays from noon to 5:00 P.M. The suggested admission is $5 for adults and $2.50 for seniors and students.

TRAVEL TIP

If you make a day of art in Queens, you might want to try some of the restaurants along the way. There's a good Greek restaurant, S'Agapo Taverna, at ✉34–31 Thirty-fourth Avenue; a lovely restaurant with a view, the Water's Edge, at ✉44 Drive and the East River; and a nice little fish and chips shop, the Chipper, at ✉41–28 Queens Boulevard.

Isamu Noguchi Garden Museum

✉32–37 Vernon Boulevard

☏718-204-7088

☏718-721-1932

🖰 *www.noguchi.org*

After undergoing a massive renovation, this beautiful garden museum dedicated to the life and work of this talented Japanese-American sculptor (1904–1988) has just reopened. Noguchi designed one of the most popular coffee tables in America—a smoked teardrop over a curved black wood base. The site is the home of a former engraving plant purchased in 1975 by the artist, architect, and sculptor as a place to display his work. More than 250 pieces of his (often large) work can be seen throughout the space and in the open air garden.

Location and Hours

The Isamu Noguchi Garden Museum is located on Vernon Boulevard at 33rd Road in Long Island City. It is accessible by subway via the N or W train (Broadway station). It is open

Mondays, Thursdays, and Fridays from 10:00 A.M. to 5:00 P.M. and on weekends from 11:00 A.M. to 6:00 P.M. The suggested donation is $4. The museum reopened in June 2004; call to check hours after that date.

MoMA QNS

✉ 45-20 33rd Street

✆ 718-389-4729

🖱 *www.moma.org*

While the Midtown site is undergoing its renovation, this former Swingline Staple Factory is home to one of the premier modern art collections in the world. You can see MoMA QNS, as the temporary location is known, from the subway station as it has been painted blue. Inside, the museum offers large spaces. Its white walls and concrete floors give it a true industrial feel, very different from the glass-and-steel architecture of the Philip Johnson building on 53rd Street—it's quite an interesting contrast. Highlights from the permanent exhibit are on display here—you can still see Rousseau's *Sleeping Gypsy* and Mondrian's *Broadway Boogie Woogie,* as well as all those Cézannes, Matisses, Johns, and Warhols. When the 53rd Street museum renovation is completed in November 2004, this space will become the site of research and storage. There is a small café on the premises for snacks and a light lunch, as well as a full museum shop.

Location and Hours

MoMA QNS is located on 33rd Street at Queens Boulevard. It is accessible by subway via the 7 train (33rd Street/Rawson station).

MoMA QNS is closed Tuesdays and Wednesdays. It is open the rest of the week from 10:00 A.M. to 5:00 P.M., with hours extended on Fridays to 7:45 P.M. Admission for adults is $12, $8.50 for seniors and students. After 4:00 P.M. on Fridays, admission is pay-what-you-wish.

P.S. 1 Contemporary Art Center
✉ 22-25 Jackson Avenue at 46th Street

✆ 718-784-2084

⌨ *www.ps1.org*

P.S. 1 was one of the first contemporary art exhibition spaces outside Manhattan to draw the mainstream art world off the island. It is considered one of the cool, hip art spaces in the city. Once an abandoned 100-year-old school building, it is now a partner with the Museum of Modern Art. P.S. 1 offers a large exhibition space, indoors as well as out on the rooftop. Exhibitions often feature local art and artists, such as the Greater New York Show, which showcased 140 New York artists, or the annual "Young Architects" exhibit.

Location and Hours
P.S. 1 Contemporary Art Center is located on Jackson Avenue at 46th Street in Long Island City. It is accessible by subway via the 7 train (45 Rd./Courthouse Square station). The center is open Thursday through Monday, noon to 6:00 P.M., and admission is $5.

Things to Do in the Bronx

A day in the Bronx can be quite a fun family affair, with a visit to the Bronx Zoo, Yankee Stadium, the New York Botanical Garden, and dinner in one of the fabulous Italian restaurants along Arthur Avenue.

The New York Botanical Garden
✉ Kazimiroff Boulevard and 200th Street

✆ 718-817-8700

⌨ *www.nybg.org*

The most beautiful 250 acres you'll find in the Bronx, and possibly in all of New York City, are in the New York Botanical Garden. A serene refuge from the big city, the garden is worth the trip to the Bronx, especially if you also visit the neighboring Bronx Zoo.

The site was selected back in 1891 and developed as a place for the public to enjoy the beautifully landscaped outdoors. Today, the facility incorporates dramatic rock outcroppings, wetlands, ponds, a waterfall, and a forty-acre forest, along with sixteen specialty gardens including a rose garden and a rock garden. A Victorian-era glasshouse has been home to indoor plants since 1902 (the orchids are world-renowned), and there is a museum building and stone cottage. The garden is also in the scientific research game, with their new Plant Studies Center and a new plant studies library, one of the biggest in the country, with more than 1.26 million print and nonprint items.

 TRAVEL TIP

If you plan to go shopping, schedule it for later in the day. Major sights have gift shops, and your purchases can add up; consider opting for inexpensive mementos or postcards. If you plan to take photos (allowed at most attractions), check your camera batteries in advance and bring an extra roll of film. Some stores don't carry batteries and film, and those that do may charge high prices. Pharmacies, such as CVS and Rite Aid, are a good place to buy inexpensive film, batteries, and water.

Included among the gardens, you'll find the Peggy Rockefeller Rose Garden, with a central iron gazebo and thousands of varieties of roses. Along with a 2.5-acre rock garden, you'll enjoy a native plant garden with nine different habitats displaying plants indigenous to the northeastern United States. More than 150 herbs are found in the Nancy Bryan Luce Herb Garden, and the Demonstration Gardens offer a variety of gardens that visitors can re-create in their backyards, including fragrance, country, and cutting gardens. There's even a children's garden, where youngsters can learn about tending to plants.

From bulbs to daffodils to daylilies to chrysanthemums, if it's a plant or part of a garden, it's most likely found in the New York

Botanical Garden. There is even a forest with birds and wildlife in one of the oldest tracts of uncut nature remaining in the city. The outdoor children's garden is a delight, where kids can build a bird's nest, look at pond life with a magnifying glass, and wander through mazes and topiary gardens. There is a wonderful botanical research center and workshops.

The garden shop is a great place for buying anything you need for a garden, from seeds to watering cans; it also has a great selection of gardening books. You'll find a children's shop in the Everett Children's Adventure Garden, and on the weekends there are wonderful workshops for kids.

There are special events and several tours are offered, including a tram tour for $1 ($.50 for children), a golf cart tour (no putting allowed), and walking tours of the gardens or the forest. The Garden Café and picnic tables are available. A visitors' center provides maps as you enter—you will need one to find your way around.

Location and Hours

The New York Botanical Garden is located on Kazimiroff Boulevard and 200th Street. It is accessible by subway via the B or D train (Bedford Park Blvd. station).

The garden is open Tuesday through Sunday from 10:00 A.M. to 6:00 P.M., April through October, and from 10:00 A.M. to 5:00 P.M. from November through March. Admission is $3 for adults, $2 for seniors and students, and $1 for children 2 through 12. Parking is available for $5.

The Bronx Zoo
✉ Fordham Road and Bronx River Parkway
✆ 718-220-5100
✍ *www.bronxzoo.com*

Just past celebrating its 100th birthday, the Bronx Zoo has for a century been a marvelous adventure for children and adults alike. The zoo, now officially known as the International Wildlife Conservation Center, is home to more than 4,000 animals in a variety of settings designed to re-create the natural habitats of the 600 species that reside here.

For families, it can be a full day of activities, with numerous exhibits including the recently added Gorilla Forest, which covers more than 6.5 acres and re-creates an African rain forest with more than 300 animals.

Other exhibits include Jungle World, an indoor tropical rain forest exhibit, complete with Asian gibbons and numerous other fascinating creatures. The zoo also features the Bengali Express, a monorail ride through (or over) the re-created forests and meadows of Asia. It's complete with all the creatures of those nature documentaries on public television, including elephants, deer, antelope, and, of course, Bengal tigers. The Baboon Reserve is a simulated archeological dig tracing the evolution of the Gelada baboons, complete with numerous baboons playing on the side of the miniature mountain range.

Kids love the World of Darkness, which gives you a glimpse into the nocturnal creatures of the night, including various bats and rats. The Himalayan Highlands exhibit features red pandas, endangered snow leopards, and other animals of the Himalayas.

The Children's Zoo allows the kids to meet, greet, and feed a variety of animals and to have fun with various kid-friendly activities. Closed during winter months, the Children's Zoo costs a few dollars more for admission. Still other exhibits include Mousehouse, Skyfari, World of Birds, African Plains, and much more.

There is also a gift shop plus snack stands, the Lakeside Café, the African Market, and other eateries. Several rides are also open in the summer.

Tickets are sold up until an hour before the zoo closes, but you should allow yourself at least three hours to see some of the massive zoo. Also, check the weather before you plan a day at the zoo.

Location and Hours

The International Wildlife Conservation Center of the Bronx Zoo is located at Fordham Road and Bronx River Parkway. It is accessible by subway via the 2 or 5 train (Pelham Parkway station). Parking at the zoo is $7 for cars.

The Bronx Zoo is open 365 days a year, although several exhibits close down during the winter months. The hours are 10:00 A.M. to 5 P.M. (4:30 P.M. during the winter). Admission is $9 for adults and $5 for seniors and children 2 through 12. Most of the year, Wednesdays are free. Zoo rides cost extra, including the Skyfari ($2), camel rides ($3), and the Zoo Shuttle ($2). The Bengali Express guided monorail tour is open from May to November and costs $2 extra per person. Prices are lower between November and March.

Wave Hill
✉ 675 West 252nd Street
✆ 718-549-3200
⌨ *www.wavehill.org*

This is one of those beautiful, quiet spots in the big city. It's the site of a former mansion overlooking the Hudson River with undisturbed vistas of the Jersey Palisades. Artists, writers, and readers come here just to sit and think. This twenty-eight-acre public garden houses a greenhouse and a conservatory as well as herb, wildflower, and aquatic gardens. There are wonderful art workshops for kids every Saturday, free concerts in the summer months, and a delightful café with good sandwiches and soups. There is also a terrific gift shop. Celebrity weddings are often held here.

Location and Hours
The entrance to Wave Hill is located on West 249th Street. It is accessible by subway via the 1 or 9 train (to 231st Street station) and then the No. 7 bus to 252nd Street. You can also take MetroNorth to the Riverdale station. Parking is available.

Wave Hill is closed Mondays. April through October, the estate is open Tuesday through Saturday, 9:00 A.M. to 5:30 P.M. Admission is $4 per person. March through November, it is free to get in on Saturday and Tuesday mornings, and admission is free from

December through February. The estate closes an hour earlier mid-October to mid-April. In July and August, Wave Hill stays open till dusk.

☰FAST FACT

Take your kids to Edgar Allan Poe's cottage at Kingsbridge Road and the Grand Concourse (with more information available online at ✑www.bronxhistoricalsociety.org). This is where Poe and his sick wife lived between 1846 and 1849, and it is believed that he wrote "The Bells" about the church bells of St. John's College (now Fordham University) while living there.

City Island

A small bridge connects this 230-acre, four-block-wide island in the Long Island Sound with the northeast section of Bronx. Less than an hour from Manhattan by car, City Island is a worthwhile excursion that even some longtime New Yorkers don't know about. It's quaint, it's fun, and if you love seafood, bring your appetite. The best way to get there is by car. Or, if you prefer public transportation, take the 6 train to Pelham Bay Parkway, and then the Bx29 Bus. April through October are the months to visit.

Fishing, sailing, and boat-building have been more than just a pastime of the island since its founding days in the eighteenth century. A little museum called the Northwind Undersea Museum can be found in the old sea captain's house (at ✉610 City Island Avenue). The museum is devoted to the maritime and deep-sea fishing and costs $3. It is open March through November. For information, call ✆ 718-885-0701.

An attractively laid out miniature golf course, Turtle Cove, is located next to a full-sized driving range, where you can stop to play along the way as you head to City Island Bridge. Once over the bridge, the smell of fresh seafood will remind you of New

England. Essentially, City Island has all the great seafood that can be found on the shores of Maine or Massachusetts. The tiny island is also chock-full of boats, and you can rent one and take a ride.

As you drive along the one main road on the island, you'll encounter a slew of restaurants. With names like Crab Shanty, King Lobster, Lobster Box, Lobster House, Sammy's Fish Box, and Sea View, you'll immediately get the idea that it's time to don a bib and prepare for some great seafood. Portions in most of these eateries are large, the food is fresh, and the dining experience at most of the twenty-plus restaurants is first rate.

Yankee Stadium

✉ East 161st Street and River Avenue

✆ 718-293-6000 (box office)

✆ 718-579-4531 (stadium tours)

✑ *www.yankees.com*

Built in 1923, the year the Babe hit his first home run, and remodeled in 1976 (during the less notable Bobby Mercer era), Yankee Stadium is home to the winning-est baseball franchise in major league history. The Yankees have fans nationwide and worldwide, and a roster of Hall-of-Famers matched by no other team, including Babe Ruth, Lou Gehrig, Joe DiMaggio, Mickey Mantle, Whitey Ford, and Yogi Berra.

The stadium itself sits on 11.6 acres and is actually the third home of the Yankees, who played in the Polo Grounds in Upper Manhattan (1913 to 1922) and before that in Hilltop Park (1903 to 1912), also in Upper Manhattan.

With very little foul territory, seats are as close to the field as you'll find anywhere. The ambiance is still that of "real baseball," without artificial turf, skyboxes, waterfalls, or massive electronic scoreboards overshadowing the game itself. If you arrive early, you can visit Monument Park, just over the centerfield fence. The park features monuments and plaques for great Yankees, including the Hall-of-Famers already mentioned plus Bill Dickey, Phil Rizzuto, Roger Maris, Thurman Munson, Elston Howard, Casey Stengel, and others. A special walkway honors those players whose numbers have been retired.

 TRAVEL TIP

Yankee Stadium holds 57,545, but getting a ticket is not easy when the Yankees are playing well, so plan in advance. The regular season runs from early April to the end of September, though the Yankees usually get to play a few weeks longer. Tickets can be purchased at Ticketmaster (call ✆ 212-307-1212) locations throughout the city and at the Yankee Stadium box office.

Location and Hours

Yankee Stadium is located on the corner of East 161st Street and River Avenue. It is accessible by subway via the B, D, or 4 train (161st Street/Yankee Stadium station). For day games, the subway is quick and gets you right to the stadium. If you'd prefer not to travel the subways at night, you can park in any of several lots around the ballpark (avoid those that say valet parking; they cost more and you're kept waiting in line to get your car after the game). Self park in a lot, and walk with the crowds. This is not a neighborhood for seeking out street parking or wandering away from the stadium area. Stadium tours are offered at noon during the week.

Take the Ferry to Staten Island

Staten Island is one of the best-kept secrets of New York City. The ferry ride is wonderful—and you get a great view of Lower Manhattan and the Statue of Liberty—and there's some wonderful history to discover!

Historic Richmond Town

✉ 441 Clarke Avenue
✆ 718-351-1611
✍ www.historicrichmondtown.org

The twenty-seven buildings of Historic Richmond Town cover 100 acres and represent three centuries of Staten Island life. The village saw its first buildings in 1690 and expanded over the centuries. These structures survived the American Revolution and the modernization of the city around them. A museum was added and is open to the public, along with fourteen of the twenty-seven historical structures.

Included in the historic town, you'll find the oldest surviving elementary school, the Voorlezer House, from 1695; a stately Greek Revival courthouse from 1837 (transformed into a visitors' center); a 1740s farmhouse; and an 1860s general store museum. Located in the former county clerk's office, the museum's exhibits feature items made in Staten Island and a "Toys!" exhibit.

Other exhibits within the quaint setting include early American crafts. Attractions feature demonstrations of quilting, carpentry, spinning, and weaving, fireplace cooking, and other aspects of colonial life. Along with guided tours of the buildings, the unique historical setting is host to a fair every Labor Day weekend. Throughout the year you'll find other events, like flea markets, an annual summer re-enactment of Civil War battles, a nineteenth-century outdoor dinner (complete with plates and utensils of a bygone era), Saturday-night concerts, an autumn celebration, and Christmas festivities.

The museum store sells reproductions, items made by the village craftspeople, and books on Staten Island history. A Victorian-style full-service restaurant offers casual dining.

Location and Hours

Historic Richmond Town is located at La Tourette Park, on Clarke Avenue. Once you take the ferry over to Staten Island, you can take a city bus or drive—there's plenty of free parking! Admission is $5 for adults, $4 for seniors, and $3.50 for children ages 6 through 18. Historic Richmond Town is open Wednesday through Sunday from 1:00 to 5:00 P.M. and is closed on major holidays.

Fort Wadsworth

✉ Wadsworth Avenue and Bay Street

✆ 718-354-4576

From 1795 through 1945, this was a navy-run fort that protected New York Harbor. Today, the 226-acre site is run by the New York Park Service and is home to U.S. Coast Guard personnel and the U.S. Army Reserve. Fourteen historic defense structures still stand, overlooking the harbor and the neighboring Verrazano Bridge. Views are outstanding!

The center has a film on the history of the fort, plus other exhibits. You can buy books and other items in the gift shop. Ranger-led tours are also available. Within the park itself, you can fish, hike, or follow a trail by foot or by bike. Special events include lantern-tour nights, living history re-enactments of rifle or musket demonstrations, special hikes, and more.

A deli on the grounds is open every day except Sunday, or you can pack a picnic lunch and enjoy a day of history and fun in the great outdoors. Bring a camera for shots of New York Harbor.

Location and Hours

Fort Wadsworth is located on the corner of Wadsworth Avenue and Bay Street. Admission is free, and the park is open from dawn to dusk. The visitors' center is open Wednesday through Sunday from 10 A.M. to 5 P.M.

 TRAVEL TIP

Need information? The Visitor Information Center at the Embassy Theater (at ✉1560 Broadway, between 46th and 47th Streets in Manhattan) has ticket centers for Broadway shows and other New York City events, MetroCards, computer terminals for Internet research, and helpful staff who can answer your questions. The center is open from 8 A.M. to 8 P.M. every day.

Snug Harbor Cultural Center

✉ 1000 Richmond Terrace

✆ 718-448-2500

🖱 *www.snug-harbor.org*

A small historical city within a city, Snug Harbor houses some twenty-eight historical structures and acres of public parkland, with meadows, wetlands, and gardens. Greek Revival and Victorian architecture characterize many of the buildings, which include a music hall built in the late nineteenth century and a main hall dating back to 1833. Five Victorian artists' cottages and a Veterans Memorial Hall from 1856 are also among the classic structures you'll find here. While Historic Richmond Town has a greater focus on history, Snug Harbor is a home for culture and the arts.

Just a ten-minute bus ride from the Staten Island Ferry, Snug Harbor has a variety of attractions for varying interests. Included, you'll find the John A. Noble Collection of Maritime Art and the Visual Arts/Newhouse Galleries. This collection features cutting-edge contemporary art creatively displayed in vivid contrast to the nineteenth-century main exhibit hall. All in all, the structures house some 15,000 square feet of exhibit space, forty visual and per-forming arts studios, three dance studios, and three assembly halls.

The Staten Island Botanical Garden is also part of Snug Harbor. The complex is home to several smaller gardens, including a White Garden with white flowers, a bird and butterfly observatory, a fragrance garden, a rose garden, an herb garden, a greenhouse, and the English Garden. A Chinese Scholar's Garden and operating vineyard are also on the premises. The garden serves as a living, working, growing scientific and educational center.

The Staten Island Children's Museum, also found in the Snug Harbor Cultural Center, offers kids under twelve a variety of hands-on exhibitions in five interactive galleries, along with storytelling, workshops, and performances. There is a gift shop with books and souvenirs.

Open from dawn to dusk, 362 days a year, Snug Harbor hosts numerous outdoor events, including classical, pop, and jazz concerts in their south meadow and in the music hall. There is also an art lab with classes, workshops, and mini-camps at the Children's Museum. The Snug Harbor gift shop sells jewelry, original art, posters, and books. Melville's Café serves sandwiches, entrees, and desserts.

While touring the site is fun, seeing one of the numerous performances will really enhance your visit. Visiting Snug Harbor is a great way to sightsee, enjoy a concert, and even have a picnic. Also, it's not very expensive and is great for the whole family.

Location and Hours

Snug Harbor Cultural Center is located at 1000 Richmond Terrace. The site is open free to the public from dawn to dusk. The Newhouse Center for Contemporary Art is open Wednesday through Sunday from noon to 5:00 P.M. The suggested donation is $3. Admission to the Staten Island Botanical Garden is free. Call ✆ 718-273-8200 for hours and information. Admission to the Staten Island Children's Museum is $5 per person (free for children under 2). Call ✆ 718-273-2060 for hours and information.

CHAPTER 12

Shopping in New York

WHO COULD POSSIBLY GO TO NEW YORK without accumulating bags of stuff to take home? New York is the city of the ultimate shopping experience, with myriad shopping options to choose from. There are designer shops along Madison and Fifth Avenues, outdoor flea markets in the Village, the most incredible department stores in the world, and hundreds of fabulous, unique little stores that make shopping in New York a one-of-a-kind experience.

In addition to clothing, jewelry, music, and books, New York City boasts some of the most amazing food stores in the world, such as Zabar's and Citarella's, as well as many ethnic stores and markets where you can buy imported foods from all over the world.

And don't forget the street vendors and souvenir shops, either. To some they may be tacky, but nothing says New York better than a $3 "I Love New York" T-shirt!

🧳 TRAVEL TIP

Many New York restaurants have online catalogs and will ship you their wares (Junior's Cheesecake, for instance). The food sections of department stores such as Macy's also offer a similar service.

Department Stores

No city in the world has more department stores than New York. There's quite a variety, from the upscale one-of-a-kind shopping experiences of Bendal's and Bergdorf's to the fashionable Bloomingdale's and the Mecca of New York shopping, Macy's.

Barney's New York
✉ 660 Madison Avenue
✆ 212-826-8900
✉ 236 West 18th Street
✆ 212-593-7800
✉ 116 Wooster Street
✆ 212-593-7800
✍ *www.barneys.com*

This store is full of top-of-the-line men's and women's clothing. The best of the hottest designer lines can be found at Barney's. Although prices are quite high, Barney's holds sales twice a year that are worth watching for. The window displays are fabulous. They change frequently and are an attraction unto themselves.

Barney's is open seven days a week. The Madison Avenue location is at 60th Street. Take the 4, 5, or 6 train to the 59th Street station. The West 18th Street branch can be reached via the 1 or 9 train (18th Street station). To get to the Wooster Street branch, take the Q or W train to the Prince Street station.

Bergdorf Goodman's
✉ 754 Fifth Avenue
✆ 1-800-558-1855
✍ *www.bergdorfgoodman.com*

Bergdorf's is a boutique department store, where each designer's shop has its own look and feel. Elegant and trendy with lots of chandeliers and mirrors, Bergdorf's is a very New York experience. There's a beauty bar on the basement level where you can march right in for a manicure (no appointment necessary) and the

Susan Ciminelli spa on the eighth floor offers facials and treatments that will make you forget you are in a department store in one of the largest cities in the world.

Bergdorf Goodman's is on Fifth Avenue at 57th Street. It is accessible by subway via the A, D, 1, or 9 train (59th Street and Eighth Avenue station) or the 4, 5, or 6 train (59th and Lexington station). The men's store is across the street.

TRAVEL TIP

Some of the department store restaurants are so good that New Yorkers make them a regular luncheon spot. Le Blue Train in Bloomingdale's is one of the best-kept New York secrets, Macy's Bar & Grill is one of the best bargains in town (especially for happy hour), and Café SFA (in Saks Fifth Avenue) serves a delicious lobster risotto. Always make reservations, as these places can get quite busy.

Bloomingdale's
✉ 1000 Third Avenue
✆ 212-705-2000
🖱 www.bloomingdales.com

One of the last remaining New York City department stores to occupy an entire city block, Bloomingdale's is known to New Yorkers affectionately as Bloomie's. The main floor is busy, with salespeople spraying shoppers with perfume and offering makeovers. But if you can see past the glitz and glitter, Bloomingdale's has a tremendous selection of designer clothing for men, women, and children, and they run sales regularly.

Strolling the wide aisles, you will see all the latest fashions as well as marvelous displays. Bloomingdale's also sells linens, furniture, electrical appliances, jewelry, and much more. Personal shoppers are also available. There's a wonderful restaurant, Le Blue Train, serving French fare in an authentic small railroad car. The food is good, and the atmosphere is to die for. Make reservations.

Bloomingdale's is located on Third Avenue at 60th Street. Take the 4, 5, or 6 train to the 59th Street station. The store is open seven days a week.

Macy's Department Store

✉ 34th Street at Herald Square

✆ 212-736-5151

✐ *www.macys.com*

Macy's is known as "the world's largest department store." Expect to get lost at least twice while navigating your way around this huge place. The main floor is designed in a beautiful marble art deco style, a perfect setting for the fine jewelry and extensive leather departments located on this level. Macy's caters to the mainstream shopper; it carries a variety of reasonably priced clothing, although all the top designers can also be found. Macy's Cellar houses what might be the city's finest collection of cookware, housewares, and gourmet delicacies. You'll also find a Macy's "New York store," where you can buy all sorts of signature items like T-shirts and bags (as well as a special stuffed animal during the Christmas season). Macy's also has the Bar & Grill Restaurant, a hair salon, a branch of the Metropolitan Museum of Art's gift shop, a post office, and an American Express travel office.

The store is open seven days a week. It's located on 34th Street at Herald Square. It is accessible by subway via the A, D, R, N, F, Q, 1, or 9 train (34th Street station).

☂ RAINY DAY FUN

Macy's is always a great place to shop, but during Holy Week—the week before Easter Sunday—the entire first floor of the store is flooded with flowers. It is delightful and like nothing you'll ever see or smell again. During Christmas time, there are wonderful window displays not to be missed.

Henri Bendel

✉ 712 Fifth Avenue

✆ 212-247-1100

✎ www.henribendel.com

At Bendel's, you will encounter the cutting edge of fashion, with quite a few brand-new and only-in-New York designers. Bendel's features its own in-house lines of clothing as well as some of the more exclusive designer brands. The prices are very high, as is the quality of the offerings.

Henri Bendel is open seven days a week. It's located on Fifth Avenue at 55th Street. It is accessible by subway via 4, 5, or 6 train (59th Street station).

Lord & Taylor

✉ 424 Fifth Avenue

✆ 212-391-3344

✎ www.lordandtaylor.com

Probably your mother's favorite store in New York City, this is the department store that caters to classic taste. Their signature merchandise, from sleepwear to French milled soaps to sweaters, is always a good buy for the mature woman in your life. When they have sales, it's packed. Lord & Taylor is located on Fifth Avenue at 38th Street; take the 4, 5, or 6 train to the 33rd Street station.

Saks Fifth Avenue

✉ 611 Fifth Avenue

✆ 212-753-4000

✎ www.saksfifthavenue.com

Saks Fifth Avenue is one of New York City's most prestigious and most famous department stores. Located across the street from St. Patrick's Cathedral and just east of Rockefeller Center, Saks is very easy to spot—just look for the flags.

Saks is perhaps the most spacious store of its genre in New York City and takes pride in having a luxurious environment and elegant displays. The main floor offers numerous counters filled with accessories. Designer clothing for men, women, and children can be purchased. Saks' own house line, SFA, features more affordable prices. Saks also carries jewelry, cosmetics, and fragrances. In addition, there is a bridal salon, offering the latest in bridal fashion displayed in a gorgeous setting.

Cafe SFA serves gourmet lunch and light fare. Saks also offers free delivery to any Manhattan hotel. This is first-rate shopping at its finest. If you're not buying, you should at least browse. Saks is located on Fifth Avenue at 50th Street. It is accessible by subway via the F or D train (Rockefeller Center station).

≡FAST FACT

You may think New York has a lot of department stores now, but there used to be a lot more. New Yorkers will regale you with tales of those that closed in the 1970s and 1980s. Alexander's was the poor man's department store, as were the legendary Gimbels, Korvette's, and May's. S. Klein and A&S were also in this everyman's field. Bamberger's was a little higher up on the clothing store food chain. And New Yorkers actually wept when B. Altman's closed.

Discount Stores

There is such wonderful discount shopping in New York that you can buy this week's hottest designer clothes at just a few dollars above wholesale. Every hardworking New Yorker knows where to shop, and now you will too!

Century 21

✉ 22 Cortlandt Street
✆ 212-227-9092
🖳 www.c21stores.com

The Century 21 Department Store is one of the best places to get top designer clothes, for both men and women, at a fraction of the price. Because it's in Lower Manhattan, they have a lot of business attire. Suits, handbags, and shoes are always worth shopping for. They also have lingerie, cosmetics, luggage, and housewares in the basement. Century 21 is located on Cortlandt Street between Broadway and Church Streets. Take the A or C to the Broadway/Nassau station.

Daffy's

✉ 34th Street and Sixth Avenue
✉ 135 East 57th Street
✉ 111 Fifth Avenue at 18th Street
✉ 462 Broadway at Grand
✍ www.daffys.com

Daffy's is a hardcore designer bargain shopper's delight with men's, women's, and children's clothes for sale. It's the kind of place where you can shop for hours and buy $1,000 worth of designer clothes and accessories for $100, if you work hard at it. You'll find shoes, bags, and lingerie here, too. Daffy's is open seven days a week, with several branches in New York. To get to the store on 34th Street and Sixth Avenue, take D, F, Q, N, or R train to the 34th Street station. To get to the Midtown store, at 135 East 57th Street, take the 4, 5, or 6 train to the 59th Street station; to get to the Chelsea store, at 111 Fifth Avenue at 18th Street, take the 4, 5, or 6 train to Union Station; and to get to the Lower Manhattan outlet, at 462 Broadway, take the J or the M train to the Canal Street station.

Loehmann's

✉ 101 Seventh Avenue at 16th Street
✍ www.loehmanns.com

Loehmann's is a bargain-shopper's paradise for women's sportswear and designer clothes, as well as shoes, handbags, jewelry, and even swimwear. You can also find some men's clothing as well as lingerie for sale. Loehmann's offers shoppers a 15-percent birthday discount (up to four days before or after the special date). On some seasonal items that are already discounted by up to 70 percent, that can mean an 85-percent total discount. Loehmann's is open seven days a week. To get to the store on Seventh Avenue at 16th Street, take the 1, 2, 3, or 9 train (14th Street station); there's also a store in Riverdale in the Bronx—take the 1 or 9 train to the 225th Street station.

 TRAVEL TIP

It is hard to find a bathroom in midtown New York, so most New Yorkers know where the bathrooms are in department stores and drop in. At the time of this writing, there were two Paris-style outdoor toilettes at Herald Square, which you can use automatically for coins. If the results are promising, the city plans on installing more. Until then, use department store bathrooms, or visit a Starbucks or McDonald's (they are everywhere and the bathrooms are usually quite clean).

One-of-a-Kind Shops

There is nothing like window shopping or browsing along Fifth Avenue and stopping to gaze at all the fabulous upscale jewelry shops. If you take the time to browse, you won't be disappointed.

Fortunoff
✉ 681 Fifth Avenue
✆ 212-758-6660

One of the premier affordable jewelry and china stores in the city. This multilevel store has an entire floor dedicated to silver, and Fortunoff also carries a fine display of crystal, Waterford, Lennox, Lalique, and other brands. It's one of the best places for wedding gifts. Fortunoff is located on Fifth Avenue at 53rd Street; take the E or V train to the Fifth Avenue/53rd Street station.

Cartier

✉ 653 Fifth Avenue at 52nd Street

☎ 212-472-6400

According to legend, Pierre Cartier acquired this mansion on Fifth Avenue in exchange for two perfectly matched pearl necklaces. There are necklaces and jewelry here for models and royalty, but there are also some surprisingly affordable items for the rest of us. Cartier is located on Fifth Avenue at 52nd Street; take the E or V train to the Fifth Avenue/53rd Street station.

Harry Winston

✉ 718 Fifth Avenue

☎ 212-245-2000

Another one of New York's legendary jewelers to the stars and royalty, Harry Winston's gems are known worldwide. (The Smithsonian's Hope diamond was once owned by Mrs. Harry Winston.) The jeweler was immortalized by Marilyn Monroe in the song, "Diamonds Are a Girl's Best Friend."

It's always a pleasure to window shop at Harry Winston. The store is located on Fifth Avenue at West 56th Street; take the B train to the 57th Street station.

Tiffany & Company

✉ 727 Fifth Avenue

☎ 212-755-8000

One of the city's most prestigious stores, Tiffany's was founded in 1837 and was known as Tiffany & Young until 1853. It is considered America's leading house of design and the world's premier jewelry retailer; the store on Fifth Avenue is probably its most famous. The main floor is where Tiffany's finest jewelry can be bought for a hefty price. Just walking around and looking at the showcases is a lot of fun. On the second floor, you will find the silver collection, offering some beautiful pieces at more reasonable prices. On the third floor, one can purchase crystal and fine china; the bridal registry is also located there.

Tiffany's offers other classically designed products, such as watches and clocks, flatware, scarves and ties, stationery, pens and pencils, leather goods, and fragrances. Any purchase you make will entitle you to the instantly recognizable Tiffany blue box. A major tourist stop, visitors from around the world enjoy strolling through this famous store. You can buy a key chain as a memento. Tiffany & Company store is located on Fifth Avenue at 57th Street; take the N, R, or W train to the Fifth Avenue/59th Street station.

Takashimaya New York

✉ 693 Fifth Avenue

✆ 212-350-0100

Takashimaya is a unique, cross-cultural, six-story gift and souvenir boutique that offers a cross between designs of the east and west. Once you pass into this lovely atmosphere, you will be immediately enchanted by the beautiful aroma of fresh-cut flowers.

Takashimaya offers a rare and distinctive selection of merchandise. The displays are equally unusual, expressing the sensitivity of Japanese craftsmanship. It is definitely worth a stroll down Fifth Avenue to visit and wander around in this relaxing setting. In the Tea Box, in the lower level, bento box lunches are served. Takashimaya New York is located on Fifth Avenue at 54th Street; take the E or V train to the Lexington Avenue/53rd Street station.

Flea Markets

New York City also offers lots of opportunities for flea-market bargain hunting. Annex Antiques Fair and Flea Market (at ✉ 26th Street and Sixth Avenue) is a popular Chelsea flea market. It's open year round on the weekends; take the C, E, 1, or 9 train to the 23rd Street station.

Chelsea Antiques Building (at ✉ 110 Eighth Avenue) is an indoor flea market that is open year round. You'll find lots of wonderful offbeat stuff here. Take the C or E train to 23rd Street.

The Green Flea Market is a wonderfully quirky New York flea market, with clothing, jewelry, and even neon beer signs from the 1950s. It's held on Saturdays at P.S. 183 (at ✉84th Street and Columbus Avenue); take the B, C, 1, or 9 train to 86th Street. On Sundays, the flea market is at Intermediate School 44 (at ✉Columbus and 77th Street); take the C or B train to 79th Street, or the 1 or 9 train to 81st Street.

☂RAINY DAY FUN

Visit the Manhattan Mall, located between 33rd and 34th Streets on Sixth Avenue. The Mall is accessible via the 1, 2, 3, 9, A, C, D, E, F, V, Q, N, and R trains (there are two different stations on 34th Street). This is the only mall in Manhattan, a good location for one-stop shopping. There's an adequate food court on the lower level with the likes of Nathan's and Subway, and there's a great sale section at the back of the store where you can sometimes get jewelry and underwear for as little as $1. There's also a good-sized KB Toys store. The mall is open seven days a week.

Secondhand Bargains

New York has some of the best thrift and secondhand shops in this country, with many of the items for sale coming from clothes-hounds cleaning out their designer closets.

Alice Underground
✉481 Broadway
✆212-431-9067
Alice Underground is a funky and fun thrift shop with great 1970s clothes, as well as vintage jeans and T-shirts, and the requisite bowling and Hawaiian shirts. Always clean and nicely arranged, Alice Underground is located on Broadway between Broome and Grand Streets; take the L train to the Grand Street station.

Cheap Jacks

✉ 841 Broadway

✆ 212-995-0443

Cheap Jacks offers about anything you could imagine in vintage clothing, from the 1920s to the present, with the stock all arranged fairly neatly. Want a smoking jacket, old belt buckles, a 1960s Chanel suit (or a knock-off), love beads, or a cigarette holder? This is the place. You'll find an awesome collection of old jeans and T-shirts, but it's often pricey for classics. Though you won't find great bargains here, it's worth it if you know what you're looking for.

Cheap Jacks discourages credit cards, so bring cash. The shop is located on Broadway between 13th and 14th Street; take the 4, 5, 6, L, N, or R train to Union Station.

Love Saves the Day

✉ 119 Second Avenue

✆ 212-228-3802

At Love Saves the Day, you'll find great wacky clothes and all the vintage lunchboxes and highball glasses you could ever want. This is a great place to hunt for a Halloween costume or cat's eye glasses. Love Saves the Day is located on Second Avenue off St. Marks Place; take the 4, 5, 6, V, or L train to the Broadway-Lafayette station.

JUST FOR PARENTS

If you have the time, you might want to sit in on one of the famous auctions at Sotheby's (✉ 1334 York Avenue at East 72nd Street; on the Web at ✑ www.sothebys.com) or Christie's (✉ 20 Rockefeller Plaza at 49th Street ✑ www.christies.com). Aside from million-dollar impressionist paintings, these auction houses often have celebrity memorabilia and animation collections, so go online and see what's coming up.

Trash & Vaudeville

✉4 St. Marks Place

✆ 212-982-3590

Rumored to have been started in the late 1970s by one of the former New York Dolls, this spacious thrift shop is almost like a costume collection. Here's where to find great vintage threads from the 1970s and 1980s. Trash & Vaudeville is located at St. Marks Place; take the 4, 5, 6, V, or L train to the Broadway-Lafayette station.

Books, Perfume, Food, and More

New York is book country. The publishing industry is centered there, and writers have made pilgrimages to the city for centuries. Even street vendors sell books there!

Books of Wonder

✉216 West 18th Street

✆ 212-989-3475

One of the last independently owned children's bookstores in New York City, this wonderful store has the most amazing collection of *Wizard of Oz* books and paraphernalia. The staff is wonderful and, of course, very child-friendly. Books of Wonder is located on West 18th Street; take the 1 or 9 train to 18th Street.

Forbidden Planet

✉840 Broadway

✆ 212-475-6161

You can find almost anything you could want in science fiction, fantasy, horror, comics, and graphic novels here. There's a great collection of models, as well as figurines from television shows and movies. No matter what time you go, the store is always filled with teens.

Forbidden Planet is located on Broadway at 13th Street; take 4, 5, 6, N, R, or L train to the 14th Street/Union Square station.

Midtown Comics

✉ 200 West 40th Street

✆ 212-302-8192

Old comics, new comics, graphic novels, and everything in between are on sale here. Figurines and collectibles are on the second floor. Midtown Comics is located on West 40th Street; take the A, C, 1, or 9 train to 42nd Street.

The Strand

✉ 828 Broadway

✆ 212-473-1452

One of the largest bookstores in the world, the Strand claims to have eight miles of books. There are always books on sale outside for $1, but it's the rows and rows of new and used books inside that will amaze you. Book reviewers sell their advance copies here, so you can sometimes get a popular title before it's officially published. The Strand is located on Broadway at East 12th Street; take the 4, 5, 6, N, R, or L train to the 14th Street/Union Square station.

 TRAVEL TIP

New York is famous for its designer sample sales, which are private and unpublished. Sometimes you can find a sign announcing a sample sale while walking through the Garment District in the west 1930s, but the best way to find one of these sales is to go online and search using the keywords "sample sale New York." Designers sell their overstock at a fraction of the cost.

Lush

✉ 33rd Street and Sixth Avenue

✆ 212-564-9120

The only New York branch of a fabulous British soap and beauty store, Lush sells the most divine chunks of soap and bath products at fairly affordable prices. The store is located on 33rd Street and Sixth Avenue; take B, D, F, V, N, R, 1, or 9 train to the 34th Street station.

Sephora

✉ 130 West 34th Street

✉ 555 Broadway, between Prince and Spring Street

✉ 119 Fifth Avenue

✉ 1500 Broadway at 44th Street

✑ *www.sephora.com*

Opened a few years ago on the Champs Élysées in Paris, and now in the United States as well, this cosmetics department store offers the wares of almost every makeup manufacturer in the world. You'll find hundreds of perfumes (arranged alphabetically) as well as lipsticks, eye shadow, mascara, and eyeliners to choose from here. There are bath products as well, and Sephora has its own brand. There are always samples to try on with plenty of cotton balls and swabs.

In New York, you've got four options to choose from. To visit the Sephora store on 34th Street, between Sixth and Seventh Avenues, take the B, D, F, V, N, R, 1, or 9 train to 34th Street. For the Broadway branch, located between Prince and Spring Streets, take the E train to the Spring Street station. The Fifth Avenue shop is at 19th Street—take the N or R train to 18th Street. For the Broadway store, Midtown at 44th Street, take the A, B, C, D, 1, or 9 train to 42nd Street.

Citarella

✉ 2135 Broadway

✑ *www.citarella.com*

Cheeses, foie gras, meat, homemade pastas—this is a gourmet food-lover's paradise. Fill a shopping bag and carry it home on the plane with you. Citarella is located on Broadway at West 75th Street; take the B train to 72nd Street or the 1 or 9 to 72nd Street.

Zabar's

✉ 2245 Broadway

✆ 212-787-2000

This store is one of the reasons that some people won't leave the Upper West Side. Again, cheeses, deli meats, breads, home-made salads, desserts, and even chocolates are available. Kitchenware is on sale upstairs. Zabar's is located on Broadway at 81st Street; take the B or C train to 81st Street or the 1 or 9 train to 79th Street.

Museum Shops and Souvenir Stores

The city's museums have some of the best and most unusual sou-venir shopping in the city. You can pick up great one-of-a-kind gifts for friends and family, too.

Museum of Modern Art Design Store

✉ 44 West 53rd Street

✉ 81st Spring Street

✆ 212-767-1050

This store offers visitors a wonderful opportunity to sample the museum's wares. There's an extensive offering of interesting jew-elry, classic modern furniture (even miniature versions for doll houses, but very pricey), and great housewares. This is a great museum store to browse for a wedding or housewarming gift.

The Museum of Modern Art Design Store has two locations, with a branch on West 53rd Street (take the V or E train to Fifth Avenue) and one between Broadway and Spring Street (take the C or E train to Spring Street).

New York City Transit Museum Shop

✉ Vanderbilt Place and East 42nd Street

✆ 212-878-0106

The Transit Museum has the ultimate New York gift shop. You can get that distinctive transit map on just about everything from

T-shirts and bags to ties, and the jewelry made out of old tokens (including women's earrings and cuff links for men) is always a conversation starter. The shop is located inside the Grand Central Terminal and is accessible by subway via many trains, including the 4, 5, or 6 (Grand Central station).

 # JUST FOR PARENTS

Babysitting in New York is expensive. If you are staying with a reputable hotel chain like Hilton, Sheraton, or Marriott, you can call ahead of time and ask them to reserve a sitter, who will be bonded, at a cost of at least $15 an hour. There is usually a two or three-hour minimum, and you do have to tip. If your hotel does not provide sitter services, you can also try the Babysitters Guild. Call ✆ 212-682-0227 for information.

City Store
✉ 1 Centre Street
✆ 212-669-8246

Discover the history of New York City. All sorts of books and maps, lapel pins, and even taxi cab memorabilia are on sale here. City Store is located on Centre Street at Chambers Street; take the 1, 9, 2, 3, A, or C train to the Chambers Street station.

New York Firefighter's Friend
✉ 263 Lafayette Street
✆ 1-800-229-9258

After September 11, everyone was wearing NYFD hats. Here's the place to buy them and give the money back to the real heroes—a portion of the proceeds goes to the widows and orphans of New York City firefighters. Tons of T-shirts, sweatshirts, and toys are available too. New York Firefighter's Friend is located on Lafayette Street between Prince and Spring; take the Q or W train to the Spring Street station.

Bargain Shopping

Because it is such a shopping center, New York City has some of the best bargains in the world. You can buy licensed sport and kid's items for as little as a dollar, if you really hunt for bargains.

Jack's 99-Cent Stores

✉ 110 West 32nd Street
✉ 16 West 40th Street
✆ 212-268-9962

The ultimate ninety-nine-cent store, Jack's on 32nd Street is the flagship store with two stories—the second floor has slightly more expensive items, such as gifts, linens, toys, and furnishings. Anything you might have forgotten at home—batteries, stockings, gloves, toothpaste—can be picked up for a buck, instead of paying over-priced hotel lobby convenience store prices. But the bargains are amazing too. You might even be able to pick up New York souvenirs for a dollar. There's an entire wall of kids' toys, many of them last year's hot Disney property (lots of Harry Potter and Lord of the Rings gadgets, and even clothes).

Jack's is located on West 32nd Street, between Seventh and Sixth Avenues; take the 1, 9, D, F, V, N, or R train to 34th Street. The second branch is on West 40th Street; take the D, F, V, N, R, 1, or 9 to 42nd Street.

Odd Job Trading

✉ 465 Lexington Avenue
✉ 350 Fifth Avenue (Empire State Building)
✉ 149 West 32nd Street
✉ 12 Cortlandt Street
✉ 66 West 48th Street
✉ 299 Broadway
✐ *www.oddjobstores.com*

There are quite a few Odd Job stores throughout the city, and they are usually packed. The business of Odd Job Trading is to buy closeout lots of clothing, housewares, cosmetics, and linens and offer the goods at a fraction of their original price. These stores are also a great source of seasonal knick-knacks.

You can get to the six Odd Job Trading branch locations as follows:

- Lexington Avenue: Take the 7, 4, 5, 6, or L train to the Grand Central station.
- Empire State Building, on Fifth Avenue: Take the D, F, V, Q, N, or R train to 34th Street.
- West 32nd Street, across the street from Jack's and Webber's: Take the A, C, E, 1, or 9 train to 34th Street.
- Cortlandt Street: Take the N or R train to City Hall.
- West 48th Street: Take the D or F to Rockefeller Center.
- Broadway: Take the A, C, J, Z, 2, or 3 to the Fulton Street or Broadway Nassau station.

TRAVEL TIP

Confused about all the cross-street addresses? There's a great Web site for locating the cross streets in Manhattan, as well as the nearest subway stop. Go to ✍ *www.manhattan address.com*.

Webber's Closeout Center
✉ 116 West 32nd Street
✉ 475 Fifth Avenue
✆ 212-564-4545

Webber's is a discount store similar to the Odd Job Trading chain. Their recent offerings have included a popular handbag—that sells for $30—on sale here for $8 and terrific shoes for $5 a pair. A pair of purple suede knee-high boots was once purchased here for $10. You have to hunt through a lot of merchandise, but it is definitely worth it if you like that type of shopping. Webber's Closeout Center has two branches. To get to the store on West

32nd Street, take A, B, C, D, E, F, N, R, 1, or 9 train to 34th Street; for the Fifth Avenue location, take the D or F train to Rockefeller Center.

Woodbury Commons

Another shopping option is to take a day trip outside the city to Woodbury Commons. This outlet mall is where many New Yorkers do their holiday shopping. There are more than 200 stores here, but some favorites are Off the Rack Saks and the Neiman Marcus store, where $1,000 gowns can go for less than $100. The Natori lingerie outlet always has great merchandise, and the Betsey Johnson store often has a rack of $10 to $15 dresses (usually in small sizes). The Pottery Barn outlet has discontinued items for a fraction of their original price. At the Frette linen outlet, where $400 imported bedroom sets can go for $150, a $400 silk skirt was purchased for $15. The Sony store has reconditioned merchandise at bargain prices.

To get to Woodbury Commons, the best option is to drive. Take the New York State Thruway (I-87) to exit 16, Harriman. Another option is to take MetroNorth on weekends, or the GrayLine or Shortline bus lines (✆ 845-928-4000) from Port Authority. The trip is about an hour and a half each way, but it's worth it.

If you take one of the buses, you get a coupon book worth the price of the bus ticket, with discounts of at least 10 percent at every store, or a free piece of merchandise with your visit, like Godiva chocolates. You can get a different coupon book by registering online at ✍ *www.primeoutlets.com* and picking it up at the customer service desk in the food court area.

CHAPTER 13

Parks, Recreation, and Sports

VISITORS TO NEW YORK are often surprised to find that it is such a great place to spend time outdoors. This is easy to do with all the terrific parks and public spaces, both in Manhattan and in the outer boroughs. There are great parks and playgrounds, gardens, beaches, and recreational facilities such as golf courses, horseback riding, and roller-skating. New Yorkers jog all year long, but it's an especially popular pastime from spring until late fall—the strip along Riverside Drive and around the reservoir in Central Park is always teeming with runners. And once the weather gets warm, the Great Lawn and Sheep Meadow turn into a giant sun-bathing arena.

The Hudson, the East River, and the Long Island Sound give New Yorkers a wonderful wealth of water activities, from boating and sailing to fishing in the warmer months.

For the sports fan, New York is a great town. There's the incredible Yankees franchise, as well as the world-class underdogs, the Mets. There's professional football, basketball, hockey, soccer, the U.S. Open, and some of the greatest golf courses in the country in nearby Westchester.

A Day at the Beach

New York City is surrounded by beaches, most of which are open to the public for free. The beaches do get very crowded during the summer months, but it's still a lot of fun to take a break from the city for a day and spend the day at the beach. Many beaches are flanked by a thriving boardwalk, with food, rides, and games.

 TRAVEL TIP

If you're planning a beach trip out of the city, leave early. If you get there late, you'll have trouble finding a spot to put your blanket down anywhere near the ocean. For information on beach hours, call the city information number at ✆311 (or ✆212-NEW-YORK, from outside the city).

Brighton Beach

This Russian neighborhood in Brooklyn has wonderful delis. Though clean and miles long, Brighton Beach is one of the city's most crowded, so get there early to stake out your territory. Take the Q train to Brighton Beach, the last stop. The ride will take at least an hour.

Coney Island

Here you'll find the legendary amusement park and boardwalk, as well as the original Nathan's. The waves here are mild. Like nearby Brighton Beach, Coney Island is often crowded, with slightly more families than teenagers because of the nearby amusement park and attractions. Take the D train to the Coney Island station; you can also take the D, F, or Q to the end of the line and catch a shuttle or bus to Coney Island.

Rockaway Park Beach

Rockaway Park is one of the least crowded beaches, found north of the last subway stop on the A line (at 116th Street). This is a year-round beach community with some die-hard surfers, so you'll see them suited up in wet suits to ride the waves. Take the A train to Rockaway Park Beach; the 116th Street station is at the end of the line.

Orchard Beach

Orchard Beach, a manmade beach on Long Island Sound in the Bronx, is affectionately known as "the Riviera of New York." It's close to City Island, so it's a popular beach destination. The nature center is open 11:00 A.M. to 5:00 P.M., as are the twenty-six baseball, basketball, volleyball, and handball courts. Snack bars are run by the Parks Department. There is ample parking for a fee. If you prefer public transportation, take the 2 or 5 train to Pelham Parkway and then the #12 bus to Orchard Beach.

Jones Beach

Because it takes longer to reach, and you must either go by car or MetroNorth, Jones Beach is much less crowded than the city beaches. During the week, you could actually spread out and play Frisbee. Take the Long Island Railroad to Freeport, where you can get a shuttle to this manmade beach. For more information, call ✆ 718-217-5477 or visit ✑ *www.mta.nyc.ny.us.*

A Stroll in the Park

Of course, Central Park is the center of the Park Universe in New York City. Many New Yorkers consider it their backyard. But there are other parks that residents love and use with almost equal passion.

Battery Park

This twenty-three-acre park is at the southern tip of Manhattan, where colonial New Amsterdam was first established. The park is home to a rose garden planted in honor of the many who have died from AIDS. There are also memorials in this historic park for World War II veterans and those who fought in the Korean War.

Fort Tryon Park/Inwood Hill Park

Located on the northwest side of Manhattan, bordering on Broadway and the Henry Hudson Parkway at Dyckman Street, this park is sixty acres of wooded hills surrounding The Cloisters museum, with a marvelous view of the Hudson River. Originally a fort in the American Revolution, this park's country atmosphere allows you to forget you are in Manhattan. In the Inwood section of the park, you can find a Native American trash dump, where American Indians once discarded their shells. People still find arrowheads every year in the park. If you walk through the park's paths, also designed by Frederick Law Olmsted, you may see wild rabbits, raccoons, and pheasants that still populate the park. Urban park rangers give tours throughout the spring and summer, and, if you are planning on being in Upper Manhattan, it's worth the trip.

≡FAST FACT

In the 1950s, when Frank Lloyd Wright was looking for a home for his new museum, Fort Tryon Park was considered (and rejected) as the site for the Guggenheim.

Riverside Park

Located between Riverside Drive and the Hudson River, from 72nd Street all the way up to 158th Street, the four-mile long Riverside Park is a popular place for strolling, dog walking, bird watching, and more, including sleighing and cross-country skiing in the winter. Designed by Frederick Law Olmsted (of Central Park fame) and opened in 1910, the long waterside park features a bird sanctuary, community garden, a marina, and an adjacent rotunda. From posh Upper-West-Siders to Columbia University students to numerous joggers, the park has a wide variety of daily visitors.

Carl Schurz Park

Running along the East River between 84th and 90th Streets, this park was once a fortification for the Continental Army in the

American Revolution, and it was later taken over by the British. Today it is taken over primarily by Upper East Siders. The park is on several levels, with marble stairways and beautiful paths. Playgrounds, basketball courts, and dog runs are part of this secret little gem. Tucked away in a cozy east side corner of the city, the park is bordered on the upper tip by the mayor's residence, Gracie Mansion. The most noteworthy aspect of this inviting little park is the John Finley Walk, a wide riverside walkway with spectacular views of Roosevelt Island, Queens, and the boat traffic along the East River. The serenity and tranquility make for a delightful afternoon.

Union Square Park

Between 14th and 18th Streets, and Broadway and Park Avenue, this small park is home to a giant green market (featuring fresh fruits and vegetables) and a flea market selling a variety of craft items. The popular 14th Street/Union Square subway station deposits many travelers on the park's borders, as the park remains the centerpiece of Union Square. The surrounding area has been refurbished in the past several years, with cafés and trendy restaurants now highlighting the increasingly popular neighborhood.

Washington Square Park

At the foot of Fifth Avenue in Greenwich Village, Washington Square Park is home to a giant white marble arch built in 1892, along with two statues of George Washington that were added in the early part of the twentieth century. The nearly ten-acre park, used in the early nineteenth century for military parade drills and public hangings, is nestled between brownstones and New York University. For decades it has been a favorite stomping ground for an eclectic variety of locals. Hippies, yuppies, punks, poets, artists, bohemians, Frisbee players, chess players, students, panhandlers, and a variety of street performers all come to enjoy themselves here. Visiting the park is a "let your hair down" experience and has been for many years. Outdoor art shows are very popular before and after the summer.

Flushing Meadow Corona Park

Take the 7 train to 111th Street in Flushing, Queens, to this full service park on the grounds of two former World's Fairs. The Unisphere is here, but people also come for the Queens Zoo and the Pitch and Putt. The grounds have softball, baseball, soccer, and cricket fields, and a new boathouse is being completed.

Prospect Park

Take the F train to Prospect Park, Brooklyn's answer to Central Park. If you lived near it, you would never go into Manhattan. There is an Audubon Center and café on the premises. The Celebrate Brooklyn Performing Arts program has events scheduled at the band shell all summer long, with fantastic performances of music, dance, and movies. The Prospect Park Zoo is here. Facilities include ice skating in the winter, as well as tennis courts. The park features the only forest in Brooklyn.

Van Cortlandt Park

Take the 1 train to 242nd Street, the last stop on the line. Van Cortlandt Park is the Bronx's answer to Central Park. You'll find horseback riding, tennis courts, and a public pool (always very crowded). The Van Cortlandt Mansion is a house museum on the premises, and it's an interesting way to spend an afternoon looking at how life was lived after the American Revolution. There are free concerts in the park in summer.

RAINY DAY FUN

Spend an afternoon at Van Cortlandt Park touring the Dutch Colonial museum house, the first of its kind in the city. In addition to restored interiors, the house was also the site of a gristmill. There's a nice gift shop there, and colonial fairs are held in the spring and the fall on the premises. For more information, call ☎ 718-271-8981 or visit ✎ www.van cortlandthouse.org.

Arenas and Stadiums

New York is the center of the entertainment industry, so every major concert will tour here. There's nothing like seeing Bruce Springsteen or Bob Dylan on their home turf. Watching the Yankees play at home is a real New York experience.

Madison Square Garden

✆ 212-465-6741

✍ *www.thegarden.com*

This is where the Rangers and the Knicks play on a regular basis. Madison Square Garden is also the venue for many large rock concerts. The Garden is located on Seventh Avenue between 31st and 33rd Streets and can be reached via the N, R, A, B, C, D, or F train, as well as the 1 or 9 to 34th Street. For event tickets, contact Ticketmaster: ✆ 212-307-7171, ✍ *www.ticketmaster.com*

Meadowlands Sports Complex

✉ 50 State Route 120

✆ 201-935-8500

✍ *www.meadowlands.com*

Also known as the Continental Airlines Arena and Giants Stadium, the Meadowlands Complex is located in East Rutherford, New Jersey. The New Jersey Nets, Jets, and the Devils play here, and the Giants play at Giants Stadium. There are always great rock concerts in the summer months.

If you can drive, take Rte. 3 and the New Jersey Turnpike to Exit 16W. Buses run from the Port Authority Bus Terminal when there are games and events.

Shea Stadium

✉ 123-01 Roosevelt Avenue

✆ 718-507-8499

✍ *www.mets.com*

The Mets play here in the stadium they once lent the Beatles.

Tickets are easy to come by, but they are cheaper at the box office—there's a heavy surcharge if you order through Ticketmaster. Shea Stadium is located on Roosevelt Avenue off Grand Central Parkway in Flushing, Queens; the stadium is accessible from the 7 train (Shea Stadium station).

Yankee Stadium

✉ 161st Street

✆ 718-293-6000

🖮 *www.yankees.com*

Yankee Stadium is home to the team with the most World Series victories, the New York Yankees. Yankee Stadium has a lot to offer. There's a food court that serves the usual chicken and hotdogs, but Chinese food is available, too. The Yankee store has been completely remodeled. There's also a Yankee Stadium tour available. Tickets can be obtained, but order ahead for special days like opening day or Red Sox/Yankee games. The stadium is located on 161st Street and River Avenue; take the 4 or D train to the 161st Street station.

TRAVEL TIP

The sports store and vendors just outside Yankee Stadium have some terrific merchandise. The official Yankee store in the stadium has been recently expanded and is also a fun way to kill some time, but it's often crowded. Get there a few minutes earlier if you'd like to browse.

KeySpan Park

✉ 1904 Surf Avenue

✆ 718-449-8497

🖮 *www.brooklyncyclones.com*

The Brooklyn Cyclones are the farm team for the Mets. They play thirty-eight games a season. KeySpan is a great park. It overlooks the Atlantic and is right next door to Nathan's. It is located on Surf Avenue. Take the D train to the Coney Island/Stillwell Avenue station.

Richmond County Bank Ballpark

✉ St. George, Staten Island

✆ 718-720-9265

The Richmond Country Bank Ballpark is home to the Staten Island Yankees, the minor league farm team for the Yankees. The stadium can be reached by the Staten Island Ferry and has incredible views of the Statue of Liberty and Lower Manhattan. This is a truly great way to see a ballgame!

Athletic Activities

If your idea of sports doesn't involve sitting on the bleachers and cheering for your favorite team, consider the many athletic activities New York City has to offer. Go biking, play tennis or golf, try ice skating or horseback riding—you can do it all here.

Bike Rides and Rentals

New Yorkers bike all over the city, from the bike paths of Central Park and Riverside Drive through Prospect Park. You can rent bikes in Central Park at the Loeb Boathouse (✆ 212-517-2233) or at the Toga Bike Shop (✆ 212-799-9625) on the Upper West Side.

Bike New York offers organized rides with other bikers; contact them at ✆ 212-932-2300, ext. 111, or visit ✎ www.bikenewyork.org. The Five Borough Bicycle Club also offers day and weekend rides—call ✆ 212-932-2300, ext. 115, or visit ✎ www.5bbc.org.

A Tennis Match

There are twenty-six public tennis courts at Central Park (✆ 212-280-0206) and Riverside Park (✆ 212-496-2006) has ten courts, but you should call ahead for availability and fees. The parks and recreation office will also give you a list of other outdoor tennis courts if you call ✆ 311 (from outside the city, call ✆ 212-NEW-YORK).

A Game of Golf

New York has a few public golf courses, including Van Cortlandt Park (✆ 718-543-4595) and Split Rock (✆ 718-885-1256) in the Bronx; Forest Park in Queens (✆ 718-296-0999); and Silver Lake Gold in Staten Island (✆ 718-447-5687). Call the city information number at ✆ 311 (✆ 212-NEW-YORK from outside the city) for directions and fees.

 **TRAVEL TIP**

There's an eighteen-hole miniature golf course at Pier 25, on Hudson River and Reade Street (✆ 212-336-6400), which has a beautiful view of the river and may be a fun way to spend an afternoon.

Ice Skating

The city's outdoor ice-skating rinks are open mid-October through April. All facilities offer skate rentals. There are two rinks in Central Park: Lasker Rink (✆ 212-534-7639) is located near 106th Street, and the Wollman Rink (✆ 212-439-6900) entrance is at 59th and Sixth Avenue.

The Rockefeller Center Rink (✆ 212-332-7654) is located on 50th Street and Fifth Avenue. It is often crowded, but skating there is a classic experience. Another Wollman Rink (✆ 718-287-6431) is located on the lake in Prospect Park.

Horseback Riding

There's wonderful horseback riding in Central Park at the Claremont Riding Academy (✉ 175 West 89th Street, ✆ 212-724-5100), but it's packed after school and on weekends, so call ahead. There's also park riding at Van Cortlandt Park in the Bronx, on 246th Street and Broadway. Call ✆ 311 (✆ 212-NEW-YORK from outside the city) for more information.

Visit Chelsea Piers

✉ 12th Avenue and 23rd Street

✆ 212-336-6400

🖰 *www.chelseapiers.com*

Chelsea Piers Sports and Entertainment Complex offers thirty acres of fun along Manhattan's Hudson River. In addition to the traditional amenities of a sports center, Chelsea Piers also boasts the largest indoor rock-climbing wall in the Northeast, one of the few indoor Olympic pools in the city, the only indoor sand volleyball court in New York City, and a quarter-mile running track, as well as the city's only all-year, indoor ice-skating rink.

☂ RAINY DAY FUN

Take your family to the Sky Rink, the only year-round indoor ice-skating arena in the city. General skating is offered every afternoon and is priced around $13 for adults and $9.50 for children and seniors.

The Gold Club at Chelsea Piers is a popular favorite. For about $20, you can hit 100 balls in one of fifty-two heated and weather-protected putting stalls on four levels with fully automated tee-up services. There is also virtual golfing, with "Full Swing Simulators," for about $45 an hour. Players can choose from thirty-six different championship courses worldwide.

The Chelsea Brewing Company has a restaurant on the premises that offers an extensive variety of pizza and burgers as well as beer; the restaurant overlooks the marina. There is also Miss Rita's and Famous Famiglia.

Going to Chelsea Piers is a nice way to spend an afternoon, especially if the weather turns bad and you've had enough of the museums.

CHAPTER 14

Broadway and the Performing Arts

NEW YORK IS THE CULTURAL CAPITAL of the country. When you visit, you should try to see at least one play and try to catch a performance of opera, ballet, or comedy. Performances like these are what the city's known for.

It doesn't have to break your budget. If you can't afford four tickets to *The Lion King,* there are off-Broadway productions with tickets for $10 per person or even summer plays at the Delacorte Theater in Central Park that are absolutely free. But it does take planning. You should go online before you arrive and see what's playing while you're here (try searching through entertainment listings of the *New York Times, New York, Time Out New York,* and the *Village Voice*). You'll also be able to find out what tickets are available and what you can afford. You won't regret planning in advance.

On Broadway

A Broadway musical can set a family back a few hundred dollars, but it's one of those rare treats you'll always remember. The long-running *Phantom of the Opera* is classic Broadway; for story and production values, you can see *The Lion King;* for more great family fare, you can see *Beauty and the Beast. New York* magazine, among other publications, will fill you in on the shows, as will the concierge in any good hotel. It's not hard to find out what shows are the talk of the town. Whether you enjoy musicals or dramas, there's always a selection of first-rate shows available. The theater in New York City is a captivating experience.

Shows are always opening and closing on Broadway, but some trends persist. There is a riveting production of some classic drama by Eugene O'Neill, Henrik Ibsen, Edward Albee, and Shakespeare in any given Broadway season. There are "classics" as well from the revivals of *42nd Street* and *Annie Get Your Gun* on up to the Tony Award–winning *Chicago*.

 TRAVEL TIP

Discount tickets can be obtained for many shows. For the most popular ones, you'll still need to plan ahead. If you can afford it, a Broadway show is something you should plan on.

Getting Tickets

Two major ticket providers are Telecharge and Ticketmaster.

Telecharge
☎ 212-239-6200   ☎ 1-800-432-7250 (outside New York City)
✍ *www.telecharge.com*

Ticketmaster
☎ 212-307-4100
✍ *www.ticketmaster.com*

Theater tickets are divided between the two ticket companies, so if tickets for the show you want to see are not sold by one, they will most likely be sold by the other. A surcharge is added per ticket; you can get the tickets mailed to you, or you can pick them up at the theater the night of the show. In some cases, you can still order tickets from the theater box office.

Same-day discount tickets are available at the TKTS Booth at 47th Street and Broadway (expect to wait at least an hour, perhaps two) or the South Street Seaport at Front and John Streets—this location is a better bet, but it's usually out of the way. Both sites sell tickets at a 25 to 50 percent discount, with a small fee per ticket, but you have to pay in cash. The downtown booth also sells tickets for the next day's matinee performances. You can buy tickets online at the Web site *www.TKTS.com*, but they are usually for the perennials and not the last minute "hot" tickets.

Broadway Shows

Here is a list of some of the perennial and long-running Broadway shows that you might consider seeing. These are only those that were running for at least a year at the time of this writing.

Aida, at the Palace Theatre
✉ Broadway and 47th Street
✆ 212-307-4747
www.disneyonbroadway.com

This 2000 Tony Award–winning musical/opera written by Elton John and Tim Rice, is a classic for slightly older children who are comfortable with opera. The musical features fabulous sets and costumes.

Beauty and the Beast, at the Lunt Fontaine Theatre
✉ Broadway and 46th Street
✆ 212-307-4747
www.disneyonbroadway.com

This is a wonderful production based on the animated Disney film. Clever and beautiful, it is appropriate for all ages and definitely worth seeing.

Chicago, at the Ambassador Theatre
✉ 219 West 49th Street
www.chicagothemusical.com

A terrific production, but its content about adultery and deceit make this a musical for slightly older kids, 12 and up. Tickets are available at Telecharge.

≡FAST FACT

Of course, there's some terrific theater history along Broadway. The Music Box (⊠239 West 45th Street) was built by Irving Berlin and opened in 1921. The New Amsterdam Theatre, a grand theater built in 1903 with an elaborate interior, was refurbished by Disney and is now home to *The Lion King*. The Shubert Theater (⊠225 West 45th Street), just off Shubert Alley, the famous theater stomping ground, was built in 1913.

Hairspray, at the Neil Simon Theatre
⊠250 West 52nd Street

✑*www.hairsprayonbroadway.com*

A wonderful adaptation of a wacky John Waters cult film, this Tony Award–winning musical is fun, but some of its subject matter makes it inappropriate for younger kids. Tickets are available at Ticketmaster.

42nd Street, at the Ford Center
⊠213 West 42nd Street

✆212-307-4100

✑*www.42ndstreetbroadway.com*

This 2001 Tony Award–winning revival is a terrific Broadway spectacle for the whole family.

The Lion King at the New Amsterdam Theatre
⊠Broadway and 42nd Street

✆212-307-4747

✑*www.disneyonbroadway.com*

If you can afford it, and you can get the tickets, this is the family show to see. It's an adaptation of the terrific animated Disney film, and the sets and costumes are spectacular. Your kids will be singing and dancing in the aisles. Get tickets at least a month ahead of time.

Mamma Mia, at the Winter Garden
✉ 1634 Broadway at 50th Street
✎ *www.mammamia.com*

This musical is about a woman who invites three men, any of whom might be her daughter's father, to her daughter's wedding. The musical score is comprised of ABBA songs. This is a good option for young and old fans of ABBA, but it is not for young children. Tickets are available from Telecharge.

 # JUST FOR PARENTS

Some shows are for grownups only. Get a babysitter and catch *I Love You, You're Perfect, Now Change* (at the Westside Theatre, ✉ 407 West 43rd Street, with tickets available at Telecharge). This is a hilarious, long-running musical about dating. Another good option is *Menopause: The Musical* (at the Playhouse, ✉ 91, 316 East 91st Street, with tickets available at Ticketmaster), which does for menopause what Weird Al Yankovic did for MTV.

Movin' Out, at the Richard Rodgers Theatre
✉ 226 West 46th Street
✎ *www.movinoutonbroadway.com*

This is a play about six people coming of age in the 1960s and 1970s, using the music and lyrics of Billy Joel and the dance of Twyla Tharp. It's one of those incredible New York Broadway experiences. If your kids like music and dance and can follow a mature theme (such as death and divorce), bring them along. Tickets are available from Ticketmaster.

The Phantom of the Opera, at the Majestic Theatre
✉ 247 West 44th Street
✆ 1-800-BROADWAY
✑ *www.thephantomoftheopera.com*

This is the ultimate Broadway experience, and it's appropriate for almost all ages, except the very young. If you can afford it, ask for seats under the chandelier.

The Producers, at the St. James Theatre
✉ 246 West 44th Street

This musical, based on Mel Brooks's classic film, is about one of the worst musicals ever made. It is a good production, but it's a show for slightly older children. Tickets are available from Telecharge.

Rent, at the Nederland Theatre
✉ 208 West 48th Street

This show is one-of-a-kind theater, illustrating life in New York in the 1990s, and is definitely worth seeing. It features great music and performances, but the content is definitely for children over 16. You will have to be comfortable discussing AIDS and death with your children. Tickets are available from Ticketmaster.

Off-Broadway Shows

Not quite as glamorous as Broadway, this is where the Broadway plays start, often for half the ticket price. You'll also find some really unusual and/or quirky theater here.

Blue Man Group, at the Astor Place Theatre
✉ 434 LaFayette Street
✑ *www.bluemangroup.com*

This is performance art with sound and various props, fun and engaging and very New York. The Blue Man Group shows are appropriate for children over 8. Tickets are available from Ticketmaster.

De La Guardia, at the Daryl Roth Theatre

✉20 Union Square East

Another one-of-a-kind New York theater experience, this Argentinean aerial group performs over your head. Very engaging, but for slightly older children. Tickets are available from Telecharge.

Forbidden Broadway, at the Douglas Fairbanks Theatre

✉432 West 42nd Street

This is an annual send-up of the current Broadway and off-Broadway offerings with four seasoned performers in a nightclub atmosphere. It is tremendous fun for those who have followed the season. Since it's a nightclub setting, it is for slightly older children. Tickets are available from Telecharge.

TRAVEL TIP

The *Radio City Christmas Spectacular* has been going strong for over sixty-five years. Complete with the "Parade of the Wooden Soldiers" and the "Living Nativity," it's an exciting seasonal spectacle. If you're in town between November and early January, it's worth seeing. Call ☎212-247-4777.

Stomp, at the Orpheum Theater

✉Second Avenue and 8th Street

✐*www.stomponline.com*

This eight-person musical review uses only found objects, such as sinks and newspapers and hubcaps, to make a funny, entertaining evening of noise and dance. It is fun for the whole family—about a third of the audience is kids. This show is worth every penny. Tickets are available from Ticketmaster.

Tony & Tina's Wedding, at Ceremony St. Luke's

✉308 West 46th Street

✐*www.tonylovestina.com*

Now in its seventeenth year, this is an "interactive" play that offers dinner with spectacle. Tickets are available from Telecharge.

Performing Arts

No trip to New York should be without a visit to the opera or ballet or a concert of some sort, as the finest performers in the world all play or perform here.

Carnegie Hall
✉ 881 Seventh Avenue
✆ 212-247-7800
🖅 *www.carnegiehall.org*

Carnegie Hall has been the standard for performance excellence in New York City and the world for more than 100 years. Legendary musicians, vocalists, dancers, and even speakers including authors and politicians, have graced the hallowed stage of this international institution. The history of the hall and the esteemed artists who have played here have created a tradition greater than the building itself.

Construction began on Carnegie Hall in 1890 at a cost of more than $2 million. The six-story structure was designed to encompass a main hall seating 2,800, a recital hall (now the Carnegie Hall Cinema) seating 1,200, and a chamber hall (now the Weil Recital Hall) seating 250. The building opened in 1891 with five days of performances that attracted New York's high society. In the audience were the Rockefellers, Whitneys, and Fricks, all listening to Peter Tchaikovsky play for them opening week!

While many people associate Carnegie Hall with classical music, it has broadened its performance scope in the past decades to include jazz (Fats Waller, Louis Armstrong, Count Basie, Ella Fitzgerald, Miles Davis, John Coltrane, and Benny Goodman have all played here), as well as rock (Paul McCartney, Roger Daltrey) folk (Woody Guthrie, Pete Seeger, and Arlo Guthrie), and popular (Frank Sinatra, Judy Garland, Ethel Merman, and even the Beatles). Young people's concerts, radio and television programs, and speeches by Winston Churchill, Mark Twain, Booker T. Washington, and Woodrow Wilson are also part of this legacy.

☰FAST FACT

Carnegie Hall was almost demolished in the 1960s, when the New York Philharmonic Orchestra moved uptown to Lincoln Center. Fortunately, it was saved and even refurbished in the 1990s.

There is a gift shop on the premises, as well as a small exhibit—the Rose Museum—that features noteworthy items from performers who have graced the great stage.

Location and Hours

Carnegie Hall is located on Seventh Avenue, on the corner of 57th Street. It is accessible by subway via the N, R, or Q train (57th Street station). Tours of the premises are available Mondays through Fridays at 11:30 A.M. and 2:00 and 3:00 P.M. and will take you behind the scenes. Tours are $6 for adults, $5 for seniors and students, and $3 for children under 12. There are also tour and dining packages; for more information, call ✆ 212-903-9765.

Lincoln Center

✉ 140 West 65th Street
✆ 212-875-5370
🖱 www.lincolncenter.org

The premier performing arts complex in the world, Lincoln Center for the Performing Arts occupies sixteen acres of Manhattan's Upper West Side. Home to eleven performing arts companies and educational institutions, the renowned multibuilding complex attracts more than 5 million visitors annually.

Originally conceived in the 1950s, the complex is a result of a search for a new home for the New York Philharmonic and the Metropolitan Opera Company, and it opened in the fall of 1962. On opening night, Leonard Bernstein and the Philharmonic Orchestra played in front of a live audience of 3,000 people, plus a television audience of 26 million.

The Lincoln Center is located on Broadway between 62nd and 66th Streets. It is accessible by subway via the A, B, C, D, or 1 train (59th Street station). For more information, call ✆ 212-875-5370 or visit ✐ *www.lincolncenter.org*. The companies that call Lincoln Center home are world-renowned. If you are not seeing a performance, you can still visit the premises and even take a tour.

The New York Philharmonic
✉ Avery Fisher Hall, 10 Lincoln Center Plaza
✆ 212-875-5656

The nation's oldest orchestra was founded in 1842. The New York Philharmonic plays more than 150 concerts a year to audiences totaling more than a million people. This includes the annual visit to Central Park for a special performance under the stars, where the *1812 Overture* is performed amid fireworks. The philharmonic's schedule also includes young people's concerts, Saturday matinee programs, and other specially scheduled performances.

The New York City Ballet
✉ 20 Lincoln Center Plaza
✆ 212-870-5570

The New York City Ballet has a performing season of only five months and features the choreography of its founders, George Balanchine and Jerome Robbins. The annual performance of *The Nutcracker* is one of the season highlights. Tickets sell out quickly, so order a few months in advance if you are hoping to see this with your family. The New York City Ballet performs at the New York State Theater.

The Metropolitan Opera
✉ Columbus Avenue between 62nd and 65th Streets

The Metropolitan Opera performs nearly twenty operas annually, and state-of-the-art individual viewing is available at each seat. This is a good venue to introduce your kids to opera as there are subtitled translations throughout the entire performance.

The New York City Opera

✉ 20 Lincoln Center Plaza, New York State Theatre

✆ 212-870-5570

🖰 *www.nycopera.com*

Not as well known as the Metropolitan Opera, this is the city's more innovative opera company. The New York City Opera performs new and offbeat operas, such as the acclaimed *Dead Man Walking*. Both Beverly Sills and Placido Domingo began their careers there. The season runs from September through November and again in March and April.

 RAINY DAY FUN

TADA! Theater, with just under 100 seats, features performances for kids and their families, presented by kids ages 6 through 17. The theater is at ✉ 15 West 28th Street between Sixth and Seventh Avenues. Call ✆ 212-252-1619.

The Chamber Music Society of Lincoln Center

✉ 70 Lincoln Center Plaza, Alice Tully Hall

✆ 212-875-5788

Founded in 1969 by Alice Tully, an opera singer in the 1920s who became a philanthropist in her nineties; William Schuman, the first recipient of the Pulitzer Prize in Music; and Charles Wadsworth, whom the *New York Times* credited with starting the chamber music boom, this society is the premier in the field. If you love chamber music, this is the place to go.

The New York Public Library for the Performing Arts

✆ 212-870-1630

The New York Public Library is a terrific research facility where every play that has been on or off Broadway for the past three decades can be seen on videotape. There is also an extensive collection of audio recordings. The library is occasionally the site of performances as well.

Other Attractions

Also on the Lincoln Center grounds are the small Walter Reade Theater, which shows award-winning independent and foreign films, run by the Film Society of Lincoln Center; the Gallery at Lincoln Center, both an art shop and gallery; the Juilliard School, complete with the Juilliard theater, Paul Recital Hall, and Drama Workshop; Lincoln Center Plaza; and the Guggenheim Band Shell at Damrosch Park, which hosts outdoor concerts and events for up to 3,000 people.

While strolling the grounds, you will see the brilliant murals in the lobby of the Metropolitan Opera House, the architecture and grandeur of these buildings, and the fountains that are the Lincoln Center's centerpiece (and a wonderful family photo op). You can buy gifts at the Lincoln Center gift ship (often music- and theater-related). You can dine at Lincoln Center or grab a light snack at Café Vienna with its fountain plaza setting, or you might prefer to enjoy a full sit-down dinner at the Met's Grand Tier Restaurant overlooking Lincoln Center.

Most performances take place between September and May, when the opera season, Great Performances series, and ballet companies are running. Mostly Mozart takes place during the summer; other events take place throughout the year, from outdoor concerts and meet-the-artist nights to the New York Film Festival. There are events for children of all ages. For group events, such as Sea and Symphony, which includes lunch on a yacht and a meet-the-artist program, call the Lincoln Center Visitors' Services at ✆ 212-875-5370.

Several tours are offered at Lincoln Center. The guided tour includes the Metropolitan Opera House, Avery Fisher Hall, and New York State Theater, taking you backstage where you may get a glimpse of a rehearsal in progress. Tours cost $12.50 for adults, $9 for students and seniors, and $6 for children under 12 and are offered every day at 10:30 A.M. and 12:30, 2:30, and 4:40 P.M. Call ✆ 212-875-5350 for information. There are also specialty tours, such as Tour with a Bite, which includes a light meal at Café Vienna, and the Art and Architecture tour, which features the background

and history of how the theaters and performing arts centers origi-
nated (by reservation only).

TRAVEL TIP

Lincoln Center is an ideal destination year-round. During the
warmer months in the evening you are likely to find outdoor
entertainment under the stars, such as the fun-filled
Midsummer Night Swing in July, featuring dancers from
around the world.

Catch the Taping of a Television Show

Television shows are free if you want to watch a taping. The
problem is that tickets are very hard to get for most shows. Most
shows do not allow children under 18, so if you get a real person
on the phone, ask what the cutoff is. Shows also have standby policies; you can spend a great portion of your day in line in hopes of
getting one of the few tickets that become available prior to taping.
Or you could do something more productive with your day and then
watch the show on television that night or the following night.

Among the growing number of shows taped in New York City
are the following:

- *The Daily Show* stars Jon Stewart and includes pretaped
  segments. Call ✆ 212-468-1700.
- The *Late Show with David Letterman* tapes at the famous
  Ed Sullivan Theater on Broadway and 53rd Street. This is
  the best television taping in the city and hardest to get
  tickets for. Tickets can be obtained in advance on their Web
  site, ✐ *www.lateshowaudience.com*, or in person at the
  box office Monday through Friday 9:30 A.M. to 12:30 P.M.,
  Saturday and Sunday from 10:00 A.M. to 6:00 P.M. Standby
  tickets for day of show are available by calling ✆ 212-247-
  6497 after 11:00 A.M. You can also call ✆ 212-975-1003 for
  more information.

- *Late Night with Conan O'Brien* tapes at ✉30 Rockefeller Plaza. Call ✆212-664-3056 for advance and standby tickets, as well as other information.
- *Saturday Night Live* accepts e-mail ticket requests for a lottery drawing held once a year, in August. Please note that applications are limited to one e-mail per household for up to two tickets and viewers must be at least sixteen years of age. The e-mail address for sending your request is ✍*SNLtickets@nbc.com.*
- *The View*, featuring Joy Behar, Elisabeth Hasselbeck, Star Jones, Meredith Vieira, and Barbara Walters, is a daily talk show on ABC. The best way to get tickets is to write or e-mail a request via the Web site at ✍*www.abc.com.* Do it a least a month ahead of time. Standby tickets are offered the day of the show, but you have to show up at 8:30 A.M. and wait until 10:00, and then wait some more.

If you don't feel like chasing after tickets to New York's few hot television tapings, you can always stroll by the *Good Morning America* studios (on the corner of 44th and Broadway), the *Today Show* (across from 30 Rock on 49th Street), or *The Early Show* (on 59th and Fifth Avenue). The glass-enclosed studios let you watch while they do the show, and when you've had enough, you can simply stroll away.

Going to the Circus

Visiting New York in the springtime? Consider taking the whole family to the circus. Ringling Brothers Barnum and Bailey Circus hits Madison Square Garden every spring. After well over 100 years, it's still "the Greatest Show on Earth." It features a full-fledged extravaganza with three rings of animals, clowns, and jugglers, plus acrobats swinging overhead. Stuff your face with cotton candy and enjoy. Call the Madison Square Garden box office at ✆212-465-6741 or visit ✍*www.ringling.com* for information.

Another option is the Big Apple Circus, dedicated to classical circus acts. It is a one-ring circus under a big-top tent, featuring world-renowned acrobats, clowns, aerialists, tightrope walkers, jugglers, hoop divers, and more. Also in the lineup are some dogs, birds, horses, and elephants. The international circus rolls into town in May and can be found in Queens at Cunningham Park and, later in the month, on Long Island at Long Island University's C. W. Post Campus. The extravaganza hits Manhattan in October at Damrosch Park, behind Lincoln Center on West 65th Street. On a smaller, more personal scale than Ringling Brothers, the Big Apple Circus lets you get closer to the action. Call ✆ 212-268-2500 or visit ✎ *www.bigapplecircus.org* for more information.

TRAVEL TIP

Visiting New York during the Christmas season? *The Nutcracker* plays Lincoln Center every holiday season. It's a marvelous performance for all ages. Call ✆ 212-875-5000 for more information.

New York after Dark

Although New York is famous for its nightlife, it's not for kids. Included here is a limited list of the better nightclubs and comedy clubs in the city. Keep in mind that these clubs serve alcohol; no one under twenty-one is admitted.

Jazz Venues

Some call the Birdland the nicest jazz room in New York—it's comfortable and features great talent. The Blue Note is another popular tourist destination that hosts some of the biggest names in jazz.

Birdland
✉ 315 West 44th Street
✆ 212-581-3080

Blue Note
✉ 131 West 3rd Street
✆ 212-475-8592

Rock and Other Popular Music

There are also a lot of options for going to hear popular music at a smaller venue.

B.B. King's

✉ West 44th Street at Times Square

☎ 212-997-4144

✍ www.bbkingblue.com

This is a wonderful, intimate nightclub with stellar performances by artists such as Aretha Franklin, Etta James, and Greg Allman, as well as tribute bands.

≡FAST FACT

Studio 54, on 54th Street, recently home to *Cabaret*, is known less as a Broadway theater and more as a disco, famed in the late 1970s and early 1980s. It's at 254 West 54th Street.

Beacon Theater

✉ 2124 Broadway at 74th Street

☎ 212-496-7070

The Beacon is a small venue for rock concerts. You can purchase tickets at the theater box office or through Ticketmaster.

CBGB

✉ 315 Bowery (at Bleecker Street)

☎ 212-982-4052

CBGB is a legendary club that spawned the Talking Heads, Ramones, and others. Enjoy the atmosphere and sound system.

Irving Plaza

✉ 17 Irving Plaza (at 15th Street)

☎ 212-777-6800

✍ www.irvingplaza.com

Showcasing major bands, this is one of the prime locations to play in the city. It's smaller than the Roseland but bigger than most other venues, and it has a good sound system and stage.

Knitting Factory

✉ 74 Leonard Street (between Broadway and Church Street)

✆ 212-219-3055

Enjoy eclectic music in this venerable institution; it's a New York musical sanctuary and offers multiple stages with a variety of bands.

Roseland

✉ 239 West 52nd Street (between Eighth Avenue and Broadway)

✆ 212-249-8870

A huge old place, Roseland attracts acts that aren't quite big enough for Madison Square Garden but that can still draw big crowds.

Comedy Clubs

If you can leave your kids in the hotel and see a late comedy show, you've got several options.

Caroline's Comedy Club

✉ 1626 Broadway (between 49th and 50th Streets)

✆ 212-757-4100

✑ *www.carolines.com*

This first-rate club features headliner and stand-up comics including Rich Jeni, Margaret Cho, and other frequent guests on late-night television. It's a top comedy room. Call for reservations on weekends.

The Comic Strip

✉ 1568 Broadway

✆ 212-861-9386

✑ *www.comicstriplive.com*

This longtime club—starting ground for Eddie Murphy and others—features a solid array of hot new comics, some seen on Letterman and Conan. Weeknights feature numerous performers. Call for reservations on weekends.

Gotham Comedy Club

✉ 34 West 22nd Street (between Fifth and Sixth Avenues)

✆ 212-367-9000

✐ *www.gothamcomedyclub.com*

The Gotham Comedy Club is one of the newer rising clubs, with good up-and-coming comics and a monthly Wednesday-night Baby Boomer Humor Show (political comedy). Call for reservations on weekends.

Pips

✉ 2005 Emmons Avenue

✆ 718-646-9433

Pips is a longtime Brooklyn comedy club in Sheepshead Bay, where people such as David Brenner and many others started out. Call for reservations on weekends.

Stand Up New York

✉ 236 West 78th Street (just off Broadway)

✆ 212-595-0850

✐ *www.standupny.com*

This attractive Upper West Side club has nightly shows featuring working comics, plus amateur "occupation" contests, such as Funniest Accountant, Funniest Lawyer, and other such gimmicks.

CHAPTER 15

Family Dining

EVERY NEIGHBORHOOD in the city has restaurants. Because you're likely to spend most of your time in midtown Manhattan, that's where we'll start. The restaurants listed in this chapter are for sit-down dining, with children who like to eat and be served. If your kids are too energetic or young for this kind of meal, try any of the restaurants listed in Chapters 16 and 17, which offer more casual dining.

As with all things in New York, price is relative to where you are eating. An expensive meal is one that runs at least $30 per person. A moderate meal will run between $15 and $30 per person, and a reasonable meal would be under $15 per person. Remember to ask for a children's menu, and don't be ashamed to share a meal or to order an appetizer portion for a young gourmet.

So Many Options

Wow! What a city to eat in! There is so much to choose from, from the absolute finest dining in the world to food that tickles the palate. There are thousands of choices, and new restaurants are opening every day. World-renowned chefs open their signature restaurants here, while New Yorkers flock to old favorites that have been on the block for generations. There are charming and eclectic cafés and bistros, and amazing combination restaurants that could have only come about in this city of immigrants.

 JUST FOR PARENTS

Food is serious business in New York. Most waiters are professionals, or performers with a college degree who work the late shift. You must tip, and you should tip like a New Yorker. Since tax in the city is 8 percent, most New Yorkers just double the tax, which leaves your server a 16-percent tip. If you have a coupon (10 percent off or buy one, get one free), remember to tip for the meal before the discount.

The Manhattan restaurant market is highly competitive, with three or four restaurants on a single block. With all this choice and competition, you should not have to put up with bad service, although it's often hard to determine what you'll find once inside. The nicer restaurants should afford you the finest service, but that is not always the case.

Midtown West

Midtown Manhattan, between 30th and 59th Street, is the most popular section of town because so many of the big New York attractions are here, from the Empire State Building to Times Square. There are some wonderful restaurants in this area, so there's no need to wing it.

American Festival Café
✉ 20 West 50th Street
✆ 212-332-7620
American Festival Café is located at Rockefeller Center. It is a very popular lunch spot all year round, so always make a reservation. If you dine here in the wintertime, you can watch the ice skaters; in the summer, there's outdoor dining available.

The menu is contemporary American, with good sandwiches and salads. There is a prix fixe meal for all the holidays—the Thanksgiving, Christmas, and Easter menus are wonderful, and the atmosphere is one-of-a-kind. Prices are moderate. The American Festival Café is accessible by subway via the B, D, F, or V train (47th-50th Street/Rockefeller Center station).

B. Smith's

✉ 320 West 46th Street

✆ 212-315-1100

B. Smith, a legendary entertainment diva (former Oil of Olay beauty and now a lifestyle expert with a syndicated show) moved her signature restaurant a few blocks closer to Restaurant Row. Celebrity photos line the wall, and Smith has added a lot more French influence to her exquisite American soul food. She loves her restaurant, so she may be on the premises when you come by. The macaroni and cheese is great for both kids and adults, as are the sweet potatoes (as a side dish or in pie, as well), and people come back again and again for the crab cakes, the ribs, and the stuffed chicken.

Desserts are awesome, and they can be served later in the evening. The Sunday brunch is spectacular, with wonderful waffles and sweet potato pancakes. There's also a branch of the restaurant in Sag Harbor, where the emphasis is on seafood. Prices are moderate. B. Smith's is accessible by subway via the N, Q, R, 1, 2, or 3 train (Times Square station).

The Bull and Bear

✉ 49th and Lexington

✆ 212-872-4900

The Bull and Bear is located inside the Waldorf-Astoria Hotel. It is a remarkable restaurant—beautiful, exquisite, and quiet, with wonderful seafood and steak. Men must wear a jacket, and women should wear a cocktail dress, so it's not really for young children. The chocolate martinis are wonderful (and clear), the portions are large (you can share the seafood salad appetizer), and the Angus steak is delicious and smooth. Service is impeccable. You are never rushed. Reservations are advised. The Bull and Bear is expensive. It is accessible by subway via the 6 train (51st Street station).

 **TRAVEL TIP**

Along 44th Street are the blocks known as "Restaurant Row." There are at least twenty places to eat along the way, all there for the theater crowd. There are often prix fixe meals, and everyone knows there's an 8:00 P.M. curtain call. Broadway Joe's is an institution, and B. Smith's is a delight.

Carnegie Deli
✉854 Seventh Avenue at 55th Street
✆ 212-757-2245

A famous and popular Midtown deli, this well-known eatery is often crowded and hectic, especially during lunch, but it's also a great off-hours spot (late lunch after 2:00 P.M. or even a late dinner after 9:30 P.M.). Portions are huge, so feel comfortable asking to share. The pickles are great. Prices are moderate. Carnegie Deli is accessible by subway via the B, D, or E train (Seventh Avenue station).

Docks Oyster Bar
✉633 Third Avenue at 40th Street
✆ 212-986-8080

This establishment is a New York favorite, so, of course, it's often packed. The oysters are divine, and the clam chowder's pretty good, too. Docks serves fresh seafood and features a raw bar and clambakes. The atmosphere is upbeat and fashionable. Prices are moderate. (There is a second location at ✉2427 Broadway at 89th Street.) The main Docks location is accessible by subway via the 4, 5, or 6 train (Grand Central station); the second location is accessible by subway via the 1 or 9 train (86th Street station).

Ellen's Stardust Diner

✉ 1650 Broadway near 51st Street

✆ 212-956-5151

The location is perfect, so, again, it's often crowded. Ellen's is nothing to knock your socks off, but the place is fun and familiar. It features American fare in a recreation of a rockin' 1950s diner, so kids will love the burgers, fries, and shakes. Prices are reasonable. Ellen's is accessible by subway via the 1 or 9 train (50th Street station).

Keen's Steakhouse

✉ 72 West 36th Street

✆ 212-947-3636

This is one of the best-kept secrets in New York. It's where New Yorkers go for steaks and chops, but it's also the perfect place for beer and snacks before or after almost any game at Madison Square Garden. Kids will love the pipes on the ceiling (the pipes are for decoration only—there is no smoking anywhere on the premises) and the hot-fudge sundaes are divine. The salads here are ample and delicious, and the fried chicken with Stilton is a real pleaser. The Bloody Marys are made according to Keen's house recipe, but they're also happy to serve Virgin Bloody Marys to kids. The limeade in the summer months is wonderful. Prices are moderate. Keen's is accessible by subway via the B, D, F, N, Q, or R train (34th Street/Herald Square station).

Le Perigord

✉ 405 East 52nd Street

✆ 212-755-6244

This is a New York classic, where Richard Burton and Elizabeth Taylor once came for a little privacy and an exquisite French meal. The owner, Georges Briguet, is a true gentleman, and he will entertain you with wonderful stories about the restaurant's forty-year history. There is a sumptuous hors d'oeuvres display when you enter. The pâté de foie gras and artichoke soup are terrific, the rack of lamb is perfectly French, and the fish selections are always special. The soufflés are particularly delicious, and children who enjoy fine dining are encouraged to come. There is also a private dining room for small parties.

Because of its proximity to the United Nations and Sutton Place, this is a restaurant visited by international dignitaries and some of the richest people in the world. With that in mind, it is surprisingly affordable, but it's still expensive nonetheless. There is both a dinner and lunch prix fixe. Le Perigord is accessible by subway via the 6 train (Lexington Avenue/51st Street station).

 JUST FOR PARENTS

The Four Seasons (at ✉ 99 East 52nd Street, between Lexington and Park Avenues; ✆ 212-754-9494) is one of the most expensive and most difficult restaurants to get into in the city. Ever since it opened its doors, it has been the place to be seen in New York, for decades the home of the "power lunch." Unless your kids are really comfortable in this atmosphere of business suits and cocktail dresses, this is one you should visit alone. You have to make a reservation at least three weeks in advance.

Le Bernardin

✉ 155 West 51st Street, between Sixth and Seventh Avenues
✆ 212-489-1515

This is perhaps the best French restaurant in New York. The emphasis here is on seafood, which is why the walls display large paintings of the sea and fishing. And although there is a divine tasting menu that runs well over $200 per person (with matching wines), it is surprisingly affordable, especially at lunch (with a prix fixe for $44). The staff is superior, and if you bring an older child who knows how to eat with dignity, you will find that this is one of the best and most memorable places in the city to dine with your family. It is perfect for a special occasion or a celebration.

The sauces are so perfect, you will wish they had a cookbook. Le Bernadin is expensive (but worth every penny). Make reservations before you arrive in the city. The restaurant is accessible by subway via the B, D, F, or Q train (47th–50th Streets/Rockefeller Center).

Macy's Bar and Grill

✉ 34th Street at Herald Square

✆ 212-736-5151

Who would believe that this is one of the best family restaurants in the city? The location is fantastic, the décor is fun—there are displays of great moments in Macy's history from a diorama from *Miracle on 34th Street* to old ads and appliances from the turn of the century—and the food is very good and affordable. They have an extensive children's menu (with a large portion of macaroni and cheese), but the real bargain is the dinner for two at $24.95 for chicken or $34.95 for steak or shrimp. Every day after 3:00 P.M. there are $5 drinks at the bar (in a separate room) and there is a hot-fudge sundae that could feed an entire family for $7.95. For an additional $9.95, you can take home the giant glass it comes in, decorated with the New York skyline, a wonderful souvenir. Prices are moderate. Macy's Bar and Grill is accessible by subway via the B, D, F, N, Q, or R train (34th Street/Herald Square station).

 TRAVEL TIP

As of 2003, New York is a smoke-free town, at least when it comes to dining. Smoking is prohibited in most New York City restaurants, except in outdoor seating. There is even no smoking in bars!

Manhattan Ocean Club

✉ 57 West 58th Street between Fifth and Sixth Avenues

✆ 212-371-7777

The Manhattan Ocean Club is another New York institution known for its seafood at its finest and for its collection of Picasso ceramics. Always wonderful are the daily specials, as well as the array of enticing appetizers and a long wine list. Prices are expensive. The Manhattan Ocean Club is accessible by subway via the A, B, C, D, 1, or 9 train (59th Street/Columbus Circle station).

Mickey Mantle's

✉ 42 Central Park South, between Fifth and Sixth Avenues

✆ 212-688-7777

Mickey Mantle's is an absolute favorite among kids; New Yorkers have birthday parties here. The French fries are incredible, and the souvenir mugs and glasses are worth considering. There's a gift shop on the premises, and in the summer or spring it's really lovely to sit outside and eat your burger and fries and watch the horse-drawn carriages go up and down Central Park South. The restaurant is filled with kids every day of the week, although weekend nights do draw an older, sports-watching male crowd. Prices are moderate. Mickey Mantle's is accessible by subway via the A, B, C, D, 1, or 9 train (59th Street/Columbus Circle station).

Mars 2112

✉ 1633 Broadway at 51st Street

✆ 212-582-2112

Mars 2112 is a not-to-be missed kid pleaser on any trip to New York. This is a one-of-a-kind theme restaurant that also draws a large New York kid's birthday party crowd. You enter the premises by a "ride" to the planet Mars—there's a side entrance if your kids are easily scared, or someone in your party gets motion sickness— and are seated at a table deep inside the red rock. There are a number of alien servers, and a screen shows the moon launch on a regular basis. Bring a camera to take pictures with the costumed aliens, who make the rounds quite regularly. There's an excellent kids' menu that offers the burgers and pizza and also a root-beer float and fun desserts. The adult cocktails are delicious and fun, and the meals are surprisingly hearty. There's an arcade for the kids to play in, and the bar (great for the adults) was the site of the opening party for the third *Star Wars* movie. There's also a gift shop with all sorts of Mars-related gizmos and gadgets. Prices are moderate. Mars 2112 is accessible by subway via the 1 or 9 train (50th Street station).

Oscar's

✉ 50th and Lexington

✆ 212-872-4920

This is a surprisingly good and affordable restaurant housed in the lap of luxury, the Waldorf-Astoria Hotel. Kids will pass out over the dessert selection (especially if you go for the buffet). Oscar's was named after the legendary hotel maitre d', Oscar Tschirky, who worked at the Waldorf for more than fifty years. He was such a character that everybody just referred to him as "Oscar of Waldorf." Signature menu items include the Waldorf salad (there's a recipe in Chapter 20) made of apples and walnuts, and the veal Oscar, but the best bet on this menu is always the daily buffet, where you get a bit of everything. The setting is lovely, as well, with etched glass panels and a wide-open interior. Prices are moderate. Oscar's is accessible by subway via the 6 train (51st Street station).

Petrossian

✉ 182 West 58th Street at Seventh Avenue

✆ 212-245-2214

This is a beautiful restaurant in a landmark building serving exquisite Russian food. With the Russian Tea Room gone, it is hard to get a reservation. It's for children who love to dine well and like things like borscht and caviar. The marble and mink-trimmed room and pink tablecloths set the tone. It's lovely and continental. Prices are expensive. Petrossian is accessible by subway via the A, B, C, D, 1, or 9 train (59th Street/Columbus Circle station).

Planet Hollywood

✉ 1540 Broadway

✆ 212-333-7827

Located in the heart of Times Square, Planet Hollywood offers the usual chain-restaurant food fare of huge burgers, salads, sandwiches, and fun cocktails. But visitors don't come to Planet Hollywood for the food. They come for the atmosphere and all that movie memorabilia. Burgers and sandwiches run about $10, as do the specialty cocktails. There's a great kids' menu for $7.95. Prices are moderate. Planet Hollywood is accessible by subway via the N, R, S, 1, 2, 3, 7, or 9 train (42nd Street/Times Square station).

RAINY DAY FUN

For kids, visiting Planet Hollywood is like going to a museum. In the Times Square restaurant, you can find John Travolta's black leather jacket from *Saturday Night Fever,* the original keyboard from *Big,* Julia Robert's outfit from *Pretty Woman,* Ben Affleck's senior yearbook, and original costumes from Britney Spears's music videos.

Redeye Grill

✉ 890 Seventh Avenue at 56th Street
✆ 212-541-9000

A good, fun Midtown restaurant with an excellent assortment of appetizers (wings are good), as well as seafood galore and a good raw bar. It's spacious and fashionable, so it does fill up with a weekend crowd. This place is best for a family lunch or late afternoon fare. Prices are moderate to expensive. The Redeye Grill is accessible by subway via the N or R train (57th Street station).

Seppi's

✉ 123 West 56th Street
✆ 212-708-7444

Right next door to Le Parker Meridien Hotel, this delightful French restaurant serves an array of creative meals in a distinctly French/Swiss style. The terrine of foie gras is perfect, as are the escargots; the shrimp and artichoke risotto is a signature dish. There are daily specials of foie gras, omelets, pasta, and fish. On Sundays Seppi's serves a chocolate brunch, where every dish has a hint of chocolate (even chocolate mimosas). Desserts are awesome. The white chocolate soufflé is perfect, and the ice creams and sorbets are all homemade. There are prix fixe menus for lunch and dinner. Prices are moderate. Seppi's is accessible by subway via the 4, 5, or 6 train (59th Street station).

Smith & Wollensky

✉ 201 East 49th Street at Third Avenue
✆ 212-753-0444

One of New York's finest steakhouses with its famous green and white décor, Smith & Wollensky is a good place to bring a family for a good, old-fashioned, traditional meal. Prices are expensive. Smith & Wollensky is accessible by subway via the 6 train (51st Street station).

21 Club

✉ 21 West 52nd Street
✆ 212-582-7200

Who would believe that the site of New York's most infamous speakeasy would be one of the best restaurants to take children who know how to dine? This is one of the best and classiest restaurants in the city (jacket and ties for all men, no matter what the age, and positively no jeans for either men or women), and yet New York's families often celebrate their great moments here. Sit in the main dining room, where sports memorabilia and toys from the rich and famous hang above your head. The foie gras is among the best in the city, and the steak and chops are wonderful, but the chicken hash is absolutely divine and worth every penny. Be sure to order a Shirley Temple for the kids. If you ask (and you should ask), your server will arrange a tour of the wine cellar, where you and the kids will be shown Richard Nixon's personal stash, and you can push the big brick door that was used to hide the speakeasy during raids. This is a classic New York experience. The food is excellent, and so is the service. Prices are expensive. The 21 Club is accessible by subway via the E or F train (Fifth Avenue station).

Chelsea and the Village

There's great food in these neighborhoods, from the funky—because there are so many NYU students eating here—to the sublime (it's quite an expensive neighborhood to live in).

Alfama
✉ 551 Hudson Street
✆ 212-645-2500

Alfama is an exquisite Portuguese restaurant. Its white interior makes you think you are on the beach. It's intimate and cozy, yet surprisingly kid-friendly. The seared garlic steak is like no other. There's a fun cocktail list, as well as a good selection of Portuguese wines. Each month the menu profiles a different section of Portugal. There is a lovely and creative Sunday brunch. Prices are moderate. Alfama is accessible by subway via the 1, 2, 3, or 9 train (Christopher Street station).

Cowgirl Hall of Fame
✉ 519 Hudson Street at West Tenth
✆ 212-633-1133

This is a kid favorite—the restaurant even features a "cowgirl" candy shop at the front of the store. There are paintings of cowgirls all over the walls, and the chandeliers are made of antlers. The kids' menu is excellent. Breakfast items are included, and crayons are available for coloring in the cowgirls on the menu. But the surprise is the delicious frozen margaritas (maybe one of the top five in the city). The homemade blueberry/peach cobbler is worth saving room for, but it's huge, so prepare to share it. The chili is excellent, and the taco salad is one-of-a-kind, and the pulled pork sandwiches are worth trying. You'll come back here a few times because your kids will love it (Chelsea Clinton is a regular, when she's in New York). Prices are moderate. The Cowgirl Hall of Fame is accessible by subway via the 1, 2, 3, or 9 train (Christopher Street station).

 TRAVEL TIP

Go online and check out restaurant reviews at *New York* magazine, *Time Out New York, Where,* or the *New York Times.* Ask friends who have recently visited the city to recommend restaurants, too!

Gotham Bar & Grill

✉ 12 East 12th Street, between Fifth Avenue and University Place
☎ 212-620-4020

Gotham Bar & Grill is a very popular place—one of the city's most highly rated eateries, so you'll need a reservation. The food is a little fancy and on the expensive end because of the restaurant's celebrity chef (Alfred Portale), but some of it is very clever, and the offerings are always seasonal. Gotham Bar & Grill is accessible by subway via the L, N, R, 4, 5, or 6 train (14th Street/Union Square station).

Gramercy Tavern

✉ 42 East 20th Street, between Broadway and Park Avenue South
☎ 212-477-0777

Gramercy Tavern is an exquisite restaurant, where you definitely need a reservation. Food is presented gorgeously, and it is often quite hearty. In the winter, there's a lot of elegant meat and potatoes in sauces and gravies, which is popular with children. Prices are expensive. Gramercy Tavern is accessible by subway via the N, R, or 6 train (23rd Street station).

Rocco's on 22nd

✉ 12 East 22nd Street

✆ 212-353-0500

This is the restaurant where NBC's reality-TV show, *The Restaurant,* was filmed. Celebrity chef Rocco DiSpirito is often on the premises, as is his equally famous mom. You can buy an auto-graphed copy of his cookbook, *Flavor,* when you dine here. There's a faux newspaper menu, printed weekly, that offers the day's specials, and it's surprisingly affordable and good. This isn't gourmet Italian food with fancy touches, but consistent stick-to-your-ribs fare that should make any visitor feel really satisfied. During lunch time, you can usually just walk in and get a table. The three-course prix fixe meals are excellent, and so are the meatballs and cheesecake. Prices are moderate. Rocco's is accessible by subway via the N or R train (23rd Street station).

Old Homestead

✉ 56 Ninth Avenue, between 15th and 16th Street

✆ 212-242-9040

What lover of steak could resist a restaurant with a giant steer above its front door? This is a classic New York steakhouse from 1868. It's just the slightest bit off the restaurant path, so you can get a table without weeks of planning. The portions are huge, so sharing is strongly suggested with kids. There's a wonderful gourmet shop next door. Prices are expensive. The Old Homestead is accessible by subway via the A, C, or L train (14th Street/Eighth Avenue station).

Zoe

✉ 90 Prince Street, between Broadway and Mercer

✆ 212-966-6722

This is possibly the best restaurant to take your children to dine in style. The owners, a husband-and-wife team, have children of their own, and they understand that kids love to eat just like their parents. The signature crispy calamari is a must and can be shared (also featured on the fabulous kids' menu), and the pizzas and tuna burger are wonderful. Desserts are so good that many people come by for after-dinner goodies and drinks. The children's menu is one of the best in the city, and kids love to watch food prepared in the open kitchen. It's a popular neighborhood place, so make reservations on the weekends. Prices are moderate. Zoe is accessible by subway via the N or R train (Prince Street station).

Lower Manhattan

There's great food and shopping in these neighborhoods, which include Chinatown and Little Italy.

Aquagrill
✉ 210 Spring Street and Sixth Avenue
✆ 212-274-0505
Aquagrill is a lovely small restaurant that is always packed. It serves a creative presentation of seafood and fine cuisine. Make reservations, as this is still considered one of the trendy "in spots." Prices are expensive. The restaurant is accessible by subway via C or E train (Spring Street station).

Balthazar
✉ 80 Spring Street, between Crosby Street and Broadway
✆ 212-965-1414
Balthazar is one of the hottest restaurants in New York City, so make a reservation. For many, this is considered the picture-perfect French bistro, with great food. They serve breakfast lunch, late lunch, dinner, and after dinner. The steak frites is always popular. You'll find a good wine list and desserts. Sunday brunch is also offered, and there's a bakery. Prices are expensive. Balthazar is accessible by subway via the N or R train (Prince Street station) or the C or E train (Spring Street station).

Chanterelle

✉ 2 Harrison Street at Hudson

📞 212-966-6960

Chanterelle is considered one of the best restaurants in the city, so, again, make a reservation. The walls are bare and there's no music, so you can concentrate on the food. This is not a restaurant for loud or rambunctious children. The food is French and exquisite. The atmosphere is impeccable, as is the service. There is a $95 tasting menu. Prices are expensive. Chanterelle is accessible by subway via the 1 or 9 train (Franklin Street station).

Frances Tavern

✉ 54 Pearl Street

📞 212-968-1776

This is a must-see New York attraction and dining experience. Eat in the Revolutionary War tavern where George Washington celebrated victory over the British. There's nothing else like it. The food is pretty good and affordable, though, of course, very American. This is a good place to go for roast turkey and gravy or chicken pot pie, food you won't find at many of the fancier restaurants. There's also a great selection of salads and sandwiches during the day and an excellent clam chowder. You'll find a museum on the premises where you can look at Revolutionary War artifacts. Should anyone you know be in need of a place to hold a colonial-style wedding, this is the place to go. Prices are moderate. Frances Tavern is accessible by subway via the A, C, 2, 3, 4, or 5 train (Broadway/Nassau station).

One If by Land, Two If by Sea

✉ 17 Barrow Street

📞 212-228-0823

Considered one of the most romantic restaurants in Manhattan (many marriage proposals have taken place here), this seventeenth-century townhouse with fireplaces and resident pianist is also a favorite of celebrities. The food is excellent American and French.

Beef Wellington is a favorite dish. Prices are expensive. One If by Land, Two If by Sea is accessible by subway via the 1 or 9 train (Christopher Street station).

≡FAST FACT

Frances Tavern's changing exhibits tell the story of this landmark tavern that was once the "war room" of the revolution and the headquarters of General George Washington. There's a 215-year-old flag on display, as well as portraits of Washington, and the Long Room—where he celebrated with his victorious army—has been re-created for eighteenth-century authenticity. This is definitely a fun educational site for kids.

Upper East Side

Some of the best restaurants in the city are located in this part of Manhattan because some of the most expensive housing in the city can be found on the Upper East Side.

Aureole

✉ 34 East 61st Street, between Park and Madison

✆ 212-319-1660

This is one of the hottest new restaurants on the Upper East Side. It has classic food, with a nice twist such as curried lobster. Aureole is always packed, so make a reservation. There is live jazz on Tuesday nights. Prices are expensive. Aureole is accessible by subway via the 4, 5, or 6 train (59th Street station).

Mimi's Macaroni

✉ 718 Amsterdam Avenue at 95th Street

✆ 212-866-6311

What kid could not love a restaurant with a name like this? There is pasta for one and all in this extremely kid-friendly restaurant (toys and all). Wait staff is good with kids and will bring bread as soon as you sit down. Prices are reasonable. Mimi's Macaroni is accessible by subway via the 6 train (96th Street station).

Park Avenue Café
✉ 100 East 63rd Street at Park Avenue
✆ 212-644-1900

This is both a neighborhood favorite and a busy business lunch restaurant. It serves rustic American bistro fare. The food combinations are creative (salmon pastrami) and the service is excellent. There's also the classy "Park Avenue" setting. Prices are expensive. The Park Avenue Café is accessible by subway via 4, 5, or 6 train (59th Street station).

Serendipity 3
✉ 225 East 65th Street, between Second and Third Avenues
✆ 212-838-3531

This is such a kid palace that you should put it near the top of your list! There are cheddar burgers to die for, and the frozen hot chocolate is a signature dish. Also other fun kid drinks. The restaurant has a wonderful ambiance that reminds you of *Alice in Wonderland* and *Grease* and a sweet-sixteen party all at once. Save room for dessert. This is a great place to go after a day of shopping at Bloomingdale's. Serendipity 3 is accessible by subway via the 6 train (68th Street station).

Tony's Di Napoli
✉ 1606 Second Avenue, between 83rd and 84th Streets
✆ 212-861-8686

Tony's Di Napoli is a family favorite, much like Carmine's (see page 261). Bring a big appetite and share. There's a balloon man who makes balloon animals on some nights. It's crowded, so get there before 6:00 P.M., or expect to wait. Prices are reasonable. The restaurant is accessible by subway via the 4, 5, or 6 train (86th Street station). There's another branch Midtown at ✉ 147 West 43rd Street.

West Side

Many Manhattan families live on the Upper West Side, so there's great family dining in this neck of the city woods.

Barney Greengrass

✉541 Amsterdam Avenue, between 86th and 87th Streets

✆ 212-724-4707

This is a popular Jewish deli that serves the usual suspects, but its nickname since 1908 has been "the Sturgeon King." People line up for the smoked fish. You should get lox on an H&H bagel, or herring. Prices are moderate. Barney Greengrass is accessible by subway via the 4, 5, or 6 train (86th Street station).

JUST FOR PARENTS

For something special, you can order wine and drinks with your meals, but don't forget your kids! Shirley Temples are always popular in fancy New York restaurants, and you can ask the server to serve your child's cranberry juice in a martini glass. It makes the kids feel sophisticated.

Carmine's

✉2450 Broadway, between 90th and 91st Streets

✆ 212-362-2200

Carmine's is almost always crowded, but for good reason—what a delicious meal! Everything is served family style, which means it serves at least two. The stuffed artichokes are great, as is the fried calamari. The shrimp scampi is terrific, and the meat platter is almost enough to feed a family of four. Carmine's tiramisu is wonderful. A good house wine is available. There are no reservations for parties of less than six, and there's always a wait by 6:00 P.M. This is the real thing: family-style Italian, spacious, crowded, and good food. Bring your appetite! Prices are moderate. Carmine's is accessible by subway via the 1 or 9 train (86th or 96th Street station). (There's a second location on 44th Street.)

Fiorello's

✉ 1900 Broadway, between 64th and 65th Streets

✆ 212-595-5330

Almost across the street from Lincoln Center, this Italian restaurant has wonderful Jerusalem artichokes, rack of lamb that is heavenly, pizzas that will blow your mind, and great fish, as well as terrific tortellini. People have been coming here for generations (especially the opera crowd), so make a reservation. In the summer and spring, you can sit outside and people-watch. It's also a good spot for celebrity sightings. Last time we were there, we saw Sean Connery. The service is speedy, and this is a great place for lunch. Prices are moderate. Fiorello's is accessible by subway via the 1 or 9 train (66th Street).

Tavern on the Green

✉ Central Park West, between 66th and 67th Streets

✆ 212-873-3200

This is a must-see experience for families visiting the city. Kids are always charmed by this unusual restaurant that is one of the most sought-after wedding and event spots in the city. There is an excellent children's menu, but meals are so generous that you can share. The wait staff is gracious, and they are truly pleased to serve children who appreciate the finer things. The lobster bisque is an institution, the crab cakes are fabulous, and the mushroom linguini is surprisingly delicious if available. Ask for the glass-enclosed Crystal and Terrace Rooms. The chandeliers, in all colors, are beautiful. The Topiary Garden is legendary too. There's dancing for grown-ups on the weekends and a fabulous Sunday brunch. Tavern on the Green also serves incredible holiday prix fixe meals (Easter includes a petting zoo for the kids). Prices are expensive. Tavern on the Green is accessible by subway via the B or C train (72nd Street station).

Brooklyn

Don't think you have to rush back to Manhattan for another trendy lunch or dinner. Brooklyn has some wonderful places to eat.

Junior's

✉386 Flatbush Avenue at DeKalb Avenue

✆ 718-852-5257

This delightful deli is a classic that Brooklynites have been coming to for generations. Many a graduation and celebration have been heralded within these orange walls and seats. The food is pretty good. Surprisingly, the burgers are excellent (not what you'd expect in a deli), but the blintzes are definitely worth traveling for, and the pastrami is classic. Save room for those cheesecakes. Put this restaurant on the menu for a day at the Brooklyn Museum or the Botanical Garden. Prices are reasonable. Junior's is accessible by subway via the Q or R train (DeKalb Avenue station).

Peter Luger's Steakhouse

✉178 Broadway at Driggs Avenue

✆ 718-387-4700

Peter Luger's is the Taj Mahal of steakhouses—the best! Be sure to make reservations, and bring a pocketful of cash; credit cards are not accepted. Don't forget to try the creamed spinach at this landmark eatery. Some say the shrimp cocktail features the biggest crustaceans in the city. The restaurant is surprisingly kid-friendly, right down to the gold-covered chocolate coins that come with the bill. Prices are expensive. Peter Luger's is accessible by subway via the J, M, or Z train (Marcy Avenue station).

River Café

✉1 Water Street

✆ 718-522-5200

The view at the River Café is spectacular, so you must make reservations, and it is often full of out-of-towners. This restaurant is not overly family-friendly, but don't let that stop you from treating your kids to a spectacular New York experience. A three-course prix fixe meal is $70. There's usually a pianist on the premises. Prices are expensive. River Café is accessible by subway via the A or C train (High Street station).

 TRAVEL TIP

Can't live without Junior's cheesecake? There's a much smaller version of the legendary deli/cheesecake restaurant on the lower floor of Grand Central Station. You can also get the terrific cookbook, which besides recipes gives the story of this family-owned and operated business. Or you can always order the cheesecake online, at *www.juniorscheesecake.com*.

The Bronx

Some of the best-kept secrets of New York dining are the wonderful Italian restaurants along Arthur Avenue and the great seafood restaurants on City Island. This is where real New Yorkers dine.

Dominick's

✉ 2335 Arthur Avenue, between East 184th and 187th Streets
✆ 718-733-2807

There is no menu. You sit family style and the waiter either asks you what you're in the mood for or tells you the day's specials. The stuffed artichoke is the best in the city (with bacon and bread crumbs) and the pastas are excellent. You can always share a meal. The house wine is delicious. There is often a wait because every one in the city comes here if they don't feel like going downtown, even Mayor Bloomberg. If you go around Christmas, they will give you a pen as a keepsake. No dessert—they expect you to patronize one of the great bakeries on the block, and you should. Prices are reasonable, but cash only is accepted—no credit cards. Dominick's is not accessible from the subway.

Jimmy's Bronx Café

✉ 281 West Fordham Road (off the Major Deegan)

✆ 718-329-2000

Because of its location in the Bronx, if you come on the right night, there's a good chance you might be dining beside Yankees. There's a showcase full of baseball memorabilia (from Pedro Martinez and Tony Pena), and the food's pretty good too, with hefty portions. The stuffed pork chops are favorites, and everyone comes back for the yucca fries. Prices are reasonable. Jimmy's is not accessible by subway.

Queens

Queens is known for the great Greek restaurants in its Astoria neighborhood.

Christos-Hasapo Taverna

✉ 41-08 23rd Street

✆ 718-777-8400

One of the best Greek restaurants in Astoria, Christos-Hasapo is a Greek steakhouse and butcher shop. The wealth of Greek appetizers is amazing, and the dessert is wonderful too. Prices are moderate to expensive. Christos-Hasapo is accessible by subway via the N train (Astoria/Ditmars Blvd. station).

Joe's Shanghai

✉ 82-74 Broadway, between 45th Street and Whitney Avenue

✆ 718-539-3838

The restaurant is famous for their soup dumplings (yes, the soup is inside the dumplings) with pork or crabmeat. The Chinese food is wonderful, and the portions are ample in this very popular Chinese restaurant. Prices are reasonable. There's another branch on Thirty-seventh Avenue in Queens and a third one on Pell Street in Lower Manhattan. The Broadway location is accessible by subway via the R train (46th Street station).

CHAPTER 16

Breakfast, Lunch, and More

THERE ARE SO MANY WONDERFUL RESTAURANTS, diners, cafés, and cafeterias throughout New York that breakfast and lunch should never put you over the top of your budget. In this chapter, you'll find a list of places to eat breakfast and lunch (although you could probably go for dinner), with most meals running between $5 and $12. The majority of these places are located downtown, with a handful on the Upper East or West Side.

Since you'll be on the go from morning until sunset, your best bet is to look for something along your route during the day, and then splurge on one of the city's unique dining experiences for dinner, when you'll need to get off your feet.

🧳 TRAVEL TIP

Don't forget that some of the major department stores have truly exceptional dining experiences, such as Macy's, Saks, and Le Blue Train at Bloomingdale's.

Lunch is a good way to experience some of the city's more expensive restaurants without having to pay top dollar. For instance, should your child be a Michael Jordan fan and want to eat in his Grand Central restaurant, lunch is the more affordable option.

Of course, there are also many delis and pizzerias, as well as Nathan's (of Coney Island), Burger Kings, and McDonalds along the way. Ask your hotel concierge for the one closest to you, if that's what you're interested in.

Breakfast Options

There are fabulous breakfasts throughout the city, but your best bet is likely to be in a diner around the corner. Hotel breakfasts in New York are very expensive and not that good. Many hotels include a continental breakfast in the price of the room.

Good Enough to Eat
✉ 483 Amsterdam Avenue

This is by far the best breakfast in New York. Every meal comes with homemade strawberry butter, orange juice is fresh-squeezed and omelets are big. The décor is cozy, and there are toys and crayons for the kids. It gets very crowded on the weekends, when West Siders line up with their Sunday *New York Times*, but weekdays are usually easy to get in. We saw Kevin Bacon eating bacon there recently! There's a pretty good cookbook you can take home with you. Good Enough to Eat is accessible by subway via the 1, 9, B, or C train (86th Street station).

Popover Café
✉ 551 Amsterdam Avenue, between 86th and 87th Streets
✆ 212-595-8555

Down the block from Good Enough to Eat is this other classic Upper West Side breakfast nook. Of course, every breakfast meal comes with delicious popovers that can be a meal in themselves. A full assortment of breakfast entrees is offered. Popover Café is accessible by subway via the 1, 9, B, or C train (86th Street station).

Sarabeth's
✉ 423 Amsterdam Avenue, between 80th and 81st Street
✆ 212-496-6280

Another Upper West Side favorite, the omelets and bread here are wonderful. There's a cookbook, too. Sarabeth's is accessible by subway via the 1 or 9 train (79th Street station). The restaurant has additional locations at the Hotel Wales and the Whitney.

Sunday Brunch

If you are going to be in town on Sunday morning and have the time to dine leisurely, you might want to schedule a Sunday brunch, as the city hosts a phenomenal variety of unique brunch experiences.

Alfama
✉ 551 Hudson Street
✆ 212-645-2500

This elegant Portuguese restaurant offers two lovely prix fixe brunches that includes a drink, salad, and dessert for either $14 (Portuguese eggs Benedict) or $25 (steak or salmon), as well as delicious à la carte selections. Alfama is accessible by subway via the 1, 2, 3, or 9 train (Christopher Street station).

B. Smith's
✉ 320 West 46th Street
✆ 212-315-1100

This is a great Sunday brunch, with ample portions of sweet potato pancakes, gourmet omelets, a smoked salmon platter, and a French toast butter brioche. B. Smith's is accessible by subway via the N, Q, R, 1, 2, or 3 train (Times Square station).

The Mark
✉ 25 East 77th Street
✆ 212-879-1864

This is a surprisingly sumptuous breakfast buffet with a carving station and wonderful pasties, and the waiters are extremely child-friendly. It's a little expensive but a real treat. The Mark is accessible by subway via the 6 train (72nd Street station).

Seppi's

✉ 123 West 56th Street

☎ 212-397-1963

Chocolate for breakfast—who could ask for more? Every meal on the Sunday brunch menu has at least a hint of chocolate, while some have even more. What a treat, in a lovely French restaurant. Seppi's is accessible by subway via the 4 or 6 train (59th Street station).

≡FAST FACT

There are many branches of popular chain restaurants in the downtown area—Applebee's, Chili's, Houlihan's, Red Lobster, TGI Fridays—that are good and dependable. They may not be classic New York dining experiences, but you know what to expect.

Tavern on the Green

✉ Central Park West between 66th and 67th Street

☎ 212-873-3200

Treat yourself to a real New York experience. Brunch at Tavern on the Green is memorable, especially in the Crystal Room. There's everything from Irish oatmeal to eggs Benedict to crab cakes. A little on the expensive side, but worth it. Tavern on the Green is accessible by subway via the B or C train (72nd Street station).

Sylvia's

✉ 328 Lenox Avenue between 126th and 127th Streets

☎ 212-996-0660

This is simply one of the best brunch deals in town. For $15, you get an authentic gospel brunch with eggs, pork chops or sausages, a drink, and two sides (black-eyed peas and sweet potatoes are our choices). Many Sundays, Sylvia shows up herself. Go to church at the Riverside Church or the Cathedral of St. John the Divine, and then come here afterwards to eat. Sylvia's is accessible by subway via the 2 or 3 train (125th Street station).

Lunchtime Fare

You will most likely eat lunch on the go, and if you are touring one of the city's major museums, you should consider eating in either their restaurant or cafeteria. Most major attractions offer a good variety of kid-pleasing menu items, such as the Metropolitan Museum of Art or the American Museum of Natural History. Because of security concerns, it is now almost impossible to bring food into a museum, as all bags must be checked when you enter.

Otherwise, the following options are excellent for lunch.

Michael Jordan's Steakhouse

✉ 23 Vanderbilt Avenue

✆ 212-255-2300

This is a very good and trendy restaurant that attracts both a New York crowd and a tourist crowd, so always make a reservation. If you are lucky enough to get a seat over the balcony, it can be fun to watch the commuters rush to and fro under the faux constellations, all recently restored. It's a little pricey (although there are three good selections for a prix fixe lunch of around $20), so if you are going because the kids want to go, shoot for lunch. There are sandwiches and burgers on the lunch menu. Unlike some other celebrity restaurant owners, Michael Jordan does not tour the premises. Located at Grand Central Station, Michael Jordan's Steakhouse is accessible by subway via the 4, 5, or 6 train (Grand Central station).

Hard Rock Cafe

✉ 221 West 54th Street

✆ 212-459-9320

The Hard Rock is a New York classic, with the back end of a Cadillac sticking out of the front of the restaurant. On Friday and

Saturday night, there are crowds, and sometimes people line up, but at lunch time it's pretty easy to get in. You'll find a good selection of salads, sandwiches, and burgers. The Hard Rock is accessible by subway via the N or R train (57th Street station).

Mars 2112

✉ 1633 Broadway at 51st Street

✆ 212-582-2112

Mars 2112 is a great place for lunch. The décor is right out of *Star Trek*, with spaceship rides and aliens—kids love it! Mars 2112 is accessible by subway via the 1 or 9 train (50th Street station).

Planet Hollywood

✉ 44th Street and Times Square

✆ 212-333-7827

This is really an excellent place for lunch in a busy downtown day. Planet Hollywood serves great wraps and burgers, and there is an excellent kids' menu for only $7.95. You can also buy souvenir cups, magnets for little kids, and those popular baseball caps and T-shirts for the teens. Planet Hollywood is accessible by subway via the N, R, 1, or 2 train (Times Square/42nd Street station).

Jekyll & Hyde Club

✉ 1409 Sixth Avenue between 57th Street and 58th Streets

✆ 212-541-9517

This four-floor horror-themed restaurant is like something out of Disney's haunted mansion. There's a show in the middle of the restaurant and a haunted elevator ride. You can take home a canteen in which your drink was placed. This place might frighten smaller children. It's packed on weekend nights, but a good bet for lunch. The pumpkin tortellini is very good. Jekyll & Hyde is accessible by subway via the F train (57th Street station). There is a second location at 91 Seventh Avenue, in the Village.

☂ RAINY DAY FUN

New York's theme restaurants are great lunch spots—the Hard Rock Cafe, Jekyll & Hyde, Mars 2112, and Planet Hollywood—and the food is pretty good at this time. They all have good children's menus, and who would ever want to return from New York without a Planet Hollywood New York T-shirt?

Uncle Nick's

✉ 747 Ninth Avenue, between 50th and 51st Streets

✆ 212-245-7992

A very nice Midtown Greek restaurant with an impressive selection of enticing appetizers (such as spinach pie and Greek meatballs) that could easily make a meal. There are many good selections in this simple setting, and there's a lovely outdoor garden. Uncle Nick's is accessible by subway via the C or E train (50th Street station).

Silver Star

✉ 1265 Second Avenue at 65th Street

✆ 212-249-4250

Silver Star is a good, classic diner on the Upper East Side—which is a hard thing to find. Standard breakfast and lunch items are served. Silver Star is accessible by subway via the 6 train (68th Street station).

The New York Deli

Delicatessen food has its beginnings on Manhattan's Lower East Side, so eating in a real New York deli should be a must-do on your list of authentic New York experiences. Everything else is a pale imitation.

Ben's Deli

✉ 207 West 38th Street

✆ 212-398-2367

Ben's is traditional deli in midtown Manhattan, with lovely art deco art throughout. It's not on the tourist map, but it's well loved by those in the Garment District, so you can always get a seat and a meal. The pickles and cole slaw are ample and delicious, and there's a surprisingly full menu. This is a good place for turkey and gravy, but the serving is huge, so share. Sandwiches are large too. Ben's Deli is accessible by subway via the 1, 2, 3, N, or R train (42nd Street/Times Square station).

Carnegie Deli

✉ 854 Seventh Avenue

✆ 212-757-2245

The classic New York deli, but it's always very crowded. It's better if you can go a little outside the regular lunch or dinner time hours. The deli serves great sandwiches and brisket. Prices are moderate. Carnegie Deli is accessible by subway via the N or R train (57th Street station).

Junior's (Midtown)

✆ 212-983-5257

Can't make it to Brooklyn? Don't worry, there's a smaller version of this popular deli in the heart of the city, in the main concourse of the Grand Central Station. The pastrami and blintzes are always terrific, and save room for the cheesecake.

Katz's Deli

✉ 205 East Houston Street

✆ 212-254-2246

This is such a classic deli, it's worth making the trip to eat there. Big and authentic, this place dates from the turn of the century. The pastrami and salami on rye is wonderful. Blintzes and knishes are great, as are the hot dogs and the desserts. Portions are ample. Katz's Deli is accessible by subway via the 1, 2, 3, or 9 train (Houston Street station).

≡FAST FACT

Along Seventh Avenue in the 30s, the streets are lined with bronze circles depicting the stars of the fashion world (a sort of Garment District version of the Hollywood Walk of Fame), where you'll find accolades to Donna Karan and Ralph Lauren. On 39th and Seventh Avenue, you'll also find a giant statue of a garment worker sewing on an old Singer sewing machine. This is a tribute to the generations of immigrant workers who made America's clothing right here (and still do). This is also the area to find designer sample sales.

Out for a Burger

Although there are Burger Kings and McDonald's throughout the city, there are still some really good places to get a burger and fries, where New York's workers dine daily.

Hamburger Harry's
✉ 145 West 45th Street
✆ 212-840-0566

One of the best burgers in town (try the cheddar) and very kid-friendly, Harry's is also pretty inexpensive by New York City burger standards (under $10). The curly fries are great. The restaurant is closed Sundays. Hamburger Harry's is accessible by subway via the B, D, F, or Q train (47th–50th Street/Rockefeller Center station).

Jackson Hole
✉ 517 Columbus at West 85th Street
✆ 212-362-5177

Jackson Hole is a little bit more than a burger joint (there are soups and salads and fries on the menu, too), but most people do come here for the burgers. It gets a little rowdy after work, but it's a great lunch spot. Jackson Hole is accessible by subway via the 1, 2, 3, or 9 train (86th Street station). There's also a brunch at the location at ✉ 1270 Madison at 90th Street, ☎ 212-427-2820; take the 4, 5, or 6 train to the 86th Street station.

 TRAVEL TIP

Another burger option is Burger Heaven, which is more than just another fast food eatery. The burgers are good (especially the blue cheese burger) and the service is quick. Nearly a dozen are scattered around Manhattan.

Only in New York

Street vendor food can be delicious and exciting. There's always the hot dog and pretzel stand (sometimes they sell knishes); in the winter, roasted chestnuts and nuts can be found in front of the department stores; and the smell of grilling meat for gyros and sausage and peppers often fills the air. In the morning, street vendors sell coffee and muffins, and there are several vendors selling hot soup. In the summer you'll find carts with fresh fruit. They're all licensed by the city, so they do pass some sort of inspection.

Gray's Papaya
✉ 2090 Broadway at 73rd Street
✉ 539 Eighth Avenue at 37th Street
✉ 402 Sixth Avenue at Greenwich Avenue
People line up for these hot dogs at a dollar a pop. They're a legend, and many former New Yorkers hit a Gray's Papaya right after arriving at the airport.

Gyro's
✉ Seventh Avenue between 33rd and 34th Street
This hole-in-the-wall gyro stand has been here for at least twenty years, and it serves the best lamb or chicken gyro in the

city for under $5. The Greek fries are pretty good too. It's a hearty meal, so young kids can share, or you can order a gyro platter. Right across from Madison Square Garden, people often come before a concert or game. Gyro's is accessible by subway via the 1, 2, or 3 train (34th Street/Penn Station).

H&H Bagels

✉ 2239 Broadway at 80th Street (open twenty-four hours)

✆ 212-595-8003

✉ 1551 Second Avenue at 80th Street

✆ 212-734-7441

✉ 639 West 46th Street, between 11th Avenue and the West Side Highway

✆ 212-595-8000

Ask any New Yorker; every one of them will tell you that H&H Bagels are the best in the city. Buy a dozen for the road and bring them back home with you (but remember to put them in a plastic bag and tie it tightly). They'll go over bigger than Empire State Building souvenirs. Take the 1, 2, 3, or 9 train to 79th Street; the 6 train to 77th Street; or the C or E to 50th Street.

Mamoun's Falafel

✉ MacDougal Street below West 3rd Street

A tiny, hole-in-the-wall that New Yorkers of Middle Eastern descent consider a sort of falafel haven. A falafel sandwich consists of roasted chickpea balls in a sesame sauce with a salad of lettuce and tomatoes served in a pita. They make a great lunch and run under $5. Mamoun's is accessible by subway via the 1, 2, or 3 train (West 4th Street).

Ray's Pizza

✉ 465 Sixth Avenue at 11th Street

This is the original Ray's pizza that you've heard about for years. Ray's is still one of the best pizzerias in the city, although there are many pizza parlors that claim its fame. Ray's built its reputation for serving extremely cheesy pizza by the slice. Ray's is accessible by subway via the 1, 2, or 3 train (West 4th Street).

 TRAVEL TIP

It's hard to travel far without finding a pizza place in New York City, especially in Manhattan. Manhattan is full of numerous new pizzerias, many making up numerous new concoctions with elaborate toppings in an attempt to top one another. While many chains have tried, they cannot top the authentic pizzerias you'll find around town. From thin crust to deep dish, lots of cheese, three cheese, pepperoni, or Sicilian, New York City is home to a lot of great pizza.

Lombardi's
✉ 32nd Spring Street
✆ 212-441-7994

This is the oldest pizzeria in America, established in 1897, and many still consider it the best. Lombardi's is accessible by subway via the C or E train (Spring Street station).

Mariella's
✉ 16th Street and Third Avenue

Some consider this the best slice of pizza in the city, especially if it's hot and fresh out of the oven. Mariella's is accessible by subway via the L, N, R, 4, 5, or 6 train (14th Street/Union Square station).

Sofia Fabulous Pizza
✉ Madison Avenue by 79th Street
✆ 212-734-2676

Sofia's is more than just a pizzeria. You can get caesar salad and stuffed mushrooms, but everyone comes for the thin crust pizza. Sofia's is accessible by subway via the 6 train (77th Street station).

Original Ray's Pizza

✉ Sixth Avenue and 11th Street

Founded in 1959, this is the original and first of the famous pizzerias. Have a slice for the history. Original Ray's is accessible by subway via the F or V train (14th Street station).

⩵FAST FACT

The coffee shop in *Seinfeld* that George and Jerry and Elaine frequent is real—it's Tom's Restaurant, located on 112th Street and Broadway. The restaurant offers regular diner food but is now a part of the New York legend.

Soup Kitchen International

✉ 259A West 55th Street between Broadway and Eighth Avenue

If your kids are old enough to watch *Seinfeld* reruns, they'll recognize this as the inspiration for the Soup Nazi. It's a hole-in-the-wall stand that sells homemade soup for $8 a pop, but it's so good people that line up around the block. Business is so good that the owner can afford to close in the summer. The Soup Kitchen is accessible by subway via the A, B, C, 1, or 9 train (59th Street/Columbus Circle station).

CHAPTER 17

Exotic Eats

NEW YORK IS A CITY OF IMMIGRANTS, so the food is a wealth of the best and the boldest from all over the world. Aside from Paris, no other city in the world has the mix of cultures and cuisines as New York. Here you can find kosher Chinese and French Japanese restaurants. It's one of the few cities in the country where there is a Chinese, Japanese, and Latin restaurant, as well as a pizzeria on almost every block—and they all deliver.

Because it is also the center of art and finance in this country, internationally renowned chefs have come here to set up their kitchens and show the world what they have to offer. And the result is staggering. This chapter is organized by cuisine, with most of the restaurants located in Manhattan below 96th Street. Enjoy!

Caribbean, Mexican, and Spanish

Latin food in New York can be a mix of Caribbean cuisines, from Dominican and Puerto Rican, to Cuban (and sometimes Cuban Chinese). But whatever the exact ethnic origin, the food is always plentiful. There's a terrific chain of Latin restaurants throughout Upper Manhattan under the name of La Caridad (look in the local phone book for one near you, or call information). You can feed a family of four on $30.

There are also excellent Mexican and Spanish restaurants all over the city.

 **TRAVEL TIP**

Ordering in a Latin restaurant is easy, once you realize that every meal will come with rice and beans—you have to decide whether or not you want red or black beans—bread, and a salad. If you don't know what to order, try the roast pork or the breaded steak. Most Latin restaurants have delicious fruit milkshakes called *batidos*, which come in such flavors as mango and papaya. Cuban sandwiches (sliced pork, ham, cheese, pickle, on a garlic roll) are truly delicious and will run about $4. Flan is always a good choice for dessert.

Victor's Café 52
✉ 236 West 52nd Street
✆ 212-586-7714

One of the oldest Latin restaurants in the city, it's one of the best, with a fairly upscale ambiance. The Cuba Libre drinks here are smooth in the summer. Fish and steak are always excellent. If you're going to the theater, it's a good idea to make a reservation so you get out in time. Prices are moderate. Victor's is accessible by subway via the N or R train (49th Street station).

MaryAnn's
✉ 2454 Broadway at 90th Street
✆ 212-877-0132
✉ 1503 Second Avenue at 77th Street
✆ 212-249-6165
✉ 116 Eighth Avenue
✆ 212-633-0877

An all-time favorite little Mexican restaurant in New York, MaryAnn's is open late and very kid-friendly (but only during the day—late at night people come in for the margaritas). The house salsa is good, too. Prices are moderate. Take the 1 or 9 train to

86th Street; the 6 train to 77th Street; or the A or C train to 14th Street/Eighth Avenue.

El Farro

✉ 823 Greenwich Street

✆ 212-929-8210

One of the oldest Spanish restaurants in the city, with a delightful mural in the back room, the garlic shrimp is awesome, as is the paella. Sangria will make you sing, and it's wonderfully child-friendly. It's a small restaurant, so you might want to make a reservation. Prices are moderate. El Farro is accessible by subway via the 1 or 9 train (Christopher Street or West 4th Street station).

El Cid

✉ 322 West 15th Street between Eighth and Ninth Avenues

✆ 212-929-9332

El Cid serves Spanish food and is known for its tapas. You can eat a meal from a number of small portions such as garlic shrimp, seasoned sausages, or the wonderful Spanish torta of egg and potatoes. Excellent sangria and wine are available, and the restaurant is cozy and unpretentious. Prices are moderate. El Cid is accessible by subway via the 1, 2, or 3 train (14th Street station).

Patria

✉ 250 Park Avenue South at 20th Street

✆ 212-777-6211

The cuisine here is New Spanish, featuring vibrant food and atmosphere, specialty drinks, and fun. Prices are moderate. Patria is accessible by subway via the 6 train (23rd Street station).

Chinese and Pan-Asian Cuisine

Chinatown on Canal and Mott Streets is where you should head for an authentic Chinese meal in New York. These streets are literally lined with good, fairly inexpensive restaurants, some offering dim sum (a kind of brunch, where a selection of small dishes can be ordered from a cart) and some offering a larger menu of specialties. It's a safe neighborhood and always packed.

 TRAVEL TIP

You can make reservations online at most of the city's restaurants by going to *www.opentable.com*. You could set up all your meals from home and make sure at the same time that you have reservations at the city's best restaurants.

Some of the restaurants recommended are the following:

The Golden Unicorn
✉ 18 E. Broadway
✆ 212-941-0991

Wong Kee
✉ 113 Mott Street
✆ 212-226-1160

Jing Fong
✉ 20 Elizabeth Street between Bayard and Canal Street
✆ 212-964-5256

Other Chinese and Pan-Asian restaurants recommended include the following.

Aja
✉ 937 Broadway at 22nd Street
✆ 212-473-8388
Aja is one of the newer, trendy pan-Asian restaurants. The ambiance is a modern fusion of unique styles. Prices are expensive. Aja is accessible by subway via the 1 or 9 train (23rd Street station).

Cendrillon

✉ 45 Mercer Street between Broome and Grand Streets

✆ 212-343-9012

The restaurant name means Cinderella in French and is run by a Filipino husband-and-wife team of self-taught chefs. However, it's really pan-Asian with a pleasant setting and interesting creative choices. The lamb dishes and the desserts are highly recommended. Prices are moderate. Take the N or R train to Prince Street or the C or E train to Spring Street.

Shun Lee Palace

✉ 155 East 55th Street between Lexington and Third Avenues

✆ 212-371-8844

This is an upscale Chinese restaurant serving delicious food with extravagant presentations. There is a great $19.99 prix fixe lunch. Prices are expensive. Shun Lee is accessible by subway via the 6 train (51st Street station).

Indian Fare

Indian food in New York is really pretty good, and there's a strip of Indian restaurants on 6th Street in the East Village (between 1st and 2nd Streets) that many New Yorkers frequent. Almost every restaurant on these blocks is good, because the competition is fierce, and many feature sitar music to accompany the meal. They are also quite inexpensive, and Indian food makes for excellent sharing among the family. The yogurt drinks should go over well with the kids. The following restaurants are recommended:

Mitali East

✉ 334 East 6th Street

✆ 212-533-2508

Gandhi

✉ 345 East 6th Street

✆ 212-614-9718

Passage to India
✉ 308 East 6th Street
✆ 212-529-5770

Other great Indian restaurants in other parts of Manhattan are also included here.

Bombay Palace
✉ 30 West 52nd Street between Fifth and Sixth Avenues
✆ 212-541-7777
Bombay Palace is one of the best Indian restaurants in Midtown. It serves excellent food, including a terrific lunch buffet in a charming atmosphere. Prices are moderate. Bombay Palace is accessible by subway via the E or V train (Fifth Avenue/53rd Street station).

Dawat
✉ 210 East 58th Street between Second and Third Avenues
✆ 212-355-7555
Another upscale Indian restaurant, Dawat is considered one of city's best. It offers creative cuisine in a sophisticated setting. Prices are moderate. Dawat is accessible by subway via the 4, 5, or 6 train (59th Street station).

 TRAVEL TIP

When ordering Indian food, it's a good idea to plan on sharing. Start with a mixed appetizer platter (the fried bananas and chickpea balls are delicious) and make sure to order some nan (a flat bread). Then order some tandoori and some curries.

Italian Cuisine

When visiting the city, you should try to catch a meal in Little Italy on Manhattan's Mulberry Street (and Grand Street). Though it's a smaller stretch of the city today, it's still full of wonderful restaurants, offering good food and desserts. Our suggestions are these:

Da Nico
✉ 164 Mulberry Street
✆ 212-343-1212

Il Cortile
✉ 125 Mulberry Street
✆ 212-226-6060

Umberto's Clam House
✉ 386 Broome Street (between Mulberry and Mott Streets)
✆ 212-431-7545

The last of the three, Umberto's, is a neighborhood institution as well as a tourist site (because of its mob history—which kids and *Sopranos* fans just love). It's also a good place to spot celebrities, from Sammy Sosa to Robert DeNiro. The seafood sauces are what Umberto's is known for (they keep coming back for the white clam sauce), and all the seafood is fresh and delicious. They now serve steaks and chops, but the restaurant was entirely seafood-based when it opened in the 1970s. The décor is simple white-and-blue and quite unpretentious, and the restaurant is surprisingly family-friendly. The only credit card they take is American Express. Definitely worth the trip, but prices here are expensive. Umberto's is accessible by subway via the 1 or 9 train (Canal Street station).

Japanese, Korean, and Thai

There is at least one Japanese restaurant on every street in Manhattan, and the food is surprisingly good, affordable, and creative. Korean restaurants can be found in the Garment District, and Thai restaurants are almost as popular with New Yorkers as Japanese restaurants.

Chosi

✉ 77 Irving Place at 19th Street

✆ 212-420-1419

Chosi serves Japanese food. The restaurant offers indoor and outdoor dining, and the menu includes sushi, sashimi, and prix fixe dinners. Chosi is accessible by subway via the 1 or 9 train (18th Street station).

Nobu

✉ 105 Hudson Street at Franklin Street

✆ 212-219-0500

This is a very trendy New York restaurant and the top-rated Japanese restaurant in the city, with a phenomenal forest setting. Reservations are a must, and it's even a good idea to make them a week or two in advance. Prices are expensive. Nobu is accessible by subway via the 1 or 9 train (Franklin Street station).

 TRAVEL TIP

There is much on a Japanese menu that is not raw fish. Kids love the miso soup and the edaname, which are steamed soy beans with salt. Tempura is deep fried vegetables and fish, and chicken or beef teriyaki always goes over well with kids.

Woochon Restaurant

✉ 8–10 West 36th Street

✆ 212-695-0676

This is an incredibly good restaurant that is open twenty-four hours a day. Adventurous kids will absolutely love the assortment of appetizers offered with every meal (some are spicy) that are served on a very large table. The winter soups are terrific, and the lunch special runs between $8 and $10. Prices are moderate. Woochon is accessible by subway via the B, D, F, N, Q, or R train (34th Street/Herald Square station).

Siam Inn

✉ 854 Eighth Avenue between 51st and 52nd Streets

✆ 212-757-4006

This is a lovely little restaurant with interesting menu choices, including traditional satays and coconut soup. It's a comfortable setting and good for theatergoers. Prices are reasonable. Siam Inn is accessible by subway via the C or E train (50th Street station).

Topaz

✉ 127 West 56th Street between Sixth and Seventh Avenues

✆ 212-957-8020

Topaz is considered one of the best Thai restaurants in the city. It gets very crowded at lunch time, so arrive early. Prices are reasonable. Topaz is accessible by subway via the B or Q train (57th Street station).

Try Moroccan

Al Baraka

✉ 1613 Second Avenue at 84th Street

✆ 866-268-6808

What a delightful surprise this restaurant is! From the outside, you would never know that you were about to enter into a somewhat authentic Moroccan garden with imported antiques and a working tiled fountain. Your hands are washed with rose water after you enter, and you can order from an appetizer menu (which is terrific for kids) or a full menu of incredible lamb and couscous meals. Sam, the proprietor, is usually on the premises, and will explain and entertain. After two hours in this wonderful place, you will forget you are in New York and will be shocked when you step back outside. Prices are moderate. Al Baraka is accessible by subway via the 4, 5, or 6 train (86th Street station).

Soul Food

Some times you just want pork chops smothered in gravy and some sweet potato pie, and guess what? You can find it in New York.

The Cotton Club

✉ 656 West 125th Street at St. Clair Place

✆ 212-663-7980

People don't come here for the food but for the experience. The cuisine is Southern at this renowned Harlem nightclub with a weekend gospel lunch. Prices are reasonable. The Cotton Club is accessible by subway via the 2 or 3 train (125th Street station).

 JUST FOR PARENTS

Two times a year (in the summer and winter), more than 100 New York restaurants participate in Restaurant Week, where lunches are offered for $20.04 per person and dinner is another $10. This is a great opportunity to eat in some of the best New York restaurants for a fraction of the price. But book ahead, because everything fills up fast.

Londel's

✉ 2620 Frederick Douglass Blvd. between 139th and 140th Streets

✆ 212-234-6114

This is a classic Southern soul food restaurant just off Striver's Row. There's music in the evening, and people come for the smothered pork chops and the blackened catfish. There's a Sunday brunch and a children's menu. Prices are moderate. Londel's is accessible by subway via the 2 or 3 train (135th Street station).

Sylvia's

✉ 328 Lenox Avenue between 126th and 127th Streets

✆ 212-996-0660

With the best soul food in New York, this is a comfortable, homey setting with patio dining available. The Sunday gospel brunch is one of the best buys in the city, and you can always buy the hot sauce or the collard greens, as well as the tie and apron. Sometimes, Sylvia herself shows up. Prices are reasonable. Sylvia's is accessible by subway via the 2 or 3 train (125th Street station).

Just for Fun

New York has some of the most unique restaurants in the world, such as Italian/Japanese.

Basta Pasta

✉ 37 West 17th Street between Fifth and Sixth Avenues

✆ 212-366-0888

This is an only-in-New York restaurant. Who would believe you could find Italian food, prepared by Japanese chefs in an open kitchen? The food is terrific, especially the sea urchin linguini and the tuna with wasabi tartar sauce. Kids will absolutely love this place, and you'll find yourself thinking about this incredibly creative food for a long time. The décor is bright and popular. Prices are moderate. Basta Pasta is accessible by subway via the F train (14th Street station).

La Bonne Soup

✉ 48 West 55th Street

✆ 212-586-7680

Named after a French comedy, this popular bistro has been offering families its traditional food for more than thirty years. Kids love the fondue—cheese, meat, and the chocolate dessert fondue—but the steak frites is very good and even the house salad dressing is memorable. Some people come for just the onion soup and salad. The chocolate mousse is pretty good as well. The children's menu is very affordable, and the daily prix fixe is always a bargain. This place is a real family favorite. They always have a delightful Bastille Day celebration (July 14th). There's also a cookbook to purchase. Prices are moderate. La Bonne Soup is accessible by subway via the E or F train (Fifth Avenue station).

Ruby Foo's
✉ 1626 Broadway at 44th Street
✆ 212-489-5600
✉ 2182 Broadway at 77th Street
✆ 212-724-6700

This is a faux Chinese restaurant—its interior is made to resemble the Chinese restaurant of the 1950s with red lacquer. The food is pan-Asian/American with everything from calamari and sushi to duck and steak. This is a menu designed for sharing. The Ruby Foo drink is delightful (but it packs a wicked punch) and the bento box dessert, in which sweets are presented as fake sushi in a bento box, is just incredible and delicious—and a real kid pleaser. Make reservations, as this is a popular restaurant with the date crowd as well as theatergoers at the Times Square location. Prices are moderate. Take the N, Q, R, 1, 2, or 3 train to Times Square/42nd Street; or take the 1 or 9 train to 79th Street.

City Island Seafood

You really need a car to get to this wonderful little island in the Bronx. In the summer, it's hopping with New Yorkers who come for the seafood. Who would ever believe that there's a boating community in the middle of the Bronx? Take the Bruckner Expressway to Pelham Parkway East to City Island.

Crab Shanty
✉ 361 City Island Avenue
✆ 718-885-1810

The Crab Shanty serves seafood. It's one of several fine City Island eateries, with big portions. Prices are moderate.

 TRAVEL TIP

If you want to find a restaurant or even a type of cuisine, go to ✍ *www.metronewyork.com* and search through the restaurant database compiled by *New York* magazine.

The Lobster Box

✉ 34 City Island Avenue

✆ 718-885-1952

The Lobster Box is another seafood restaurant. This one has been in business fifty years. It serves many variations of lobster, and the views are great. Prices are moderate.

CHAPTER 18

Where to Stay Under $150

THERE ARE HUNDREDS OF HOTELS in New York City, from those that cater to the family to some of the most luxurious suites in the nation to those for people on a very tight budget and international businesspeople.

The average hotel room runs about $150 for double occupancy, so only in a city like New York would hotel rooms that run $150 or less be considered "budget." There are also hotel taxes of about $15 a night, and parking charges run about $25 a night.

≡FAST FACT

Because New York is the nation's business capital and so many business travelers come to the city, hotel rooms are usually more expensive during the week than during the weekend.

The hotel listings in this chapter include a few in each part of Manhattan, with an emphasis on Midtown. The hotel reviews are organized by location, beginning with Midtown, which is the most popular location, and then looking at Lower Manhattan and Upper Manhattan.

How to Save

There are many ways to cut the cost of your hotel stay, from using the Automobile Association of America (AAA) and the American Association of Retired Persons (AARP) discounts, which are usually around 10 percent, to looking for a room that gives you free breakfast or even has a kitchenette. There are often discounts for summer and weekend specials and family rates, so ask for the lowest rate when you call for reservations.

Always try a number of Internet travel search engines that offer hotel rooms (some offer discounts too), as they often offer the best rates around and make a deluxe hotel very affordable for families. The following is a good selection of travel-related Web sites:

- *New York Times*: *www.newyorktimes.com*. Go to the travel section and then click onto Hotels. There is a good listing of New York hotels with simple descriptions.
- Fodor's: *www.fodors.com*. Their site offers a similar hotel index that you can use to search by name or category, as well as its own list of best hotels.
- Priceline: *www.priceline.com*. This site will allow you to make bids on discounted hotel rooms, but you don't have control over the hotel that is chosen for you (you set the price and see what comes in). They say that all their hotels are members of major chains, and you can probably get a very good rate this way, but be aware that there are parts of Upper Manhattan and the boroughs where you have to take a cab once the sun sets.
- Expedia: *www.expedia.com*. Expedia will give you a listing of hotels by location and price, and you can even see photos, but make sure you look the hotel up elsewhere, as sometimes they are adjacent to seedier parts of town.
- Orbitz: *www.orbitz.com*. This is another hotel search engine with hotel photos; be sure to double-check the listing before making reservations.

- TripAdvisor: ✑ *www.tripadvisor.com*. This is a great Web site that will give you fellow-traveler reviews as well as the best price on the Web for any hotel you are searching for.
- Travelocity: ✑ *www.travelocity.com*. This is another good Web site if you know the neighborhood and/or hotel you want to stay in.
- Preferred Hotels and Resorts Worldwide: ✑ *www.preferred hotels.com*. This site is operated by Travelweb, which is a reservation system for the hotel industry.
- Holiday Inn: ✑ *www.holidayinn.com*. At this hotel chain, with its own Web site, you may be able to find packages and last-minute deals.
- Radisson Hotel: ✑ *www.radisson.com*. This is another hotel chain with possible discounts and packages offered through their Web site.

═FAST FACT

Remember that sometimes it's worth it to pay a little more for location. Otherwise, you'll be paying to park the car all day and/or paying subway fares for the whole family, when you could just be walking from a downtown hotel.

Location and Price

The two most important elements to choosing your accommodations in New York are going to be location and price. Of course, if you are traveling as a family or visiting the city on business, there might be additional amenities that you will want (such as a pool or a fax machine). If you are not coming by car or don't plan on renting one, try to find a hotel near a subway station.

There are many hotels near the airports in Queens, but they are at least a half hour from the city by car or train. If you just need a place to stay overnight after you land, they are fine; otherwise, get something in Manhattan.

Location

The obvious location choice is Manhattan, since you want to be in the middle of the action. Within Manhattan, you need to determine which area is to your liking. Hotels in and around Times Square are busy and certainly in the middle of the hustle and bustle. Since Times Square and 42nd Street are now "cleaned up" and Disney-fied, the area is more appropriate for families than it once was. Times Square is ideal for theatergoing and sightseeing. Several Midtown hotels in both the East and West 50s put you in close proximity to the sights and excitement of the city, with slightly less hustle and bustle.

▌ TRAVEL TIP

Choosing a hotel room solely off the Internet can be deceiving. If something looks too inexpensive, be careful. Some New York hotel rooms are no bigger than closets, and are certainly not big enough for a family. Double-check the hotel's reviews before making reservations.

As you approach Central Park, you'll find more lavish accommodations, particularly on Central Park South, where the Plaza and plush neighboring hotels overlook the park. These elegant hotels are in a less touristy area than Times Square and cost quite a bit more. Here, instead of the glut of souvenir shops you'd find in Times Square, you'll find elegant stores such as Tiffany's and Saks.

Heading downtown, there are many fine hotels in the 30s, on both the east and west side. Some of these are a little quieter and less expensive, since they're not in the "middle of the excitement." Often these hotels will be surrounded by office or residential buildings. Since taxis are abundant and mass transit covers the city, it is not hard to get wherever you are going from these hotels. Streets in the downtown 30s, however, can be quiet at night, and you may not feel as safe walking around.

Further downtown in Lower Manhattan, you'll find some of the newest, most fashionable hotels in the city. While this area can be quiet at night and on weekends, it is bustling during the day. If you are planning to see the Statue of Liberty, Ellis Island, the South Street Seaport, and other Lower Manhattan sights and are not as attracted to the Midtown nightlife and Museum Mile, you may enjoy staying at these hotels, which are often frequented by business travelers in town for meetings in the financial district. You might appreciate more elbow room on the weekends as the business execs hit the road. On the other hand, if you plan evenings at the theater, want to spend days in Central Park and at the United Nations, and enjoy being in the heart of the action, this might not be the area for you.

Decide what you plan to do during your stay, your price range, and the atmosphere you are looking for when you step both into and out of the lobby, and then determine which part of town best suits your needs.

Other Considerations

Once you look through the hotel listings and determine those that fit your price range, consider these factors:

- Is there an extra charge per night for children staying in your room? Are there special children's rates or family packages?
- Is there a kitchenette in the room? A refrigerator? Microwave?
- What kind of restaurants are in the hotel? For family dining, a casual restaurant is more practical if you want to grab a quick, inexpensive breakfast or lunch. All major hotels have room service, but the prices can be steep. (You're better off in a neighborhood with stores nearby where you can buy a few items rather than ordering room service.)
- Is there easy access to public transportation?
- Does the hotel have bus or van service to the airport?

- Does the hotel have a concierge? In New York City, a hotel concierge is far more common than a hotel swimming pool. It is also more practical, as the concierge can help you with directions, reservations, and all sorts of services.
- How much does the hotel charge for phone calls? Phone calls made from hotel rooms (anywhere) can be quite costly. It's to your advantage to make calling card calls or to use a cellular phone. You might also ask about a jack for using your laptop. Most New York hotels now offer two-line phones and jacks for computers. Being able to go online and look up your next destination can be a plus.
- Is there a safe in the room? Whenever you travel, it's important to know you can protect valuables. (Of course, it's not advisable to travel with too many valuable items.)
- What is the parking situation? If you drive to the city, ask your hotel about parking availability and cost. Even some of the finest hotels don't have much to offer. Also ask what the fee is for re-entry to the lot and whether the lot is near the hotel.

Midtown Listings

If you are only in town for a day or two, Midtown is really where you should try to stay. You'll be close enough to everything you want to see and can travel by train or bus, or even a taxi.

Ameritania Hotel
✉ 230 West 54th Street and Broadway
✆ 212-247-5000

The Ameritania is a hip, trendy 207-room hotel with thirty-nine rooms with king-sized beds and thirteen suites. The interiors and guest rooms were refurbished in 1998, and the marble and fashionable décor is quite pleasing.

A stone's throw from the Ed Sullivan Theater, home to *The Late Show with David Letterman,* the Ameritania is just a short walk from

Central Park, the Theater District, and Fifth Avenue shopping. Amenities include valet laundry service, a concierge, and discounted parking. A comfortable, well-situated hotel, the Ameritania is one of several Amsterdam Hospitality Group Hotels around the city, all designed to provide quality accommodations at reasonable (for Manhattan) prices. One such property, the Amsterdam Court Hotel, is very similar to the Ameritania and sits four blocks away at Broadway and 50th Street. Call the Amsterdam Court at ✆212-459-1000.

≡FAST FACT

Pay phones in New York cost a quarter. However, many of the working phones on the street are not operated by standard phone companies, and they charge more if you call outside the (212) area code. Your cell phone should work throughout the city. Cell phones will not work on the subway.

The Ameritania features the popular Bar 54, a restaurant/bar with standard fare, serving all meals and cocktails in a sky-lit atrium. Although rates are said to start at $150, you can get a room for as low as $100 a night on an off-season night, more for deluxe suites. The Ameritania is accessible by subway via the A, B, C, D, 1, or 9 train (59th Street/Columbus Circle).

Best Western Manhattan

✉ 17 West 32nd Street between Fifth and Sixth Avenue
✆ 1-800-567-7720
✆ 212-246-8800

Best Western provides your standard clean, comfortable hotel room at a good price. The "Manhattan" is in the fashion district, which is hectic by day and quiet by night. For sightseeing, you are in the shadows of the Empire State Building and close to Times Square and the Theater District. You can also stroll over to nearby Macy's for some shopping with the money you save on your room.

The 176 rooms are basic with on-demand movies, irons, coffeemakers, and typical fare. The hotel has a fitness room, beauty salon, and laundry service and provides complimentary continental breakfast.

Best Westerns are good hotels. In Manhattan, where luxury and pricey amenities are abundant, this is comparatively a no-frills deal, but for the "get up and go" traveler who plans to get out each day and see the city, this fits the bill nicely. Another Best Western hotel, the Best Western Woodward, is located at ⊠ 210 West 55th Street (✆ 1-800-336-4110).

Restaurants include Manhattan Café, which serves American cuisine; Dae Dong, serving Asian food (located next door with an entrance from the lobby); and the Skybar, an outdoor rooftop bar that is pleasant for snacks and drinks in warm weather.

Rates start at $99 and $129 for suites. The hotel is accessible by subway via the B, D, F, N, Q, or R train (34th Street/Herald Square station).

Crowne Plaza

⊠ 1605 Broadway between 48th and 49th Streets
✆ 1-800-243-6969
✆ 212-977-4000

The Crowne Plaza enjoys a marvelous location—just north of the busy Times Square area, south of Central Park, and within a short walk of the Theater District, Rockefeller Center, St. Patrick's Cathedral, and Fifth Avenue shopping. This is a forty-six-story, upscale, 770-room hotel.

The views are terrific from the higher floors. Rooms feature an in-room refreshment center, free movie channels, makeup mirrors, ironing boards, and in-room safes. Children under 19 stay for free if sharing a room with their parents—a nice touch for families. The hotel also offers a room service kiddies menu.

The on-site health club is huge—nearly 30,000 square feet—and is run by fitness managers with trainers on hand. And yes, the health club has one of the city's largest hotel indoor swimming pools. The pool and wide array of fitness equipment are first-class amenities, as are classes offered in boxing, yoga, ballet, and water aerobics.

Crowne Plaza sports a friendly atmosphere and provides laundry service, a concierge, and on-site valet parking. Restaurants include the 136-seat Balcony Café, which is ideal for breakfast and lunch; the Sampling Bar, which is a lively bar/restaurant for pretheater fare with a wide variety of wines; and the Broadway Grill, which is a casual 120-seater with memorabilia from the Broadway shows.

Rates start at $150 and suites at $450. The hotel is accessible by subway via the 1 or 9 train (50th Street station).

Days Inn Hotel
✉ 790 Eighth Avenue between 48th and 49th Streets
✆ 1-800-572-6232
✆ 212-581-7000

Part of the Loews Hotel Group, Days Inn Hotel is a standard facility offering quality rooms at a comparatively good price. Featuring 367 recently renovated guest rooms, the hotel is within walking distance to the Theater District for Broadway shows, Rockefeller Center, and Radio City.

Rooms are sizable, with on-demand movies and plenty of cable channels and in-room climate controls, plus refrigerators in some rooms. The gift shop staff double as concierges, making tour arrangements and helping arrange for theater tickets.

🌂 RAINY DAY FUN

The Loews Loves Kids Program offers children a welcome kit with games and crayons, plus the use of a family video library. Participating hotels include the following: Howard Johnson (✆ 212-581-4100), Howard Johnson Plaza Hotel (✆ 212-581-4100), Loews New York Hotel (✆ 212-947-5050), and the Regency (✆ 212-759-4100). Call to see if this plan is still in effect at the hotel you choose.

The Days Inn Hotel is, essentially, not unlike hotels you'll find along the highways of America. This is your standard place to stay, not elegant, not fancy, but comfortable and a good choice for the family with plenty of things to see and do. The neighborhood, once an outgrowth of "seedy" 42nd Street, has improved with the Times Square cleanup and is crowded with theatergoers in the evenings. Parking is available for a fee. The Metro Deli serves standard American fare and is open from 6 A.M. to 11 P.M.

Rates start at $150 ($350 in December). The hotel is accessible by subway via the C or E train (50th Street).

Ramada Milford Plaza

✉ 270 West 45th Street on Broadway

✆ 1-800-221-2690

✆ 212-869-3000

A Ramada property, the Milford Plaza put a lot of money behind its advertising campaign, which featured the tune "Lullaby of Broadway" to appeal to the theatergoers—as the hotel is smack in the middle of the Theater District. The campaign apparently worked; Milford has established a presence amid several more luxurious hotels rich with amenities and designed for the business traveler.

Some 1,300 rooms were refurbished in 1995; they are comfortable and safe and feature cable television and in-room movies. While they are not lavish, they are sufficient if you are planning to spend the bulk of your time seeing the sights and/or taking in the Broadway shows.

A spacious lobby complete with fountains, chandeliers, and flowers awaits you as you enter. Once you're inside, the Milford features a theater ticket and sightseeing desk, a game room for the kids, a fitness center, valet services, and parking at $24 per day (if you don't use the car that day). There is also a gift shop. Restaurants include the Celebrity Deli and the Honolulu Steamship Company. Both are more than adequate.

The Milford Plaza provides no-frills rooms at a good price in a great location. Rates start at $129 for two persons, suites at $200.

The hotel is accessible by subway via the N, Q, R, 1, 2, or 3 train (Times Square/42nd Street station).

Travel Inn Hotel

✉ 515 West 42nd Street between Tenth and Eleventh Avenues

✆ 1-800-869-4630

✆ 212-695-7171

West 42nd Street underwent the first wave of revitalization on the city's major cross street. The Travel Inn sits right in the middle of that area's "new look," just a few blocks from the Javits Center and not far from Times Square.

It's nothing too fancy but a good value, with clean rooms and two very unique amenities: an outdoor pool with a deck and free parking, yes, that's free parking. The hotel's 160 guest rooms are reasonably large with the standard hotel fare. A fitness center, gift shop, and tour desk are also included within.

The River West Café/Deli, located within the hotel, is a pleasantly designed little coffee shop with standard American cuisine.

An "outside Manhattan" hotel placed in Manhattan, the Travel Inn is in a convenient location, particularly for visiting the *Intrepid* Sea, Air & Space Museum or taking a ride around Manhattan on the Circle Line or another of the many water cruises. Cross-town buses on 42nd Street are frequent, and Broadway and the major theaters are not far away. If you're not seeking luxury and, particularly, if you're driving into the city (with kids), this might be worth checking out.

Rates start at $150 for a single or double. The hotel is accessible by subway via the A, C, or E train (42nd Street station).

Lower Manhattan and Downtown

If you're in town for a holiday and all the Midtown hotels are booked, this area is your next best bet. It's also good if you are visiting New York University or doing business in the Wall Street area. You might even be able to get a good weekend deal because these hotels cater to the business crowd.

JUST FOR PARENTS

The legendary Chelsea Hotel, where 1960s and 1970s celebs partied and stayed in the tradition of artists and writers going back to the turn of the century, is just not a place for families. Its current motto is "A Rest Stop for Rare Individuals," and it still has an edgy quality that might not be right for a traveling family.

Best Western Seaport Inn
✉ 3 Peck Slip
✆ 1-800-HOTELNY
✆ 212-766-6600

One block north of the South Street Seaport and one block south of the Brooklyn Bridge, you'll find the Seaport Inn tucked away in Lower Manhattan. A comfortable hotel with modern amenities and old-world charm, the Best Western features easy access to all Lower Manhattan sites, obviously including the seaport. Rooms are large with quaint furnishings and modern amenities, including video players, voice mail, refrigerators, and safes. Some rooms include whirlpools or steam baths.

The hotel has an exercise facility and offers a continental breakfast. If you're looking for a Lower Manhattan location and are planning to see the sights and visit Chinatown, Little Italy, and the Financial Center, this is a cost-effective, clean hotel with all the basics. In the winter months, the area around the seaport can get awfully quiet, and the brisk winds from the river make walking around the shops, ships, and eateries less fun. In the warm weather, however, it's a wonderful area. Also, the hotel is not widely known, so you should get more personalized attention.

There is no on-site restaurant, but there are plenty of places to eat near the hotel. Rates start at $150. The hotel is accessible by subway via the A, C, 2, 3, 4, or 5 train (Fulton Street/Broadway Nassau station).

Holiday Inn Downtown

✉ 138 Lafayette Street, near Canal Street

✆ 1-800-465-4329

How unbelievably cool would it be to stay in Chinatown? This 215-room hotel is housed in a historic Chinatown building and is one of the very few hotels in the area. The Asian décor of the lobby and Pacifica restaurant (which offers excellent dim sum) and good price make it a favorite amongst family budget travelers and Europeans. Parking is available for a fee.

Rates start at $150, but they are sometimes less off-season and on the Internet. The hotel is accessible by subway via the 6 train to Canal Street.

≡FAST FACT

There is a great hotel in Brooklyn Heights, so if you're staying there to see family, or you want to spend a day at the Brooklyn Museum, Botanic Garden, and Junior's, try the New York Marriott in Brooklyn (call ✆ 1-800-843-4898 for more information). It has an Olympic-length lap pool and a kosher kitchen. Rooms have eleven-foot ceilings (unheard of in Manhattan), and the lobby features seats from the Old Ebbets Field. Rooms are usually under $150.

The Millennium Hilton

✉ 55 Church Street

✆ 1-800-835-2220

✆ 212-693-2001

Reopened after the September 11 terrorist attack, this sleek modern marvel rises fifty-eight stories high. Nonetheless, the 565-room Millennium has a lot to offer, including king-sized beds in most of the guest rooms, forty-two-inch plasma televisions, in-room safes, mini-bars, and fax machines, plus makeup mirrors and video checkout. Guest rooms are large and modern and offer a warm residential ambiance.

The spacious lobby is filled with the sounds of the piano. There is a new fitness center and a glass-enclosed heated pool. A concierge, laundry service, and babysitting service are also among the various amenities offered at the Millennium, a popular hotel with both business and leisure travelers.

The new Church & Day Restaurant is on the 14th Floor and offers authentic American regional cuisine. Parking is available but quite limited (and at a fee). Rates start at $135, and junior suites run from $185 to $509. There are various specials throughout the year. The hotel is accessible by subway via the 1 or 9 train (Franklin or Chambers Street station).

Washington Square Hotel
✉ 103 Waverly Place at MacDougal Street
✆ 1-800-222-0418

This has been where parents visiting New York University students, and the university's prospective students, have stayed for generations. On the corner of Washington Square Park, this small 165-room hotel offers visitors a continual breakfast, has a gym, and offers in-room data ports and cable television. There's a restaurant, C3, on the premises and the famous Blue Note jazz club is just down the street. Rooms run between $110 and $150. The hotel is accessible by subway via the A, C, E, or F train (West 4th Street).

Upper Manhattan

The hotels in this section are located above 59th Street in Upper Manhattan, a good place to stay if you are planning on spending time at the American Museum of Natural History or in Central Park.

Barbizon Hotel
✉ 140 E. 63rd Street, at Lexington Avenue
✆ 1-800-223-1020

This legendary Upper East Side hotel was once a women's-only residence (from 1927 until 1981) where Grace Kelly, Joan Crawford, and Liza Minnelli once lived. The elegant lobby features marble and limestone, with chairs covered with mohair. Guest rooms are done in contemporary blond wood and soft pastel shades. There is a spa, operated by the Equinox gym chain, which includes a lap pool. There are 306 rooms, all with cable television, mini-bars, data ports, and safes. There is room service and a restaurant, and babysitting services are available. Parking is available for a fee.

Rates start at $150. Suites are available for more. The hotel is accessible by subway via the 4, 5, or 6 train (59th Street station).

The Empire Hotel

✉ 44 West 63rd Street, between Broadway and Columbus

✆ 1-800-333-3333

This Upper West Side Hotel has been completely redone and is within walking distance from Lincoln Center, as well as an arthouse movie theater and the new Columbus Circle restaurants. There are tapestries on the lobby walls, and the 355 small hotel rooms are charming and well furnished, with big televisions and CD players. There are two restaurants on the premises. Parking is available for a fee.

Rates begin at $150 (sometimes there are Internet specials for even less) and there are twenty suites available. The hotel is accessible by subway via the A, B, C, 1, or 9 train (59th Street/Columbus Circle station).

Excelsior

✉ 45 West 81st Street between Central Park West and Columbus Avenue

✆ 1-800-368-4575

✆ 212-362-9200

The Upper West Side is a trendy neighborhood with many old apartment buildings, fashionable cafés, plenty of shopping, and "old New York charm." The area is also home to the Excelsior, a landmark hotel rich with atmosphere yet complete with the modern amenities.

A stone's throw from the American Museum of Natural History, the Excelsior has one- and two-bedroom suites, with some of the (recently refurbished) 116 rooms and eighty suites sporting balconies and in-room PCs. The hotel features a fitness room, entertainment lounge, library, and continental breakfast buffet.

This is a hotel for those who want a small, quaint hideaway in Manhattan, just north of the action, to enjoy quiet nights, an afternoon stroll, or a picnic in Central Park, a short walk away. Lincoln Center is some fifteen blocks south. There is a new restaurant and lounge. Rates start at $149 and suites at $189. The hotel is accessible by subway via the B or C train (81st Street station).

 **TRAVEL TIP**

Even the most expensive hotels have special last-minute Internet rates and other specials, so you may be able to stay at a first-class hotel for half-price if you search for a discount rate.

The Lucerne

✉ 201 West 79th Street between Broadway and Amsterdam
✆ 1-800-492-8122
✆ 212-875-1000

A treasured landmark, the Lucerne is nestled among the shops and cafés on the Upper West Side and is a short walk from Central Park, the American Museum of Natural History, and Lincoln Center. Featuring 250 large rooms and suites, the Lucerne is one of several Empire Hotel Group properties around the city.

Rooms feature marble and granite bathrooms, in-room movies, and other standard amenities; the hotel includes valet service, a concierge and tour desk, fitness center, and discount parking.

The location puts you in a busy neighborhood with easy access to numerous sights. Service is also more personalized, since the hotel is relatively small. Wilson's restaurant is a bar and grill with breakfast and dinner. Rates start at $150. The hotel is accessible by subway via the 1 or 9 train (79th Street station).

CHAPTER 19

Moderately Priced Hotels ($150–$250)

IT'S HARD TO BELIEVE, but in New York City, a moderately priced hotel means a room under $250. As everyone knows, New York is a very expensive city. When you're traveling with a family, you want to make sure that your accommodations are comfortable and safe, so you can't cut the same corners you might if you were on your own.

In 2002, New York was named the safest large city in the country by the FBI. For the past two years running it has held on to the number two spot for family vacations in the U.S. (second only to Orlando, and followed by Vegas). The city has some wonderful family hotels. With more than 80,000 hotel rooms in this city, there should be something in your budget even if you are traveling during the busiest season (the winter holidays).

Midtown Listings

As in the previous chapter, hotel listings are organized by location, starting with Midtown, the most sought-after location, and then covering Lower Manhattan, downtown, and Upper Manhattan. Midtown includes the area between 59th and 30th Streets.

Beekman Tower

✉ 3 Mitchell Place, between 49th Street and First Avenue

✆ 1-800-ME-SUITE

✆ 212-230-8018

Overlooking the United Nations and the East River, this lavish art deco style hotel is a New York City landmark. Built in 1928, it offers 172 handsomely furnished studio, one-bedroom, and two-bedroom suites.

The Beekman Tower suites feature complete kitchens with full stoves, refrigerators, microwaves, dishes, and utensils. Luxury baths, plush robes, and cable channels, plus in-room movies and in-room safes are included in your accommodations. The facility also offers a health club with saunas, a concierge, valet parking, a coin-operated laundry, a grocery shopping service, and more.

Essentially this is an opportunity to rent a luxury apartment in New York City for a week, complete with (in some cases) a terrace and a river view. In fact, you're one up on apartment dwellers—you can get room service! The kitchens can save you some money if you buy food and eat in, or you can use the valet grocery shopping service to have groceries delivered to your door.

The Zephyr Grille restaurant features continental American cuisine, while the Top of the Tower on the twenty-sixth floor overlooks the city and serves lunch, dinner, or cocktails. Rates start at $229. This hotel is accessible by subway via the 6 train (51st Street station).

 TRAVEL TIP

Other Manhattan Suites East Hotels in the city include the Dumont Plaza, Eastgate Tower, Lyden Gardens, Lyden House, Plaza Fifty, Shelbourne Murray Hill, and Surrey Hotel. They are all located between 34th and 76th Streets on the east side. The Southgate Tower is on Manhattan's west side, by Penn Station. Call ✆ 1-800-ME-SUITES for reservations at any of the properties.

Crowne Plaza at the United Nations

✉ 304 East 42nd Street, between First and Second Avenues

✆ 1-800-879-8836

✆ 212-986-8800

This forty-year-old, twenty-story high-rise is a fashionable hotel in the quaint surroundings of Tudor City, just a block away from the United Nations and a bus ride across town from Times Square. High on hospitality and comfort, the Crowne Plaza is a popular stop for tourists and for visiting dignitaries with business at the United Nations.

The hotel has a classic old-world charm, with marble floors and velvet furnishings. The tiny Tudor City area, a quiet street tucked away behind the hotel, is just off 41st Street. Most New Yorkers have probably never seen this little two-block area overlooking the United Nations.

As for the 300-room luxury hotel, which you enter from East 42nd Street, guest rooms include in-room movies, mini-bars, digital safes, large beds, Italian marble bathrooms, and a warm, comfortable, yet modern atmosphere. The hotel includes a fitness center, concierge, parking, and some marvelous views from the higher floors. For a few dollars extra you can enjoy complimentary breakfasts and cocktails in the Crowne Club Lounge. This is a first-rate facility in a prime, safe, and easily accessible location run by a worldwide hotel chain.

Cecil's Bistro, featuring both American and French cuisine, is on the premises. Rates start at $199. This hotel is accessible by subway via the 4, 5, or 6 train (Grand Central Station/42nd Street station).

Grand Hyatt New York

✉ Park Avenue at Grand Central

✆ 1-800-233-1234

✆ 1-800-243-2546 (for instant check-in)

✆ 212-883-1234

With more than 1,300 rooms, the Grand Hyatt is indeed "grand"! Donald Trump built the hotel. It opened in 1980 and was refurbished with a $100-million face-lift in 1996. The Hyatt is a short walk from Broadway theaters, the United Nations, the finest shopping on Fifth Avenue, and other attractions. Sports fans may enjoy catching a glimpse of the ballplayers who stay at the hotel when the "visiting" teams are in town.

TRAVEL TIP

Remember that when traveling with children, you can set up a lot of what you'll need ahead of time, such as a crib in your room. You can also check to see if they have in-room Nintendo or if you'll need to bring your own.

The Hyatt's rooms, including sixty-three suites, are well lit, sleek, and comfortable, with in-room movies and other amenities. A health club, concierge, laundry service, and outdoor garden are all part of the Grand Hyatt, which features a sprawling plant-filled atrium lobby, complete with a cascading waterfall. It's quite impressive, but that's the typical Trump style.

Three restaurants include the glass-enclosed Sun Garden Lounge, which serves Mediterranean fare and overlooks 42nd Street; the Crystal Fountain, which serves American cuisine and champagne Sunday brunches; and the small Cigar Room, featuring fine dining and exquisite cigars.

Rates start at $219 on weekends and $265 on weekdays. Ask about holiday rates. This hotel is accessible by subway via the 4, 5, or 6 train (Grand Central Station/42nd Street station).

Loews New York
✉ 569 Lexington Avenue at East 51st Street
✆ 1-800-23-LOEWS
✆ 212-752-7000

Built in 1961 and designed by the same architect as Miami's famed Fontainebleau, this recently renovated 728-room hotel sports an art deco lobby plus two restaurants and several stores below. While the views aren't spectacular, the stylish east side/Midtown area offers an array of shopping and restaurants. It's also convenient to all transportation.

Essentially a quality hotel without all the elegant trimmings, Loews offers a good value, comfort, safety, cleanliness, and some amenities in a good location. The Club 51 concierge level provides special amenities, including complimentary breakfasts and evening cocktails.

Rooms are comfortable, with a modern décor, and they feature an in-room safe, marble bathtub, in-room modem line, and refrigerator. Other amenities include a modern fitness center, a concierge for special requests, and reasonable parking (for Manhattan) at $30 a day. On the premises you'll find a gourmet coffee beanery, nail salon, barbershop, and a W. H. Smith newspaper and magazine shop.

The Lexington Avenue Lounge offers an intimate setting for cocktails, snacks, or supper, complete with a multitude of television screens with news, sports, and videos. The Lexington Avenue Grill is a popular location for standard American Cuisine in a warm, casually elegant environment.

Rates start at $189. This hotel is accessible by subway via the 6 train (51st Street).

Marriott East Side

✉ 535 Lexington Avenue between 49th and 50th Streets
✆ 1-800-228-9290
✆ 212-755-4000

This hotel property is a landmark Marriott Hotel. Its east side location is ideal for those interested in visiting Rockefeller Center, the United Nations, and many other popular city locations. The grand lobby, complete with columns and a lavish interior, welcomes you to this fashionable, but not ostentatious, hotel.

Some 643 guest rooms and 12 suites offer a "Servi-Bar" (snacks) and in-room movies as part of their well-appointed, fashionable accommodations. There are six deluxe concierge floors available, plus amenities for all guests, including a theater, tour and travel desk, health club, video message center, safe deposit boxes, and gift shop.

The Shelton Grille features continental dining throughout the day, and the lobby lounge provides an intimate setting for cocktails and conversation.

Rates start around $200 and suites around $400. Ask about seasonal specials. This hotel is accessible by subway via the 6 train (51st Street station).

≡FAST FACT

Once upon a time, the Marriott East Side was the Shelton Towers (built in 1924). Over the years, it has been a stomping ground for many performers, including Harry Houdini, who performed escape tricks from the pool. Bandleader Xavier Cugat, Peggy Lee, and Eddie Fisher also performed there. Shelton Towers was also the first major New York City hotel to employ female bellhops.

The Algonquin

✉ 59 West 44th Street, between Fifth and Sixth Avenues
✆ 1-800-784-1180
✆ 212-840-6800

This classic hotel is famous for its Algonquin Roundtable literary gatherings, which included such writers as Dorothy Parker and James Thurber. For many years, it was the "in" place for writers to meet, and it housed visiting actors, playwrights, and others in the arts, including Helen Hayes, Sinclair Lewis, Maya Angelou, George S. Kaufman, and many other notables. Built in 1902, the Algonquin is now a historic New York landmark. Even if you're not staying there, it might still be worth a visit.

The hotel is rich with history, and it is also fresh from a $5.5-million restoration designed to return the property to the glory of an earlier period, with furnishings from the turn of the century. The antiques that make up the Algonquin décor were carefully chosen to re-create the ambiance of a bygone era.

Today, the 165-room hotel combines the elegance and charm of the early twentieth century with the functionality of the early twenty-first century. Specialty suites are dedicated to and feature the works of Dorothy Parker, with warm, comfortable furnishings in all guest rooms, plus movies, safes, and fax machines as part of the in-room amenities.

A small twenty-four-hour fitness center might seem out of place, but if you read while on the treadmill, you will at least be maintaining the literary theme of the hotel. Concierge and laundry service are available, and also on premises is (appropriately) a library.

The Oak Room, for dining by day, becomes a cabaret at night. The cabaret features dining and entertainment Tuesdays through Saturdays, with dinner beginning at 7 P.M. and the curtain going up on first-rate entertainment at 9. The Blue Bar serves cocktails and food, and the Spoken Word is a place for literary programs that range from discussions about books to readings of short plays.

Rates start at $198. This hotel is accessible by subway via the B, D, F, Q, or 7 train (42nd Street station).

 TRAVEL TIP

> The Algonquin is a great place to have a drink, even if it runs you $12. Sit in large wing chairs and munch on salted nuts as waiters in traditional black suits serve you. The finger food is always excellent too, and there's always the hotel cat to entertain you. This is not a place for those allergic to animals.

Doubletree Guest Suites

✉ 1568 Broadway, between 46th and 47th Streets

✆ 1-800-325-9033

✆ 212-719-1600

"Suites" is the operative word here, with forty-three floors featuring some 460 suites. Like everything else in New York, the Doubletree offers you a wide range of choices, including king suites, queen suites, double/double suites, executive conference suites, family suites, handicap suites, nonsmoking suites, and two presidential suites. Each suite includes private bedrooms and separate living rooms, plus sofa beds, wet bars, microwaves, refrigerators, two televisions with cable, and more space than many New York City apartments. They are all well decorated.

The hotel features a state-of-the-art fitness center, valet service, and a family floor with child safety features—plus a dedicated Kids Quarters Club that offers video games and fun activities for children ages 3 through 12. A gift shop and laundry are also on premises.

The Doubletree towers high above the heart of Times Square and all the action, with a glitzy, modern look and an off-the-street lobby (common in the Times Square hotels) that affords privacy and safety. It is a very child-friendly hotel, featuring freshly baked chocolate chip cookies and play activities. The suites, at essentially the same rates as comparable guest rooms in the area, provide that much-needed room for family traveling.

The Center Stage Café offers American cuisine with a Broadway theater ambiance. The Cabaret Lounge provides piano music in a lavish show biz setting while you sip cocktails. Rates start at $200. This hotel is accessible by subway via the 1 or 9 train (50th Street station).

RAINY DAY FUN

Doubletree Guest Suites offer what's called the Kids Quarters Club, which features interactive video games and other things for youngsters, plus a refrigerator and microwave in every room to save you money on a few breakfasts and lunches.

Hilton New York and Towers
✉ 1335 Avenue of the Americas, between 53rd and 54th Streets
✆ 1-800-HILTONS
✆ 212-261-5870

It's hard to go wrong with a Hilton property. This massive hotel, located in the heart of Manhattan, is a city unto itself. The Hilton provides all sorts of conveniences, including a state-of-the-art fitness center, concierge service, foreign currency exchange, computerized checkout, and an AT&T language line offering 140 languages, plus elevators with CNN newscasts to keep you abreast of what's going on in the world during your ride. There are numerous shops located in this massive structure, including boutiques, a gift shop, drugstore, ticket booth, and beauty salon/barber shop.

Guest rooms are clean and roomy. They sport modern décor plus refreshment centers, pay movies, and various basic amenities. The Hilton also has fifty-two rooms specially designed for people with disabilities; the rooms are equipped to accommodate guests in wheelchairs.

⟁ RAINY DAY FUN

Stay at the Hilton, and your kids can borrow toys to play with. The 53rd Street Hotel has a "Vacation Station"—a collection of toys for borrowing, as well as a folder of activities for kids to do around the city. The Vacation Station is open during the summer months.

The Towers is a special private sector from the thirty-eighth through forty-fourth floors, featuring a private lounge for complimentary breakfast, afternoon tea, hors d'oeuvres, and more. There are various other amenities for the Towers guests.

The Hilton has long been a favorite of visitors to the city because of its first-rate service, easy accessibility, and wide range of amenities. The hotels draws families in with their "children under 18 stay free" policy (providing they share a room with their parents or grandparents).

An eight-level underground parking garage has twenty-four-hour valet parking.

Restaurants include Etrusca, the new Italian eatery, plus the New York Marketplace, a sidewalk café that is ideal for breakfasts or lunches. There are also the Bridges Bar and the Lobby Lounge for a nightcap. Double rooms start at $250 and suites start at $525. This hotel is accessible by subway via the E or V train (Fifth Avenue/53rd Street station).

Marriott Marquis

✉ 1535 Broadway, between 45th and 46th Streets

✆ 1-800-843-4898

✆ 212-398-1900

In the heart of the Theater District, and housing a Broadway theater within, the fifty-story Marriott Marquis is one of the premier hotels in the Times Square area. The modern skyscraper is accentuated by a thirty-seven-story open atrium with glass-enclosed elevators that provide a spectacular ride.

The 1,900 rooms are modern and spacious, with in-room safes and service bars, plus on-demand video and the latest in climate-control conveniences. The hotel is a small city unto itself, with shops, restaurants, lounges, three bars, a beauty salon, and a health club. Amenities include laundry service, concierge, parking (limited and for a fee), babysitting, airport service, and a tour and transportation desk.

Marriotts are usually well run, and this big, bold, bright Broadway hotel is no exception. The energy and excitement of the Theater District is prevalent throughout, but with the main lobby several floors above the street, there's also a feeling of being secure and away from the hustle and bustle of the busy area.

Restaurants include the View (a revolving rooftop restaurant), the JW Steakhouse, Encore, and the Atrium Café. While you browse the premises, which in itself can take a day, you'll also find the Top of the View Lounge, Clock Lounge, and Broadway Lounge. Pick up a map, or you might get lost!

If the city doesn't have enough to offer, the hotel has more than its share of places to visit and to stop by for a bite to eat.

Rates start at $220 and $450 for suites. This hotel is accessible by subway via the N, Q, R, 1, 2, or 3 train (Times Square/42nd Street station).

Sheraton New York Hotel and Towers

✉ 811 Seventh Avenue between 52nd and 53rd Streets

✆ 1-800-223-6550

✆ 212-581-1000

Sheraton is another highly trusted, top name in the hotel business, and this 1,750-room skyscraper is no exception. A host of suites can also be found, including special Tower Rooms, Hospitality Rooms, and VIP Suites with parlors.

In-room amenities include "refreshment centers," coffeemakers with complimentary Starbucks coffee (in some rooms), in-room movies, and video checkout. Through an affiliation with the Voyager's Collection, a hotel shopping catalog is also available, featuring hundreds of products via in-room interactive television.

JUST FOR PARENTS

One of the nicest spots for a nightcap or late afternoon drink is the Midtown Sheraton on 53rd Street. The Lobby Court Lounge and Cigar Bar offers a unique mix of martinis and appetizers. Tuesday through Saturday, a singer/pianist is there to perform from 8:30 P.M. until after midnight.

The hotel itself is a few blocks north of the Theater District, Times Square, Radio City Music Hall, and Rockefeller Center; it's just south of Carnegie Hall and Central Park. In short, it is a prime location. The Sheraton offers a theater desk and a 4,000-square-foot fitness center and health club, complete with everything from personal trainers and steam rooms to fresh fruit.

The Sheraton Towers is a hotel within a hotel, with a special "elite" group of rooms that include personal butler service, private check-in, and a lounge on the forty-ninth floor.

Restaurants include the Streeter's New York Café, a large glass-enclosed café that seats 180 people on various levels for breakfast, lunch, and dinner. Hudson's Sports Bar and Grill is home to a host of large-screen televisions, all featuring sporting events of the season.

Nearby is the renovated Sheraton Manhattan at Seventh Avenue and 51st Street. Guests of the Sheraton New York Hotel and Towers can cross the street and use the Sheraton Manhattan's fifty-foot swimming pool. The Sheraton Manhattan features Russo's Steak and Pasta Restaurant and typical Sheraton amenities.

Rates run from $179 to over $300, and suites from $450 to $700. The location, amenities, security, and history of success at Sheraton properties makes this one a good choice. This hotel is accessible by subway via the B, D, or E train (Seventh Avenue station).

The Time Hotel

✉ 224 West 49th Street between Eighth Avenue and Broadway
✆ 212-246-5252

One of the city's newer hotels, the Time Hotel is a "luxury boutique hotel" in the middle of Times Square, featuring just 164 rooms and twenty-eight suites.

Rooms are sleek and modern, decorated in bold colors. You'll find curtains in place of closet doors, canvas covers for the television set, and essays on the choice of color for the room—all part of this unique (somewhat eclectic) experience in Manhattan. If that isn't enough, the primary color (red, blue, or yellow) will continue throughout the entire room, and you'll also enjoy a special red-, blue-, or yellow-inspired scent in the bathroom.

Basic amenities include a mini-bar, an in-room safe, Web TV along with cable and movie channels, complimentary bathrobes, and in-room fax machines. The Time also offers a concierge, fitness center, personal shopper service, laundry and dry cleaning service, valet service, express checkout, and a second-floor lounge. Essentially, the hotel provides large hotel amenities in a smaller setting. While the "designer rooms and fragrances" aren't going to be for everyone, the hotel is modern. The hotel's smaller size, compared to its Times

Square counterparts, can be comforting, especially when you're waiting for an elevator.

The Palladin restaurant is, like the hotel, eclectic, with a contemporary flair from an internationally known chef. While you can order food up to your room from the Palladin, don't be discouraged if it doesn't match the room's primary color. The Time Lounge on the second floor offers a tapas menu, plus cocktails and specialty drinks.

Rates start at $200. This hotel is accessible by subway via the C or E train (50th Street station).

Downtown and Lower Manhattan

There are some truly lovely small hotels below 34th Street in Lower Manhattan. Many of them have been catering to the sophisticated traveler to Manhattan for generations.

The Carlton

✉ 22 East 29th Street, between 5th and Madison Avenues

✆ 1-800-542-1502

✆ 212-532-4100

Situated on a quiet street between the Midtown sights and Greenwich Village, this 350-room hotel is billed as "distinctive." What is especially distinctive is that the hotel does a good job at being fashionable and luxurious without charging an extraordinary price.

Rooms are simple and comfortable, with king- or queen-sized beds, in-room movies, and Nintendo. The off-the-beaten-path location (not on an avenue and not around Times Square), coupled with the size of the hotel, allows for a private, more tranquil atmosphere.

A concierge and valet parking are offered, and children under 16 can stay free if they share a room with their parents. The Café Carlton is a warm, cozy restaurant, serving breakfast, lunch, and dinner.

Rates start at $205 and suites at $600. This hotel is accessible by subway via the 6 train (28th Street station).

Chelsea Savoy Hotel
✉ 204 West 23rd Street at Seventh Avenue
✆ 212-929-9353

This is a small and funky hotel with ninety rooms. Carpets are jade-green, the wood furniture is blond, and bright pastel shades are the norm. There is a restaurant on the premises. Rooms include in-room data ports and cable television.

Rates start at $150 to $275. This hotel is accessible by subway via the 1 or 9 train (23rd Street station).

New York Marriott Financial Center
✉ 85 West Street
✆ 1-800-228-9290
✆ 212-385-4900

There are two Marriotts in Lower Manhattan. The Financial Center property houses 504 modern guest rooms complete with pay movies, mini-bars, and standard in-room fare. The hotel is located in the shadows of the World Trade Center and the World Financial Center; it's a short walk from Wall Street and the ferries to Staten Island, Ellis Island, and the Statue of Liberty. Amenities include an indoor pool, exercise room, saunas, concierge, theater ticketing center, and gift shop.

≡FAST FACT

The former Covenant House on West 16th Street, once a home for teenage runaways, has recently been converted into the Maritime Hotel, where every room has a seafaring theme inspired by the building's circular windows. Matsuri, the Japanese restaurant on the premises, is quite popular with the local Chelsea crowd.

Since this is primarily a business hotel, you may find good deals on weekends and during the summer months, when there are fewer business travelers. You will be well taken care of, and the service will always be first rate. The Lower Manhattan location puts you out of the fast pace of Midtown, which may be a plus or a minus, depending on what you are looking for and what sights you are interested in seeing. Though the hotel is close to the numerous downtown sights, there is less nightlife, and the museums of Fifth Avenue are a bit of a walk. It's a matter of choice.

Restaurants include P.W.'s, featuring American cuisine; Battery Park Tavern, which is casual; and Pugsley's Pub. Rates start at $220 and vary depending on the season, availability, and numerous specials. This hotel is accessible by subway via the R or W train (Rector Street station).

Upper Manhattan

If you want a little quiet, hotels along the Upper East or West Side will shield you from much of the hustle and bustle of the downtown streets, while still putting you in the heart of the action.

The Bentley Hotel
✉ 500 East 62nd Street between First and York Avenues
✆ 212-644-6000

Until 1998, this 197-room hotel, with its thirty-six deluxe suites, was a modern twenty-one-story office building. Views of the East River are spectacular, both from guest rooms and from the rooftop restaurant and bar. A modern facility, the Bentley offers spacious well-designed comfortable rooms. Amenities include complimentary continental breakfast, 24-hour cappuccino bar, concierge, valet laundry service, and on-site parking. The location is easily accessible to LaGuardia Airport, just off the FDR Drive, and it's a short way from the United Nations and Central Park.

Away from other hotels, the Bentley provides an opportunity to be part of the residential Upper East Side of Manhattan, with numerous restaurants and plenty of shopping. If you don't want to stay "in the middle of it all" or you've been to the heart of the city before, this is a nice change of locale.

Rates start at $200, and deluxe suites go from $455. This hotel is accessible by subway via the N or R train (Lexington Avenue/59th Street station).

Mayflower

✉ 15 Central Park West between West 61st and 62nd Streets

✆ 212-265-0060

Across the street from Central Park, the Mayflower has long been a favorite for traveling musicians and film personnel. Rooms are larger than average, and some even come with a park view—a nice bonus that's worth a few extra bucks. Almost every room has a walk-in closet. Complimentary coffee and cookies are offered in the evening.

There is a restaurant on the premises that serves a pretty good breakfast. There is also a gym, and some pets are allowed (call first).

Rates start at $150 and go to $275. Parking is available for an additional fee. This hotel is accessible by subway via the A, B, C, D, 1, or 9 train (59th Street/Columbus Circle station).

Milburn

✉ 242 West 76th Street and West End Avenue

✆ 1-800-833-9622

This Upper West Side hotel has a kitchenette in every room with a microwave and coffeemaker. This makes it a favorite for visiting parents, along with its proximity to Zabar's, Central Park, and the American Museum of Natural History. There are only fifty rooms, but they are all cozy and bright. There is no restaurant on the premises. Rates are $150 to $275. This hotel is accessible by subway via the 1 or 9 train (79th Street station).

CHAPTER 20

Luxury Hotels

THE SKY'S THE LIMIT when it comes to hotel rooms in New York City. There are so many legendary hotels in this fabulous city that you could spend a day touring them. If you have the time, drop by the Plaza Hotel and take the kids to tea, or visit the Waldorf for a drink around Cole Porter's piano (who once lived at the hotel) or Saturday tea for the kids.

These incredible hotels offer presidential suites filled with the finest antiques and the most efficient staff imaginable. There is a $15,000-a-night suite at the famed Plaza, and the apartment suites at the Waldorf Towers are swanky enough to be home to the Hilton sisters. But they are also available (and sometimes even surprisingly affordable, once you decide to spend a little extra) to the average family. There's nothing like a childhood memory of a weekend at the Plaza or the Waldorf or the Pierre, so let your imagination go!

Midtown Listings

Some of the most luxurious hotels in the city line the streets along Central Park. The view and the dining are always excellent.

Essex House

✉ 160 Central Park South between Sixth and Seventh Avenues
✆ 212-247-0300

One of the stars surrounding the Park, the Essex House is a classic New York Hotel, now owed by the Westin chain. There are 516 rooms and eighty-one suites. All rooms have genuine antique furniture, marble baths, and some have walk-in showers. There are some fabulous views of the park. French chef Alain Ducasse has opened the most expensive restaurant in New York on the hotel's premises.

Rates start at $400. This hotel is accessible by subway via the A, B, C, D, E, 1, or 9 train (59th Street/Columbus Circle station).

≡FAST FACT

The hotels along Central Park, such as the Pierre, the Plaza, and the Essex House on Central Park South, are some of the city's most luxurious and historical. The Stanhope on Fifth Avenue, right across the street from the Metropolitan Museum of Art, has seen guests for multiple generations, and rock stars love to return to the Mayflower on Central Park West.

Fitzpatrick Grand Central Hotel

✉ 141 East 44th Street between Lexington and Third Avenues
✆ 1-800-367-7701
✆ 212-351-6800

Of the two Manhattan East Side hotels run by the Irish-based Fitzpatrick Hotel Group, the Fitzpatrick Grand is newer. Of the two, this is also the larger slice of Dublin, with 155 rooms including eight suites and two garden suites. Rooms feature canopied beds, Irish linens, and plush bathrobes, and you can probably even order Irish coffee from twenty-four-hour room service.

A short walk from the United Nations and ten blocks north of the Empire State Building, this hotel's cozy lobby sports a couple of old-fashioned wood-burning fireplaces and a comfortable setting that sets you apart from the busy Midtown location.

The Grand Central Fitzpatrick is home to the Wheeltapper, a quaint "old-world Irish railroad-themed pub" with a full menu and a children's menu called "The Wee Folk."

Rates start at $325 for a double and $395 for a double suite. Special packages are offered frequently. Concierge service is also included. Perhaps the biggest drawing card of the Fitzpatrick hotels is the personalized, friendly service. This hotel is accessible by subway via the 4, 5, or 6 train (Grand Central/42nd Street station).

The Fitzpatrick Manhattan Hotel

✉ 687 Lexington Avenue, between 56th and 57th Streets

✆ 1-800-367-7701

✆ 212-355-0100

The second of the two Fitzpatrick hotels is a small inn in the heart of Manhattan, just two blocks from Bloomingdale's and close to Rockefeller Center. Consisting of fifty-two one-bedroom suites and forty guest rooms, all impeccably, tastefully furnished, the Fitzpatrick offers the personal touch. Cozy accommodations, such as carefully chosen fabrics and furnishings, terry-cloth robes, and soft lighting, help make your stay relaxing.

The hotel also provides a comfortable, charming lobby with a warm atmosphere, plus amenities that include laundry service, a health club, and a concierge. An Irish pub and Fitzers Restaurant, which serves Irish delights as well as American cuisine, are all part of this property. There are weekend rates and specials for children, including a complimentary VCR and a video library.

Rates start at $295 and $365 for suites. Perhaps the most significant features of the Fitzpatrick Manhattan, like its sister hotel, are the personalized attention and ideal location of the property. This hotel is accessible by subway via the 4, 5, or 6 train (59th Street station).

Four Seasons Hotel

✉ 57 East 57th Street, between Park and Madison Avenues

✆ 212-758-5700

Internationally renowned architect I.M. Pei designed the hotel's spire, and the interior Grand Foyer is chock-full of marble and onyx. It's lavish and luxurious and quite opulent. Soundproof rooms start at $565 and feature ten-foot ceilings, wooden walk-in closets, bedside controls for opening and closing window shades, and marble bathrooms. There are 310 rooms and sixty-two suites.

There's a restaurant, health club, and spa on the premises. Rates start at $400. This hotel is accessible by subway via the N or R train (Fifth Avenue/59th Street station).

═FAST FACT

New Yorkers are excited about a new hotel coming to the city. The Doral on Park and 38th Street has been purchased by the San Francisco Kimpton Hotel chain. The building is currently undergoing a major rehab in order to be transformed into one of the first of many of this chain's hip hotels in New York.

Omni Berkshire Hotel

✉ 21 East 52nd Street between Fifth and Madison

✆ 1-800-843-664

This is where NBC has sent its guests since the first showings of *Saturday Night Live* thirty years ago. The flagship hotel of the Omni hotel chain in New York is a surprisingly family-friendly hotel. There's an extensive kid program, and the lounge features Siamese fighting fish at every table, which can't help but captivate children's attention. The Asian-influenced rooms are large with big bathrooms. You'll find a health club, spa, and restaurant on the premises. Rates begin at $400. This hotel is accessible by subway via the E or F train (Fifth Avenue/53rd Street station).

New York Palace

✉ 455 Madison Avenue between 50th and 51st Streets

✆ 1-800-697-2522

✆ 212-888-7000

Set in a newly refurbished 1882 landmark estate, the 800-room hotel—the former Helmsley Palace—is now a luxurious facility with a lavish décor, spacious first-class accommodations, and easy access to everything Midtown has to offer. Features include three dual-line phones, in-room safes, and fully stocked refreshment bars.

Hotel amenities include a concierge and twenty-four-hour laundry service plus a 7,000 square-foot first class health club complete with television monitors and headphones at each treadmill. A separate "Towers" section has 175 guest rooms and suites with a separate check-in, butler service, and a host of other niceties, including room service from one of New York's premier restaurants, Le Cirque 2000. If all this isn't enough, high atop the Tower sit the Triplex suites—three-floor accommodations with their own private elevator, marble floors, fully equipped kitchen, master bedroom, a solarium, and private outdoor terrace for sunbathing.

The Palace is home to the world famous Le Cirque 2000, recently renovated and reopened, and Isetan, featuring Mediterranean cuisine. It also neighbors Sushusay, one of the city's best Japanese restaurants. Rates start at $475 and $900 for suites. Ask about seasonal specials. This hotel is accessible by subway via the 6 train (51st Street station).

Regal U.N. Plaza

✉ One United Nations Plaza at 44th Street and First Avenue

✆ 1-800-222-8888

✆ 212-758-1234

Part of the Regal International Hotel chain, the U.N. Plaza, directly across from the United Nations, offers quiet elegance in a building rising some twenty-eight stories high. Elegant tapestries with designs dating back as far as the ninth century adorn the property, reflecting the multinational ambiance of the neighborhood.

Several of the 427 brilliantly decorated guest rooms are suites. Some have kitchenettes, and all have great views of either Midtown or the East River and Queens. Rooms include mini-bars, HBO, and in-room movies, and the hotel offers valet parking, a concierge, a heated indoor pool, fitness center, massage and sauna, indoor tennis courts, and covered parking. A special section of rooms, the Regal Class, is available for long-term leasing.

Restaurants include the Ambassador Grille, a casually elegant (highly acclaimed) eatery, and the Ambassador Lounge, which serves light lunches and cocktails.

Rates start at $300 for guest rooms and $500 for junior suites. Children under 17 can stay free if sharing a room with their parents. This hotel is accessible by subway via the 4, 5, or 6 train (Grand Central Station/42nd Street station).

 **TRAVEL TIP**

> The Plaza Hotel has an extensive program for young guests. Called the Young Plaza Ambassadors (YPA), there are classes on manners, modeling, opportunities to go behind the scenes with the Rockettes, and shopping trips just for kids and teens. There's even special merchandise designed just for kids.

The Plaza
✉ 59th Street and Fifth Avenue
✆ 212-759-3000

There's just no place like the Plaza. Every child has read the children's classic *Eloise,* and every kid who has the time should go for the afternoon tea. The Oak Bar and Palm Court are legendary. The 692 rooms and 112 suites (even the smallest room) all have fourteen-foot ceilings and chandeliers. Rates start at $400. This hotel is accessible by subway via the A, B, C, D, 1, or 9 train (59th Street/Columbus Circle station).

St. Regis Hotel

✉2 East 55th Street, between Fifth Avenue and Madison

✆ 1-800-759-7550

✆ 212-753-4500

Declared a New York City landmark in 1988, the St. Regis offers guests an unparalleled level of comfort and luxury. Originally opened in 1904 and recently restored with a $100 million face-lift, this is the lap of luxury, complete with crystal chandeliers, velvet-covered armchairs, silk wallpaper, mahogany paneling, antique tapestries, and Tiffany dinnerware. There is even butler service in every room.

The 315 rooms, feature ninety-two suites, including amenities such as mini-bars, safes, fax machines, concierge, laundry service, beauty salon, library, health club, babysitting service, and parking. Designer stores, including Bijan, Odica, and Christian Dior, are located in the building.

The St. Regis is certainly not for your typical vacationer. It is for an extremely upscale clientele or perhaps for a very special weekend anniversary or celebratory trip. Restaurants include the King Cole Bar and Lounge, featuring the Maxfield Parrish "King Cole" mural and the Astor Court, an elegant tea lounge.

Rates start at $520, and suites can go for as high as $10,500 a night. This hotel is accessible by subway via the E or F line (Fifth Avenue/53rd Street station).

Sheri-Netherland Hotel

✉781 Fifth Avenue at 59th Street

✆ 212-355-2800

This incredible co-op hotel is actually quite affordable, if you consider it in the grand scheme of things. There are forty rooms and thirty-five suites, many of which have fireplaces, chandeliers, and great views. Suites have separate living rooms and dining areas. Harry Cipriani's is on the premises, and there is a gym. Rates are $275-$400. This hotel is accessible by subway via the N or R train (Fifth Avenue/59th Street station).

The Waldorf-Astoria

✉ 301 Park Avenue between 49th and 50th Streets

✆ 1-800-WALDORF

✆ 212-355-3000

Originally opened in 1893 on 33rd Street, the Waldorf you see today has been at its current location since October of 1931. Over the years, the classic hotel has undergone some $400 million in renovations to maintain its art deco look and New York City landmark status.

There is a great history to the grand hotel. Over the years, the Waldorf has seen its share of dignitaries, including numerous American presidents, King Hussein, Charles de Gaulle, and Queen Elizabeth II, among others. It was, for many years, the site where Guy Lombardo and his orchestra ushered in the new year. The Empire Room was home to great entertainment, including Frank Sinatra on the bill on a number of occasions. The hotel was even the residence for three five-star generals: Douglas MacArthur, Dwight Eisenhower, and Omar Bradley.

Today, the Waldorf has some 1,245 guest rooms and more than 200 suites, each designed in a slightly different manner. The rooms have luxuries ranging from marble bathrooms to the modern in-room premium cable and video, plus in-room checkout features.

 JUST FOR PARENTS

The Waldorf now has a catalog through which you can order some of your favorite mementos online. At ✑ *www.waldorf collection.com*, you can order one of those terry-cloth robes you wore in the room, or the 300-count sheets you slept on. There are even cufflinks shaped like the hotel.

The hotel also features not one, but two lobbies, one of which (on the Park Avenue side) has a 148,000-piece mosaic called *Wheel of Life.* A concierge is available, plus an international concierge service desk providing assistance in over sixty languages. There is a theater desk, a tour desk, and a Plus One fitness center with six personal trainers and full-time massage therapists, as well as a Plus One Spa. When you're finished with your thirty-minute personal training session, you can treat yourself to a thirty-minute, or longer, shopping spree at one of several posh, luxurious boutiques that are also part of the Waldorf. A gift shop and florist are also on the premises.

A highlight of the Waldorf is the dining. Three restaurants, with a shared kitchen (the catering kitchen takes up a city block), are the pride of this classic hotel. The popular Bull and Bear is known for steaks and fine seafood. You can sit at the mahogany bar and enjoy a before-dinner cocktail while watching the stock quotes pass by on an electric ticker. Oscar's is an American brasserie serving classic American dishes in a relaxed setting and serves an incredible buffet lunch that New Yorkers consider one of the best buys in the city. Inagiku is a Japanese restaurant serving a variety of classic and contemporary dishes. There is also a lounge, the Cocktail Terrace, overlooking the art deco Park Avenue lobby, featuring a Saturday tea to the strains of Cole Porter piano music from 4 to 7 P.M.

The Waldorf is not only an elegant place to stay but also a sight to visit on your trip. With that in mind, the Waldorf is in the process of putting together free guided tours, so call the hotel for information.

The Waldorf offers several packages, including the romance package with plenty of champagne, the Bounceback Weekend Package with continental breakfasts, and the Weekend at the Waldorf package. Rooms start at $300 and suites at $500. This hotel is accessible by subway via the 6 train (51st Street station).

The Waldorf Salad

Take the recipe for the famous Waldorf Salad home with you.

1 Granny Smith and 1 Red Delicious apple, julienned
3 egg yolks
4 oz. walnut oil
4 oz. crème fraiche
4 oz. plain yogurt

1 oz. fresh lemon juice
salt and white pepper to taste
1/8 tsp. chopped black truffle
micro greens or baby lettuce
chopped candied walnuts

Whisk yolks and walnut oil together to form a mayonnaise. Fold in crème fraiche and yogurt. Add lemon juice, and season with salt and white pepper. Fold in apples. Add truffles and serve on a bed of baby lettuce or greens. Garnish with candied walnuts. (Reprinted with permission from the Waldorf-Astoria.)

Downtown and Lower Manhattan

During the weekend, Lower Manhattan clears out, so it's actually a great location for both families and couples.

Soho Grand Hotel

✉310 West Broadway between Canal and Grand Streets

✎ 1-800-965-3000

✎ 212-228-1500

Originally built in the late 1800s, the posh hotel sits in the heart of the trendy neighborhood of Soho, busy with galleries and cafés and surrounded by Greenwich Village, Chinatown, TriBeCa, and Wall Street.

The fifteen stories, housing 369 guest rooms, sit atop a large lavish lobby with oversized sofas, tropical palm trees, pillars, lanterns, and draperies surrounding sixteen-foot-high windows. The hotel welcomes pets, and you can ask for a goldfish in your room.

Rooms have large beds, mini-bars with healthy foods along with the fun stuff, photographs adorning the walls, on-demand movies, in-room safes, and marvelous views of the city—the building is in an area not oversaturated with skyscrapers.

The hotel also has valet parking, a health club, and a special "Guest Satisfaction Hotline," which essentially means good concierge service. The Canal House Restaurant, serving American fare, is in the lobby, along with the Grand Bar.

≡FAST FACT

The Soho Grand and the Waldorf Towers are two luxury hotels that are very pet-friendly. The Waldorf has a pet spa, possibly because Paris Hilton is so close to her dogs. The Soho Grand's pet amenities include in-room dining, toys, grooming brushes, and complete pet care—including walking exercise, pet transportation, a pet toothbrush, and toothpaste.

This is an offbeat but quite luxurious hotel in a fashionable part of town that isn't too far from either the Lower Manhattan or Midtown activities. Rates start at $335 and $1,099 for suites. This hotel is accessible by subway via the J, N, Q, or R train (Canal Street station).

W Union Square
✉201 Park Avenue S.
✆ 212-253-9119
The exterior is a Beaux Arts building erected in 1911, but inside it's all up-to-the-minute style. This is one of Manhattan's trendier hotels. The lobby bar is always teeming with the young and hip, and the hotel restaurant, Olives NY, is also a trendy culinary spot. The 270 rooms and sixteen suites feature beds decked out in shark-skin coverlets and feature velvet armchairs. Rooms start at $275. This hotel is accessible by subway via the L, N, Q, R, 4, 5, or 6 train (14th Street/Union Square station).

Upper Manhattan

A hotel along Central Park is a particularly nice place for watching the Thanksgiving Day Parade or to see the trees blooming in the spring.

The Mark

✉ 77th Street between Madison and Fifth Avenues

✆ 1-800-THE-MARK

✆ 212-744-4300

Situated on the posh Upper East Side of Manhattan, the Mark is an elegant hotel within a short walk of Central Park, the Metropolitan Museum of Art, the Guggenheim, and other museums, prestigious galleries, and fine shops.

Neoclassic décor, fine Italian marble, and floral motifs create the luxurious feel that defines this upscale property. A concierge, limousine service, and other "luxury services" (as they are billed) are offered. Some 160 guest rooms and sixty suites include junior suites, terrace suites, and a host of other suites that make up the hotel—which enjoyed a refurbishing in 1996.

Guest rooms and suites include a number of amenities such as refrigerators and VCRs, as well as sinks and stoves in certain rooms. King-sized beds, sofas, and large upholstered chairs are all part of what defines elegance and comfort at the Mark.

The chic Mark restaurant is in the lobby, where you can have dinner or an afternoon tea for $20 and up. The Sunday brunch is wonderful, and the waiters are very child-friendly. The Mark's bar is located on 77th Street.

Rates start at $470 for single rooms and $540 for doubles. Junior suites start at $650 and go up from there. This hotel is accessible by subway via the 6 train (77th Street station).

🌂 RAINY DAY FUN

The Paramount Hotel at ✉ 235 West 46th Street (✆ 212-764-5500) includes a well-stocked children's playroom. The Plaza at ✉ 768 Fifth Avenue (✆ 212-759-3000) includes a Young Plaza Ambassador's Club, where kids from 6 to 19 receive various gifts, plus free Sunday brunch and "Plaza Dollars" for special discounts.

The Pierre

✉ 2 East 61st Street between Fifth and Madison Avenues

☎ 212-838-8000

One of the classic New York hotels and a landmark, the Pierre emits Old-World luxury from its chandeliers and the putti murals on its walls. Currently owned by the Four Seasons chain, there are 149 rooms and 54 suites all with large art deco bathrooms and traditional décor. There's still a wonderful afternoon tea here and an on-site restaurant. Rates start at $400. This hotel is accessible by subway via the N train (Fifth Avenue/59th Street station).

The Regency

✉ 540 Park Avenue at 61st Street

☎ 1-800-233-2356

☎ 212-759-4100

One of the city's most exclusive hotels, the Regency is located on Park Avenue, also in Manhattan's "posh" Upper East Side. Having just received a $35 million renovation, the luxurious hotel, which opened in 1963, is the flagship property of the Loews Hotel chain. Celebrities are often spotted in and around the hotel, which houses some 351 guest rooms, including eighty-seven suites with custom-designed furnishings.

The combination of traditional décor with contemporary styling creates an atmosphere that is warm and comfortable as well as practical and functional.

Guest accommodations include an in-room safe, kitchenette with microwave and refrigerator, mini-bar, phone with caller ID, terry-cloth robes, pay-per-view movies, goosedown duvet comforters, and (of course) televisions in every bathroom. Suites have two bathrooms—which means yet another television.

The hotel itself has a full-service concierge, overnight valet service, complimentary Evian water and towels for morning joggers, on-site limo service (at a cost), and the Nico Salon, featuring manicures, pedicures, facials, and more—for women and men. There is also a fitness center, with everything from free weights to Trotter Treadmills, Climbmax, and other state-of-the-art machines.

Michael Feinstein recently opened a nightclub at the Regency, which shares space with the 540 Park restaurant. The 540 features light lunches and dinners by a renowned chef. The Library is also on the premises, offering a residential-style lounge for breakfast and light snacks.

To give you an idea of how exquisite the Regency is, 50,000 square feet of marble was imported from Alicante, Spain, to be used in the guest bathrooms.

With suites ranging up to $3,500 per night, this is not the hotel for the family on the run or the average traveler, which isn't to say a slightly more affordable room at the Regency might not be a special place to spend a second honeymoon. There are also weekend rates, so inquire.

Rates start at $425 and $650 for suites. Ask about special rates. This hotel is accessible by subway via the N train (Fifth Avenue/ 59th Street station).

The Stanhope Hotel
✉ 995 Fifth Avenue at 82nd Street
✆ 212-288-5800

This sixteen-story landmark building has been home to families visiting New York since 1926. Recently renovated and run by Hyatt, there are 185 rooms and seventy suites available. Across the street from the Metropolitan Museum of Art and Central Park, it is a great family-friendly hotel. The lobby features antiques, marble floors, and gold leaf. There's a restaurant on the premises, as well as a great bar, Gerard's, where you can get fruit and cheese with a drink. Rates start at $279. This hotel is accessible by subway via the 4, 5, or 6 train (86th Street station).

CHAPTER 21

Day Trips Outside the City

IF YOU'VE BEEN TO NEW YORK CITY a number of times (perhaps to visit family or even on business), you might want to rent a car or hop on the Long Island Railroad or MetroNorth and see what's on the other side of the Hudson or the Long Island Sound.

New York State has long been a popular travel destination, and the beaches of Long Island have been a summer spot for New York's rich and famous since F. Scott Fitzgerald wrote *The Great Gatsby*. Across the river, New Jersey's shore has been a site of family vacations for generations, way before there was casino gambling. There's also wonderful discount shopping at the Woodbury Commons outlets, where you can spend an entire day saving money.

▮▮ TRAVEL TIP

There's an entire booklet of information on side trips in New York State that you can order for free. Call ✆ 1-800-CALL/NYS, or check it out on the Web at ✍ *www.iloveny.com*. It comes with a foldout map and wealth of information on where to stay and what to see.

Long Island Destinations

In 1524, an Italian explorer named Verrazano spotted the area now known as Long Island. The beaches were empty, and there were no gold coast mansions or shopping malls, but there were more than 1,000 square miles of uncharted land. Not an island unto itself, Long Island is attached to Queens and Brooklyn.

Today, Long Island is "the suburbs" for Manhattanites. It is a place where many former city dwellers relocated in their quest for larger homes and backyards for patios and cookouts. Many city-dwellers visit Long Island for the beaches, sporting activities, and other fun.

The Long Island Railroad is one route through Queens to "the Island," as it's known, and the Long Island Expressway (LIE) is the most traveled major road. Often crowded, the LIE has earned the nickname "the world's biggest parking lot." Other major roads, such as the Northern State and Southern State Parkways, also transport visitors and Long Islanders around the many towns that make up Long Island. In the summer, the LIE is crowded in the morning heading to the beaches.

Long Island Beaches

Long Island consists of both Nassau and Suffolk Counties, home to some 2.7 million people. Many more people visit, especially on summer weekends when the beach is the best way to beat the city heat. Of the more than 100 beaches, Jones Beach is the most popular. Built in the 1920s by developer Robert Moses, Jones has six miles of beaches, a boardwalk, a miniature golf course, old bath houses, a pitch-and-putt golf course, a public swimming pool, and an outdoor theater for big-name concerts. The beach draws large crowds during the summer months, so pack up your sunscreen and towels and set out early. From Memorial Day to Labor Day, there are parking fees. The west end and central sections are particular favorites, with long stretches of white sand. The waves are fun for playing, but this is not the place for surfing.

Continuing past Jones Beach, you'll find Robert Moses State Park; because it's just that much farther from the city, it is usually a little less crowded.

The Hamptons

The Hamptons, consisting of four small towns, are a longer ride, but they are a worthwhile destination if you want to see mansions, beautiful beaches, and perhaps even a celebrity or two. The shops are upscale, the prices can be high, parking is difficult, and you'll find an air of pretentiousness. But if you've planned well and know where you're heading, the area can be beautiful and the beaches delightful. With that in mind, many New Yorkers take shares in homes owned by the rich who rent them out to the "summer crowd" who want to "weekend in the Hamptons."

Also for fun, sun, and sand, you might try Shelter Island or Fire Island. Shelter Island is a twelve-mile island reachable by ferry only. For sunning or fishing, it's a marvelous departure from "civilization." Fire Island is also primarily accessible by ferry. The thirty-two-mile-long seashore includes the only federally declared wilderness area in New York State.

 JUST FOR PARENTS

The most notable concert hall on Long Island is the Westbury Music Fair. The nearly 3,000-seat theater-in-the-round has been around nearly forty years and has played host to numerous major-name performers running the gamut from Tommy Dorsey to Aerosmith and Kiss. Tickets are available at the box office (✆516-334-0800) and from Ticketmaster. The Westbury Music Fair is just off the Long Island Expressway in Westbury at ✉960 Brush Hollow Road, exit 40W.

Private homes, shops, and malls dominate the landscape on Long Island, which is sprawling with a wealth of very attractive neighborhoods including Oyster Bay, Kingspoint, Sands Point, Old

Westbury, Roslyn Heights, Dix Hills, and numerous others. Numerous gold coast mansions line the island; some are noted on tours, and others you'll need to find for yourself. A few, in places like Sands Point Preserve, afford you the opportunity to step inside these spacious old homes.

There is a lot to see on Long Island, and because it's so very spread out, it's advantageous to have a car and plan a day trip carefully.

Old Bethpage Village Restoration

✉ Round Swamp Road
✆ 516-572-8400
🖝 *www.oldbethpage.org*

Old Bethpage Village Restoration is a 200-acre open-air museum of sorts. It represents a historical Long Island village of the nineteenth century. The restoration project began in 1963 in an attempt to save and preserve landmark buildings. Plainview Long Island's historic Manetto Hill Methodist Church was the first building moved onto the site and restored. The current village setting now has over fifty buildings that have been carefully transported onto the vast property and restored to a specific point in their history. Thus, all the buildings are not from the same years, allowing for a more detailed look at history over a wider range of time.

There is a reception center, where you can start your tour of the village. Roads then lead past the stores, an inn, a blacksmith shop, and on to several homes and farmhouses. Each building is complete with the details you would have found inside more than 100 years ago. Up the hill sits a one-room schoolhouse and a church. Down the road is a farm with horses, oxen, pigs, sheep, and other animals.

You can take a self-guided or guided tour of the grounds. There are also educational programs, crafts demonstrations, old brass band concerts, and other various special events including a spring festival, nineteenth-century baseball games, traditional dance and music weekends, and a Long Island fair in early October.

The village offers a fun look into the past in a very relaxing setting. It's Long Island's answer to stepping into a time machine and going back to pre–Civil War days.

There is a cafeteria for a casual lunch. There is also a village shop with plenty of books, postcards, and gift items relating to the theme of yesteryear.

Location and Hours

Old Bethpage Village Restoration is located in Bethpage, Long Island. Take Long Island Expressway to exit 48 south. Unlike Manhattan, parking is plentiful.

Old Bethpage is open Wednesday through Sunday 10:00 A.M. to 5:00 P.M., March through October, and closes at 4:00 P.M. in November and December. The village is closed on Mondays and Tuesdays and also for the months of January and February. It is open on some holidays; call first. Admission is $7 for adults, $5 for children 5 to 12 and seniors, and free for children under age 5.

The Nassau County Museum of Art

✉ One Museum Drive

✆ 516-484-9338

✎ *www.nassaumuseum.org*

Only twenty minutes from the city, this is one of the best-kept secrets in New York. One of the advantages of housing an art museum on Long Island, in a mansion, is that visitors can enjoy both the works of art inside and the beautifully landscaped grounds. Nassau County's Museum of Art is in a Georgian manor that was home to Henry Clay Frick, founder of U.S. Steel. In 1969, after Frick's death, Nassau County purchased the property and ear-marked it for a museum.

Today, the museum mounts four major exhibits every year from its massive collection that includes the works of Lichtenstein, Rauschenberg, Raphael, Moses, Daumier, and many other highly acclaimed international artists. Nearly a quarter of a million people visit the museum every year and stroll the 145-acre preserve featuring lawns, wooded areas, ponds, and a permanent display of outdoor sculptures. The indoor/outdoor pairing of culture and nature makes visiting this museum a unique experience.

The museum is also home to an international gift shop with a variety of items including scented candles, crafts, and jewelry. A bookstore/art gallery has a wide variety of books about art, gardening, and other crafts; the art selection includes original works by Long Island artists as well as prints, posters, and postcards.

Location and Hours

The Nassau County Museum of Art is located in Roslyn Harbor; take LIE to Exit 39 (Glen Cove), off Glen Cove Road.

The museum is open Tuesday through Sunday from 11:00 A.M. to 5:00 P.M. Admission is $6 for adults, $5 for seniors, and $4 for children and students. Free tours are given every day (except Sundays) at 2 P.M.

RAINY DAY FUN

From the roar of Islander fans during their reign as winners of four Stanley Cups to Led Zeppelin concerts, the Nassau Veterans Memorial Coliseum has been home to all sorts of activities, including the circus in the main arena and golf or computer shows in the 60,000-square-foot exhibition hall. The Coliseum is in Uniondale, which is forty minutes by car from Manhattan. Often the same shows that are passing through Madison Square Garden will play the Nassau Coliseum, but tickets may be easier to come by here, and you may get better seats. For information and schedule, call ✆ 516-794-9300.

Old Westbury Gardens

✉ 71 Old Westbury Road

✆ 516-333-0048

✎ www.oldwestburygardens.org

Nearly ninety acres of formal gardens, tree-lined walkways, ponds, and superb landscaping feature a stunning variety of plants and flowers in this magnificent garden that surrounds a mansion built in 1906. Seven original historic buildings include Westbury House, with its grand eighteenth-century architectural features. It's furnished with English antiques and decorative arts collected by the Phipps family, who lived in the stately mansion for over fifty years. Tours of the house start in the foyer area and are free. The beautifully landscaped gardens surrounding the house include the Walled Garden, the Rose Garden, the Lilac Walk, and the Vegetable Garden. There is also a greenhouse, as well as a gift shop and picnic area. A small restaurant, Café in the Woods, offers sandwiches, salads, and other light fare. You can also take a free garden tour.

You should inquire about special events at the Old Westbury Gardens: They include the Scottish Games, complete with bagpipes, highland dancing, and various activities and events; a Picnic Pops concert; special talks and tours; and an annual Christmas celebration. Since its opening to the public in 1959, Old Westbury has gained a reputation as one of Long Island's most popular attractions, now hosting some 80,000 visitors annually.

Location and Hours

The Old Westbury Gardens can be found at ✉ 71 Old Westbury Road in Old Westbury (off the Long Island Expressway, Exit 39S, Glen Cove Road). The facilities are open every day (except Tuesday) from 10:00 A.M. to 5:00 P.M. (last visitors admitted at 4:00 P.M.), late April through October, with later hours on weekends in the summer (until 7:00 P.M.). There are some November dates and holiday dates in December. Admission for the house and garden is $10 for adults, $8 for seniors, and $6 for children 6 through 12. You can also pay less and just visit the gardens. There are lower rates in November.

Sands Point Preserve

✉95 Middleneck Road, Port Washington

✆516-571-7900

If you want to see mansions, you'll enjoy Sands Point. Once billed as "the gold coast of the Goulds and the Guggenheims," it features Hempstead House, Falise, and Castlegould. Hempstead House, built in 1912, is a spectacular gold coast mansion that features a walnut-paneled library, billiard room with a gold leaf ceiling, stone gargoyles, and artwork that includes stained and leaded glass, velvet draperies, and paintings by Rembrandt and Rubens. Falise was built by Harry F. Guggenheim in 1923 and has French eclectic architecture modeled after a thirteenth-century Norman manor house. There is a cobblestone courtyard and a round tower (which sets the medieval tone), along with Renaissance paintings. Castlegould, built in 1904, is a 100,000-square-foot castle-shaped complex that contained horse stalls, blacksmith shops, an equestrian arena, and housing for some 200 workers.

 JUST FOR PARENTS

If you like wine, Long Island has fourteen full-time wineries and more than 1,400 acres of vineyards. The island produces more than 3 million bottles of wine annually. A winery guide book can be yours by calling ✆1-800-441-4601. You can then visit or tour any of several wineries, mostly located in the town of Cutchogue, and enjoy a taste of Chardonnay, Merlot, Blanc, or other favorites.

All of this is part of the elegant past that makes up Sands Point Preserve. Hempstead House offers self-guided tours and is open Friday, Saturday, and Sunday; Falise offers guided tours and is open Wednesday through Sunday from noon to 3:00 P.M. Children under 10 are not admitted. Castlegould's schedule depends on current exhibitions. A visitor center and museum shop are located within. Special events and a medieval festival also take place within the preserve.

Basically, Sands Point offers a look at the high life of the past. You can enjoy a scenic and historic visit. Falise House costs $5 for adults and $4 for seniors; Hempstead House costs $2. Hours, rates, and policies vary between the buildings, so call to get more information.

Fire Island National Seashore

✆ 516-289-4810

✍ www.fireislandbeaches.com

Over half a million visitors every year come to Fire Island, just over an hour east of New York City. The area includes several points of interest, some with tours, such as Fire Island Light Station or Sailor's Haven, which also houses a visitors' center, boathouses, and a marina. There is also the William Floyd Estate, which is a museum. But the lure of Fire Island are the ocean-washed beaches, dunes, and tranquility. And finally, there is a wildlife preserve. Call for information on Fire Island and ferry schedules.

Atlantic City and the Jersey Shore

✍ www.atlanticcitynj.com

You can drive, take a bus from Penn Station, or even a bus from any diner or candy store in the city, and you will be in Atlantic City in under three hours. Atlantic City is jam-packed with one-day visitors to this bustling gambling destination, but in the summer months, it is a surprisingly charming boardwalk town with a lot of family entertainment. Nearby Cape May and Wildwood Crest offer lovely (and fairly inexpensive) beach excursions along the Atlantic Ocean, and they have been the summer retreat of tri-state families for generations.

If it's a nice day, pack a blanket and plan on spending some time on the beach. There's a nice boardwalk with miniature golfing and ample ice cream and cotton candy, as well as shopping. There's also a Planet Hollywood and a new Rainforest Cafe.

If you're planning on spending an overnight, you can look up hotels in nearby Cape May or Wildwood, or stay in one of the casino hotels. However, they are really not geared toward families. Many do not even have pools. Two that do are Bally's (✆ 1-800-772-7777, ✍ www.ballys.com) and Trump Plaza (✆ 1-800-677-5687, ✍ www.trump.com), where you can find an indoor arcade. There are also a number of budget chain hotels along the strip, some of which are wonderful for families.

For slightly older children, the Legends concert at Bally's might be a fun evening out, as it presents performances by such music legends as Elton John and Bette Midler.

To reach Atlantic City by car, take the New Jersey Turnpike south to the Garden State Parkway. From the Atlantic City Expressway, take exit 38.

Dia Art Center

✉ 3 Beekman Street, Beacon, N.Y.
✆ 845-440-0100
✍ www.diabeacon.com

This newly opened avant-garde art center houses the Dia Art Center's collection of work from the 1960s until the present and is located in a rehabilitated industrial space (former home of a Nabisco box plant). You will be able to see minimalist art displayed in huge spaces (240,000 square feet) which has made this a Mecca of sorts for the city art crowd. If you have kids who are at all interested in art (especially large art), this is a nice afternoon drive in an upper Hudson town that has a certain charm of its own. There is a wealth of nice restaurants in the neighboring Hudson Valley town (such as Café Maya and Piggy Bank), and it's a beautiful drive.

Location and Hours

To reach Beacon, New York, take MetroNorth from Grand Central to Poughkeepsie. By car, drive over the George Washington Bridge and take the Palisades Parkway North to the end and then 6 East/202 to 9D to the city of Beacon. It's about a ninety-minute drive.

Open Friday through Monday during the winter, 11:00 A.M. to 4:00 P.M., and on Tuesdays during the summer months (closed Wednesday and Thursdays), 10:00 A.M. to 6:00 P.M. Admission is $10 for adults and $7 for students and seniors. Free for children 12 and under. Guided tours are offered free on Saturdays. Book shop and café on premises.

Six Flags-Great Adventure

✉ Jackson, N.J.

✆ 732-928-1821

✐ *www.sixflags.com*

After days of seeing art and shopping, you might want to spend a more simple day at this chain of theme parks. There's the traditional Warner Brothers-based theme park, a delightful safari (which you should make an effort to see no matter how old or young the kids are), and a water park. You can go for just six hours, or do the entire dawn-to-midnight experience in the summer months.

TRAVEL TIP

Great Adventure has wonderful free concerts (such as the Charlie Daniels Band) all summer long, and a host of great seasonal activities in the spring and fall, so go online before you visit. Their Fright Fest, which lasts all of October, has a Haunted Hayride and cobwebs on all rides, which is great for teens. During the summer, midweek is slightly less crowded than the weekends. The safari closes at dusk, so make sure you go during the day.

There are two theme parks at Six Flags-Great Adventure (each requiring a separate admission). The main theme park is known for its awesome roller coasters—Nitro and Superman Ultimate Adventure, as well as the Batman roller coaster, but here's a nice toddler amusement park, and plenty of opportunity to be splashed and thrilled.

The water park, Hurricane Harbor, is newer and features a host of giant slides, floating tubes, and pools to play in on a hot day.

Location and Hours

To reach the park by car, take the New Jersey Turnpike to Exit 7A, then I-95 east to Exit 16A, and then 537 to the Great Adventure Exit.

The park is only open on weekends in the spring and fall, and Hurricane Harbor is only open between Memorial Day and Labor Day. Prices are $45.99 for adults, and $29.99 for juniors and seniors with a free admission to the safari. If you choose to return for another day anytime within the season, you can buy a ticket for just $12. Hurricane Harbor is $29.99 for adults and $22.99 for juniors and seniors. There is a three-park admission fee of $60.99 and $45.99 for juniors and seniors.

Rye Playland

✉ Playland Parkway, Rye, N.Y.

☎ 914-813-7000

🖱 www.ryeplayland.org

Rye Playland in Westchester County is the only government owned and operated amusement park in this country. Built in 1928, this art deco beachfront amusement park was named a National Historic Landmark in 1987. Open in both the winter and summer, it features an indoor ice-skating rink that is the training facility for the New York Rangers. From May to September, it is home to an amusement park featuring over fifty rides such as roller coasters, virtual reality thrills, water rides, and a kiddyland. There is also a beach (on Long Island Sound), a boardwalk, a swimming pool, lake boating, mini-golf, and picnic areas.

There is the Captain Hook Seafood Restaurant that offers sit-down dining with a lovely view of the Long Island Sound, as well as boardwalk food such as hot dogs and cotton candy. A number of fast food chains are also a presence.

Location and Hours

Rye Playland is located in Westchester County. Take the New York State Thruway (I-95) to Exit 19 or Metro North trains from Grand Central Station to the Rye Station.

Indoor ice skating is open from September through early May. The amusement park and boardwalk opens Mother's Day weekend, but the pool is only open from Memorial Day through Labor Day. Entry to the park is free. Rides cost $1.25 per ticket and discount ticket books can be purchased.

CHAPTER 22

Suggested Itineraries

NEW YORK CITY COULD keep you and your family entertained for weeks. There is so much to see and do that you'll never feel you've seen it all, even if you spend a month there. And you never will be able to see it all. New museums and exhibits open in the city every year, which is why it is one of the leading family travel destinations in the country.

When you're traveling with children, you really have to plan your trip and cater your activities to both the ages, and interests, of your children, as well as the adults. That means reading up ahead, going online to check schedules and timing, and making sure you have as many tickets in advance as possible. This is the best way to avoid wasting a lot of time waiting in line, or, even worse, disappointing your kids. It's a good idea to make reservations at popular or trendy restaurants ahead of time as well.

If You Only Have One Day

One day is barely enough to get a feel for the city and see what it has to offer. But if you are only in town for one day, you should try to see the Statue of Liberty and Ellis Island and (if you have children) the American Museum of Natural History, where you should either have lunch in the refurbished cafeteria or grab a hot dog from a street vendor.

Have dinner at Mars 2112, Carmine's, or Ruby Foo's, and catch a Broadway play (*The Lion King* for families with young children, *The Phantom of the Opera* for families with children over 8) and then head to the Empire State Building and the Skyride to close out the evening.

A Weekend in New York

If you and your family are in town for a weekend, which means a Saturday and Sunday, plan on shopping and doing the museums. If possible, try to find a hotel downtown (Milford Plaza, Times Square Hilton) or near the museums (Mayflower, Stanhope, Empire), so you can do as much as possible in a short amount of time. If your kids get tired, you can race back to the hotel for a nap.

Saturday

Once you check into your hotel, head toward the New York sightseeing bus center on 47th Street and Seventh Avenue and take one of the Manhattan bus tours. Sit with the kids and let the wise and entertaining bus tour guides give you and your family a grand overview of the sights, and let your kids tell you what they'd like to see. You may not be able to fit everything into the schedule, but it's nice to see what's out there and how close some of the places are to each other. You can hop on and off, and you might want to make that your day, visiting some of the museums and some of the other attractions.

If you have not elected to hop on and off, you might want to spend an afternoon in one of the museums until it closes, either the American Museum of Natural History or the Metropolitan Museum of Art. On the east side, you can have a fun dinner at Al Baraka, a wonderful Moroccan restaurant where the kids (and you) can relax. On the Upper West Side, you might want to try Tavern on the Green (always a parent and kid pleaser) or something simpler like Good Enough to Eat.

Then either go to a night bus tour of the city or catch the view from the Empire State Building. You might also just want to pass out in your hotel room or watch a movie on pay-per-view.

TRAVEL TIP

Hotel breakfast in New York is expensive, usually about $15 for continental breakfast per person and more for simple bacon and eggs. For a family with children, this can be quite pricey. But there are diners all over the city, so ask the concierge where the nearest one is, or just go to a fast food chain, which are also all over the city.

Sunday

Eat breakfast in a nearby diner, and plan on heading to Central Park. It is a must-see for families with children. Get there early so you can catch a museum later in the afternoon. If you are so inclined, you might want to catch a morning service at St. Patrick's Cathedral or the Cathedral of St. John the Divine.

Central Park is a half-day event, so plan on eating lunch there. You can make a lunch reservation at Tavern on the Green or the Loeb Boathouse, or buy hot dogs or sandwiches at one of the outdoor cafés. There are always hot dogs and pretzels at the street vendors, or you can buy sandwiches at a deli and make a picnic. Plan on seeing the Central Park Zoo, climbing on the *Alice in Wonderland* statue, riding the carousel, floating the wooden boats, and even ice-skating (if it's winter) or visiting a playground. In the afternoon, you can visit the museum you didn't catch yesterday.

In the evening, you should see a show, either *The Lion King* or *The Phantom of the Opera,* and eat nearby at Carmine's, Ruby Foo's, or B. Smith's. After the play, walk around Times Square, and drop into the flagship Toys Я Us store on 44th Street. Ride that giant Ferris wheel and see the T-Rex from *Jurassic Park.*

Three-Day Weekend in the Big Apple

This would usually be over a holiday weekend, which means that a lot of other families had the same idea. Book hotels early, and do make reservations at the restaurants you and your family really want to go to.

Day One

If you've opted for a Friday/Saturday/Sunday visit, choose the thing you want to do most for Friday morning. All sites will be packed on the weekends, especially if it's summer. Earlier in the day will be less crowded than later, so you might want to try the Statue of Liberty and Ellis Island in the morning. If that's the plan, you might want to make a later lunch reservation at the Frances Tavern and see the South Street Seaport and Museum in the afternoon. You can catch dinner at the Seaport or in the Village, and catch a performance of *Stomp* that evening in the East Village, with plenty of shopping all day long.

Day Two

Again, breakfast at a diner near your hotel, then head straight to Central Park followed by an afternoon in a museum (where you should eat lunch). Eat dinner in Midtown, and enjoy a Broadway play.

Day Three

You should have a bit more breathing room, so perhaps one of New York's wonderful brunches (Sylvia's if you plan on visiting the Cathedral of St. John the Divine or the American Festival Café if you are visiting St. Patrick's Cathedral). If you're already downtown, this might be a good time for some shopping at nearby Saks Fifth Avenue or the shops in Rockefeller Center. If your kids are the kind who are fascinated by television, you might want to drop into the Museum of Television & Radio for an hour or so. The Donnell Library is here too, so you can run in to take a quick look at the original stuffed animals once owned by Christopher Milne, whose father wrote the children's classic, *Winnie the Pooh*. This might be the day to take the NBC tour or tour Radio City Music Hall.

Eat in Midtown, perhaps at one of the great city restaurants such as the 21 Club (a surprisingly kid-friendly establishment), and then head to the Empire State Building to see the view.

If You Have Five Days

Five days gives you enough time to leave Manhattan, if you are so inclined. Follow the three-day schedule above and add a day in the Bronx, starting with a tour of Yankee Stadium (you would be surprised how delightful this is, even for the nonbaseball fan). If you feel comfortable in this ethnic neighborhood, stop in one of the Latin restaurants and have a Cuban sandwich for lunch with one of their terrific mango or papaya milkshakes.

Then head to the Bronx Zoo, where you will have an incredible day in one of the country's best and oldest zoos. The House of Darkness where the bats dwell is truly special, and the monorail and safari rides are always fun. In the summer, there's a butterfly garden that no one can resist, where butterflies literally surround you. Then head to Arthur Avenue, where there's an incredible indoor Italian market, and then head to Dominic's on Arthur Avenue for a spectacular Italian dinner served family style. Make sure you ask if they have the stuffed artichokes. Grab a cannoli or tiramisu for dessert at one of the nearby pastry shops.

A Day in Brooklyn or Queens

If you've brought the car, drive out to the Brooklyn Museum of Art, where you will see some of the best Egyptian art in this country. This is truly one of the best museums in America, but it is overshadowed by the Met. Next door is the Brooklyn Botanic Garden, where the kids can play in the children's section and you can relax and even have a lovely meal or afternoon tea. You can have lunch at Junior's, a deli and cheesecake institution. See what is being performed at the Brooklyn Academy of Music that evening. In the summer months, you might want to spend your Brooklyn day at the beach on Coney island, catch a Cyclones baseball game, lunch at the original Nathan's, and spend an afternoon in the aquarium.

If you choose to spend a day in Queens, head over to the Hall of Science, where your kids will have the time of their lives playing with science and doing experiments. This is a very interactive museum and takes at least two hours to visit.

Then head over to MoMA QNS (the temporary location of the Museum of Modern Art) and visit some of the classics of modern art, from Gauguin to Picasso. You might want to catch a Greek meal in nearby Astoria.

 ## JUST FOR PARENTS

Tired of all that walking and shopping? You need a spa treatment! Bliss, with branches in the Village and Midtown, offers an array of massages and facials, but their mud massage is a favorite. Or you can try the hot lava-stone massage at Oasis Day Spa, with branches throughout Manhattan.

Make It a Full Week

Everyone comes to New York with a different agenda, but if you are here to shop, you can put aside a day just to do that. Certainly hit one or two of the Midtown department stores, but also plan on visiting some of the unique stores in Greenwich Village and the upscale ones along 5th and Madison Avenues.

If you love bargain shopping, make sure you visit Century 21 in Lower Manhattan and Loehmann's. You can even plan a day trip to Woodbury Commons, which any New Yorker will tell you is worth the time and energy.

If you are in town in the summer, you might want to spend a day at one of the city's beaches, but a weekday would be much less crowded than a weekend. You can take a train or bus to Orchard Beach or Coney Island, or take the LIRR to Jones Beach (where you and the family might even be able to catch an outdoor rock concert at the Tommy Hilfiger Theater).

You might also want to consider spending a day at Six Flags-Great Adventure. It's a great way to let your hair down after a vacation.

New York's Annual Events

January

Restaurant Week

Twice a year (in January and July), more than 200 of New York's finest restaurants offer a prix fixe lunch and dinner menu. Lunch is offered for the price of the year (in other words, $20.04 in 2004), and dinner is about $10 more per person. This is a fabulous opportunity to sample the best of the city's cuisine, but make reservations, as the best restaurants fill up within hours of the announcement of restaurant week. Find more information on the Web at ✍ *www.restaurantweek.com*.

National Boat Show

This annual event is held at the Jacob K. Javits Center and shows the latest in boats and other pleasure craft for the water. Call ✆ 212-216-2000 for more information, or visit the Web at ✍ *www.javitscenter.com*.

Winter Antique Show

The antique show is held at the Seventh Regiment Armory on Park Avenue. This is the top antiques fair in the city, which has just celebrated its fiftieth anniversary. Call ✆ 718-292-7392 for more information, or visit them on the Web at ✍ *winterantiqueshow.com*.

February

Chinese New Year Celebration

The annual celebration is held in Chinatown over a two-week period and includes a dragon parade and special menus in most Chinatown restaurants.

Westminster Dog Show

The annual dog-show beauty pageant is held at Madison Square Garden and is considered the big time for the dog set. Call ✆ 212-465-6741 for more information, or visit them on the Web at ✍ *www.westminsterkennelclub.org*.

March

St. Patrick's Day Parade

This annual event (since 1762) is one of the biggest and best St. Patrick's Day parades in the country. The route is Fifth Avenue from 44th to 86th Streets. Call ✆ 212-484-1222 for more information.

Art Expo

Thousands of artists and collectors show their contemporary art at the expo, held at the Jacob K. Javits Center. Call ✆ 1-888-322-5226 for more information, or visit them on the Web at ✍ www.artexpo.com.

Greek Independence Day Parade

This annual parade on Fifth Avenue has been taking place since the 1930s.

April

Easter Parade

The Easter Parade takes place along Fifth Avenue, from outside St. Patrick's Cathedral from 47th Street to 59th Streets. It's a time for New Yorkers to display their Easter finery.

New York International Auto Show

The newest and weirdest cars can be seen at this show, as well as car accessories of almost any kind imaginable. Call ✆ 212-216-2000, or go online to ✍ www.javitscenter.com for more information.

Opening Day at Shea Stadium

The Mets usually kick off the baseball season in the first week of April. For more information, call ✆ 718-507-8499 or visit them on the Web at ✍ www.newyorkmets.com.

Opening Day at Yankee Stadium

Like the Mets, the Yankees usually kick off the baseball season in the first week of April. For more information, call ✆ 718-293-6000, or visit them on the Web at ✐ *www.yankees.com.*

Ringling Brothers Barnum and Bailey Circus

The three-ring circus comes to the Big Apple every April and performs at Madison Square Garden. Call ✆ 212-465-6741 for more information, or visit them on the Web at ✐ *www.ringling.com.*

Cherry Blossom Festival

Spring is spectacular at the Brooklyn Botanic Garden, Brooklyn's favorite garden. It is celebrated in this annual festival. Call ✆ 718-623-7200 for more information, or visit them on the Web at ✐ *www.bbg.com.*

Annual Macy's Flower Show

The week before Easter, the interior of this department store is taken over by exquisite floral displays. Call ✆ 212-494-5432 for more information.

New York City Ballet

The city's premier ballet troupe begins their spring repertory season in late April. Find more information on the Web at ✐ *www.nycballet.com.*

May

Bike New York

For the bicycle enthusiast, here's a chance to take a forty-two-mile bike tour of all five boroughs with 30,000 other cyclists. Call ✆ 212-932-2453 for more information, or find more information on the Web at ✐ *www.bikenewyork.org*

Fleet Week

Navy ships from all over the country come to the Hudson and berth near the USS *Intrepid*, where they are open to the public for viewing. Call ✆ 212-245-0072 for more information.

Washington Square Outdoor Art Show

Hundreds of mostly local artists display paintings, photos, sculpture, and crafts in Washington Square Park in Greenwich Village from noon till dusk. Call ✆ 212-982-6255 for more information.

Memorial Day Parade

This annual parade on Fifth Avenue culminates with a ceremony on the USS *Intrepid*.

June

National Puerto Rican Day Parade

One of the city's largest and most popular ethnic parades, this route runs along Fifth Avenue, from 44th to 86th Street. It is the nation's oldest Puerto Rican Parade, first celebrated in 1958. Call ✆ 718-401-0404 for more information.

Annual AIDS Walk

This celebrity-filled 10K walkathon starts and ends in Central Park. Find more information on the Web at ✐ *www.aidswalk.net*.

The Belmont Stakes

One of the major horseracing events of the year, this final jewel in the Triple Crown takes place at Belmont Race Track in Long Island. Find more information on the Web at ✐ *www.nyracing.com/belstakes.com*, or call ✆ 718-488-6000.

JVC Jazz Festival New York

More than forty venues feature the best of jazz in such places as Carnegie Hall, Lincoln Center, and other venues. Call ✆ 212-501-1390 for more information.

Restaurant Week

This semiannual event features prix fixe meals in more than 100 fine restaurants; see full listing for the January event.

New York Philharmonic Concerts in the Park

New Yorkers gather on the open meadows with picnic blankets to listen to music under the stars in Central and Van Cortlandt parks. Find more information on the Web at ✍ *www.newyork philharmonic.org*, or call ✆ 212-875-5656.

Bryant Park Film Festival

The park behind the New York Public Library (at ✉ 42nd Street and Sixth Avenue) is used as an outdoor theater for the screening of classic films. Bring a blanket and lounge under the stars. Find more information on the Web at ✍ *www.bryantpark.org*, or call ✆ 212-512-7200.

July

Macy's Annual Fourth of July Fireworks Display

This spectacular display takes place over the East River. Viewing sites stretch along the FDR from 14th Street to 41st Street; the Brooklyn Promenade is also a good place to watch. Call ✆ 212-494-4495 for more information.

Midsummer Night Swing at Lincoln Center

One of the most popular city summer events, this dance event takes place outside, at the Lincoln Center fountain. Find more information on the Web at ✍ *www.lincolncenter.org*, or call ✆ 212-875-5766.

Summerstage Concerts in Central Park

Free concerts are a pleasure in at the band shell, taking place in the evening and on weekend afternoons. Find more information on the Web at ✍ *www.summerstage.org*, or call ✆ 212-360-2777.

Shakespeare in the Park

These free performances of Shakespearean dramas take place at the Delacorte Theater in Central Park, usually with a cast of celebrity actors. Find more information on the Web at ✎ *www. publictheater.org*, or call ✆ 212-539-8500.

August

U.S. Open Tennis Championships

The annual tennis championship is played at Flushing Meadow Park in Queens. Find more information on the Web at ✎ *www. usopen.org.*

West Indian American Day Parade

Held over the Labor Day weekend in Brooklyn, this parade celebrates the traditional harvest carnival native to Trinidad and Tobago. Find more information on the Web at ✎ *www.nycarnival.com*, or call ✆ 212-625-1515.

Harlem Week in Upper Manhattan

This is a day-long celebration of African-American culture. Held along 125th Street, it features dancing, performances, crafts, and food. For more information, call ✆ 212-862-7200.

September

Feast of San Gennaro

This week-long outdoor amusement park with food and games of chance takes place in Little Italy on Mulberry Street. Find more information on the Web at ✎ *www.littleitaly.com*, or call ✆ 212-794-2400.

Medieval Festival

On the third Sunday in September, 40,000 people head to Fort Tryon Park and The Cloisters to see a joust and dress in medieval clothing. Find more information on the Web at ✎ *www.whidc.com*, or call ✆ 212-795-1600.

October

Columbus Day Parade

New York hosts one of the oldest and biggest Columbus Day celebrations (and always one of the most controversial) on Fifth Avenue between 44th and 86th Streets. Call ✆ 212-642-8572 for more information.

Halloween Parade

This very popular and crowded costume parade takes place in Greenwich Village, on Sixth Avenue from 23rd Street to Spring Street. Find more information on the Web at ✐ *www.halloween-nyc.com*, or call ✆ 845-758-5519.

November

Veterans Day Parade

This annual parade route runs down Fifth Avenue to Madison Square Park. Call ✆ 212-484-1222 for information.

The New York City Marathon

Covering twenty-six miles through all five boroughs, the runners even visit Staten Island before returning to Manhattan, where it starts. Find more information on the Web at ✐ *www.nyrrc.org*, or call ✆ 212-860-4455.

Macy's Thanksgiving Day Parade

Along with over eighty floats, marchers and Santa Clauses parade down Central Park West on the fourth Thursday in November, from 77th Street to Broadway and Herald Square. Call ✆ 212-494-4495 for information.

The *Radio City Christmas Spectacular*

This annual performance includes the Rockettes, a living Nativity, and Santa Claus. Find more information on the Web at ✐ *www.radiocity.com*, or call ✆ 212-247-4777.

December

The Lighting of the Christmas Tree

A few days after Thanksgiving, thousands gather to watch the lighting of the tree at Rockefeller Center. Call ☎ 212-332-7654 for more information.

The Lighting of the Giant Hanukkah Menorah

This ceremony takes place at Grand Army Plaza, on Fifth Avenue and 59th Street, across the street from the Plaza Hotel in Manhattan. Call ☎ 212-736-8400 for more information.

The Nutcracker

Every year, this ballet—a children's favorite—is performed at Lincoln Center. Tickets are a hot commodity.

Midnight Run in Central Park on New Year's Eve

Sponsored by the New York Road Runners Club, this festive run begins at Tavern on the Green. It has become one of New York's important annual events. Find more information on the Web at *www.nycrrc.org*, or call ☎ 212-860-4455.

New Year's Eve

Just like you've probably seen on the television, the ball will drop at midnight in Times Square. For more information call ☎ 212-788-2000 or visit *www.timessquarebid.org*.

First Night

On New Year's Eve, Grand Central Station becomes a ballroom, with dancing and entertainment for an alcohol-free evening. Find more information on the Web at *www.nycvisit.com*, or call ☎ 212-788-2000.

Additional Resources

Web Sites

www.nycvisit.org
212-484-1222

This Web site is essential for planning your trip. Here, you will find hotel and restaurant suggestions and discounts, a local calendar of events, as well as suggested itineraries and ways to plan and save money. You can ask to be sent a tourist package that includes a truly handy pocket-sized subway map, an essential item for any New York City vacation.

www.iloveny.com
1-800-CALL-NYS

This is the official tourist Web site of New York State, which will give you suggested hotels and tour packages, as well as itineraries and maps. You can also register and they will send you their magazine.

www.longisland.com

This Web site contains tourist information on Long Island, with seasonal attractions and railroad schedules.

www.newyorktimes.com

Your first stop on the Web should be the *New York Times* site. It covers just about everything you need to orient yourself in the city, from news highlights and a neighborhood guide to a calendar of events and even hotel and restaurant information and reviews.

www.newsday.com

This comprehensive Web site presents information on what's going on in Long Island and Queens.

www.newyorkmetro.com

This is *New York* magazine's Web site, and it is an essential tool for finding just about anything you might want in the city. The restaurant review database is extensive.

✍ *www.NY1.com*

This is the Web site for New York's twenty-four-hour television news station. In addition to updates on local news, there's a list of sites on each borough, as well as good features.

✍ *www.villagevoice.com*

This weekly alternative newspaper hosts an informative Web site. The calendar of events is one of the best in the city.

✍ *www.nyc.gov*

This is the city's comprehensive Web site, which will give you everything from access to the Department of Parks and Recreation to parking regulations. It's huge, but very complete. While in the city, you can access this information by phone by calling ☎ 311.

✍ *www.ny.com*

This site provides general information on New York, with an emphasis on frugality.

✍ *www.nyctourist.com*

One of the many unofficial Web sites about the city, this one is fairly comprehensive with a lot of shopping suggestions and links.

Suggested Reading

Nonfiction

Bykofsky, Sheree, *The 52 Most Romantic Dates in and Around New York City* (2001, Adams Media). This is a charming and entertaining title highlighting romantic spots in the city.

Caro, Robert, *The Power Broker: Robert Moses and the Fall of New York* (1975, Vintage). This is the inside story of how New York's parks and highways were built. It includes great characters and is a fascinating read. It's a page-turner at more than 1,000 pages.

Claxton, Eve, *New York's 100 Best Little Places to Shop* (1998, City & Company). A fairly wonderful guide to off-the-beaten path shopping in the greatest shopping city in the county.

Miller, J. B., *The New York Writer's Guidebook* (2001, Universe). Anyone who has ever been interested in New York in its guise as the writing and publishing capital of the country should browse a copy of this book by this published novelist.

Sietsema, Robert, *Secret New York* (1999, ECW Press). This is another good guide book to off-the-beaten-path destinations in the city.

Traub, James, *The Devil's Playground: A Century of Pleasure and Profit in Times Square* (2004, Random House). The history encapsulates all the dirt and glamour of Times Square, and everything in between, by a *New York Times* reporter.

Fiction

Doctorow, E. L., *World's Fair* (1996, Plume). This Pulitzer Prize–winning novel records a special time and place in New York City in New York's history.

Vidal, Gore, *Burr* (Vintage, republished 2000). This great novel recounts the rise and fall of New Yorker Aaron Burr.

Kid's Books

New York has been the subject or main character of many kid's books. Below are a few that my son has always loved.

Barracca, Debra and Sal, *The Adventures of Taxi Dog* (2000, Dial). This book is for toddlers and early readers and is about the adventures of Maxi, the Taxi Dog. The Children's Museum of Manhattan features some of the book's art.

Fitzhugh, Louise, *Harriet the Spy* (1990, Harper Trophy). This children's classic is set in Manhattan. It's a great one to take on the trip.

Reingold, Faith, *Tar Beach* (1996, Crown). A classic about summer on a hot city roof. The art is featured at the Children's Museum of Manhattan.

Swift, Hildegarde and Lynd Ward, *The Little Red Lighthouse and the Great Gray Bridge* (1992, Harcourt Brace). This is a New York classic about the relationship between two real-life landmarks.

Thompson, Kay, *Eloise* (1959, Simon and Schuster). This is the classic tale of the little girl who grew up at the Plaza Hotel.

White E. B., *Stuart Little* (1974, Harper). This is another children's classic set in this fabulous city.

New York City Maps

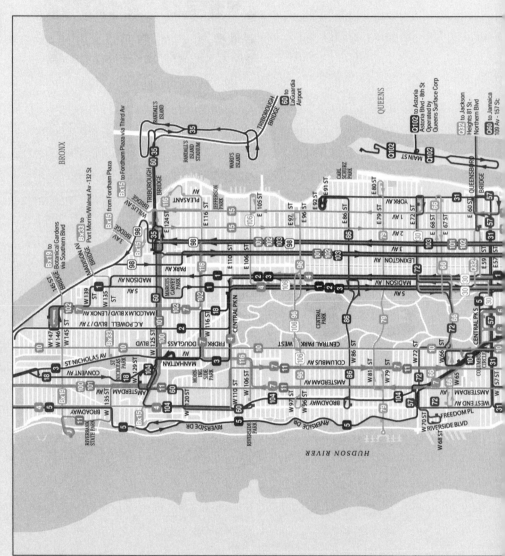

Manhattan bus map ©Metropolitan Transportation Authority is printed with permission.

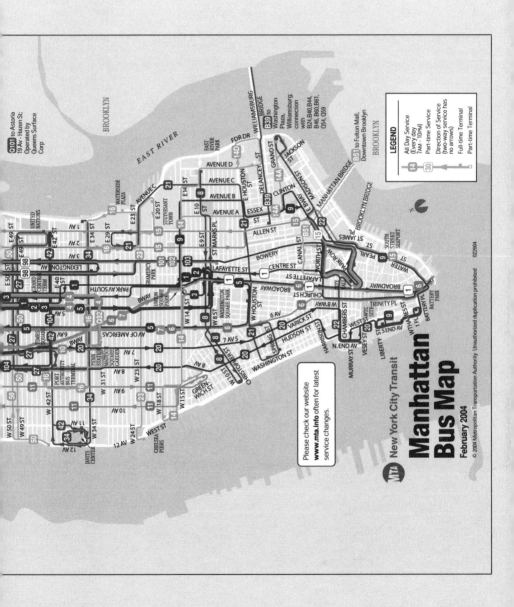

MTA New York City Transit

Manhattan Bus Map

February 2004

Please check our website **www.mta.info** often for latest service changes.

© 2004 Metropolitan Transportation Authority Unauthorized duplication prohibited 022604

LEGEND

All Day Service (Every day 7AM - 10PM)

Part-time Service

Direction of Service (two-way service has no arrows)

Full-time Terminal

Part-time Terminal

BROOKLYN

EAST RIVER

BROOKLYN

Q101 to Astoria 19 Av - Hazen St; Operated by Queens Surface Corp

B39 to Washington Plaza, Williamsburg; connection with B24, B40, B44, B46, B60, B61, Q54, Q59

B51 to Fulton Mall, Downtown Brooklyn

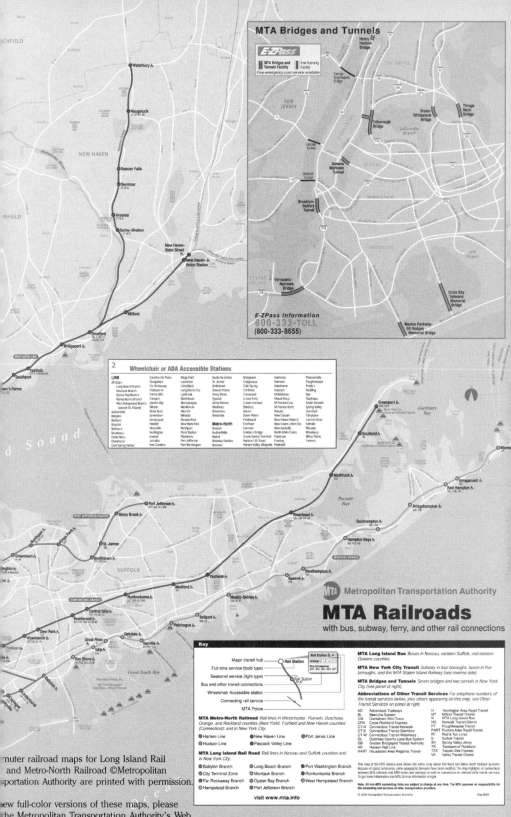

MTA Bridges and Tunnels

E-ZPass

■ MTA Bridges and Tunnels Facility   ■ Port Authority Facility
Free emergency road service available

E-ZPass Information
800-333-TOLL
(800-333-8655)

Henry Hudson Bridge
George Washington Bridge
Throgs Neck Bridge
Bronx-Whitestone Bridge
Triborough Bridge
Lincoln Tunnel
LaGuardia Airport
Queens Midtown Tunnel
Holland Tunnel
Brooklyn-Battery Tunnel
Verrazano-Narrows Bridge
Cross Bay Veterans Memorial Bridge
Marine Parkway-Gil Hodges Memorial Bridge

NEW JERSEY
NEW YORK
QUEENS
BROOKLYN
STATEN ISLAND

2   Wheelchair or ADA Accessible Stations

LIRR
All stops:
Long Beach Branch
Montauk Branch
Oyster Bay Branch
Ronkonkoma Branch
West Hempstead Branch
(except St. Albans)
Auburndale
Babylon
Baldwin
Bayside
Bellerose
Broadway
Douglaston
Dante Place
Cold Spring Harbor

Country Life Press
Douglaston
Far Rockaway
Flatbush Av
Forest Hills
Freeport
Garden City
Gibson
Great Neck
Greenlawn
Hempstead
Hewlett
Hicksville
Huntington
Inwood
Jamaica
New Gardens

Kings Park
Lawrence
Little Neck
Long Island City
Lynbrook
Mattituck
Massapequa
Merillon Av
Merrick
Mineola
Nassau Blvd
New Hyde Park
Northport
Penn Station
Plandome
Port Jefferson
Port Washington

Stadium/Yankees
St. James
Smithtown
Stewart Manor
Stony Brook
Syosset
Valley Stream
Woodbury
Woodhaven
Woodside

Metro-North
Beacon
Bedford Hills
Bedford
Botanical Garden
Bronxville

Bridgeport
Chappaqua
Cold Spring
Cortlandt
Cos Cob
Croton Harmon
Croton-Harmon
Danbury
Darien
Dover Plains
Fleetwood
Fordham
Garrison
Grand Central Terminal
Harlem-125 Street
Harlem Valley/Wassaic

Harmon
Harrison
Hawthorne
Katonah
Larchmont
Mount Kisco
Mt Vernon East
Mt Vernon West
Nanuet
New Canaan
New Haven-State St.
New Haven-Union Sta
New Rochelle
North White Plains
Pelham
Pawling
Peekskill

Pleasantville
Poughkeepsie
Purdy's
Redding
Rye
Southeast
Spring Valley
Stamford
Tarrytown
Tenmile River
Valhalla
Wassaic
Woodlawn/Jct
White Plains
Yonkers

Waterbury
Naugatuck
Beacon Falls
Seymour
Ansonia
Derby-Shelton
New Haven-State Street
New Haven-Union Station
Milford
Stratford
Bridgeport
Fairfield
Southport
Greens Farms
NEW HAVEN LINE
NEW HAVEN
FAIRFIELD
Long Island Sound
Greenport
Southold
Mattituck
Riverhead
Port Jefferson
Stony Brook
St. James
Smithtown
Yaphank
Medford
Mastic-Shirley
Ronkonkoma
Central Islip
Brentwood
Deer Park
Wyandanch
Pinelawn
Great River
Oakdale
Sayville
Islip
Bay Shore
Babylon
Copiague
Bellport
Patchogue
Westhampton
Speonk
Hampton Bays
Southampton
Bridgehampton
East Hampton
Amagansett
Montauk
SUFFOLK
Peconic Bay
Gardiners Bay
Great South Bay
PORT JEFFERSON BRANCH
MONTAUK BRANCH
RONKONKOMA BRANCH

(MTA) Metropolitan Transportation Authority

MTA Railroads
with bus, subway, ferry, and other rail connections

Key

Major transit hub ●○ Rail Station
Full-time service (bold type)
Seasonal service (light type)
Bus and other transit connections
Wheelchair Accessible station ◇ Rail Station
Connecting rail service

Rail Station
Subway
Bus Connections

MTA Long Island Bus Buses in Nassau, western Suffolk, and eastern Queens counties.

MTA New York City Transit Subway in four boroughs, buses in five boroughs, and the MTA Staten Island Railway (see reverse side).

MTA Bridges and Tunnels Seven bridges and two tunnels in New York City (see panel at right).

Abbreviations of Other Transit Services For telephone numbers of the transit services below, plus others appearing on this map, see Other Transit Services on panel at right.

MTA Metro-North Railroad *Rail lines in Westchester, Putnam, Dutchess, Orange, and Rockland counties (New York); Fairfield and New Haven counties (Connecticut); and in New York City.*

■ Harlem Line   ■ New Haven Line   ■ Hudson Line
■ Hudson Line   ■ Pascack Valley Line

MTA Long Island Rail Road *Rail lines in Nassau and Suffolk counties and in New York City.*

■ Babylon Branch   ■ Long Beach Branch   ■ Port Washington Branch
■ City Terminal Zone   ■ Montauk Branch   ■ Ronkonkoma Branch
■ Far Rockaway Branch ■ Oyster Bay Branch   ■ West Hempstead Branch
■ Hempstead Branch   ■ Port Jefferson Branch

MTA Police

visit www.mta.info

AD Adirondack Trailways	H Huntington Area Rapid Transit
BL Bee-Line System	MT Milford Transit District
CM Danbertown Mini-Trans	N MTA Long Island Bus
CRX Cross Rockland Express	NO Norwalk Transit District
CT-N Connecticut Transit-Norwalk	PT Poughkeepsie Transit
CT-S Connecticut Transit-Stamford	PART Putnam Area Rapid Transit
CT-W Connecticut Transit-Waterbury	RT Red & Tan Lines
DL Dutchess County Loop Bus System	S Suffolk Transit
GB Greater Bridgeport Transit Authority	SV Spring Valley Jitney
HR Hudson Rail Link	TR Transport of Rockland
HART Housatonic Area Regional Transit	TZX Tappan Zee Express
	VA Valley Transit District

This map of the MTA service area shows the entire Long Island Rail Road and Metro-North Railroad systems. Because of space constraints, some geographic distances have been modified. The map highlights all connections between MTA railroads and MTA buses and subways as well as connections to selected other transit services. To get travel information see MTA Service information at right.

Note: All non-MTA connecting links are subject to change at any time. The MTA assumes no responsibility for the scheduling and services of other transportation providers.

© 2004 Metropolitan Transportation Authority   May 2004

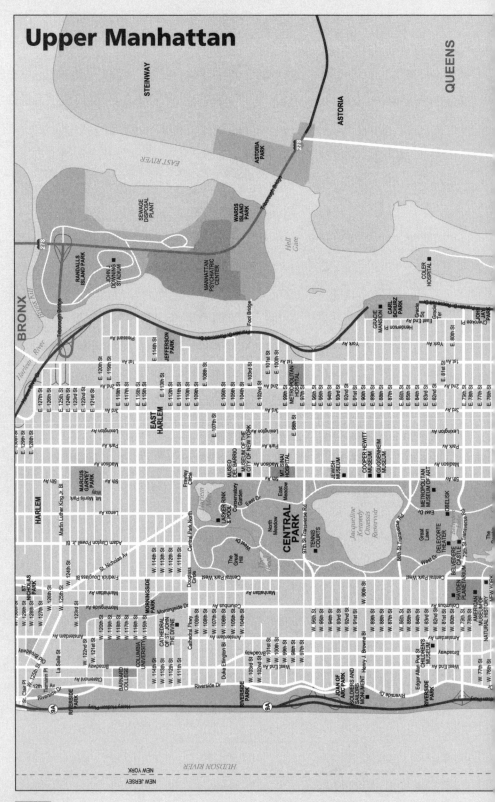

Upper Manhattan

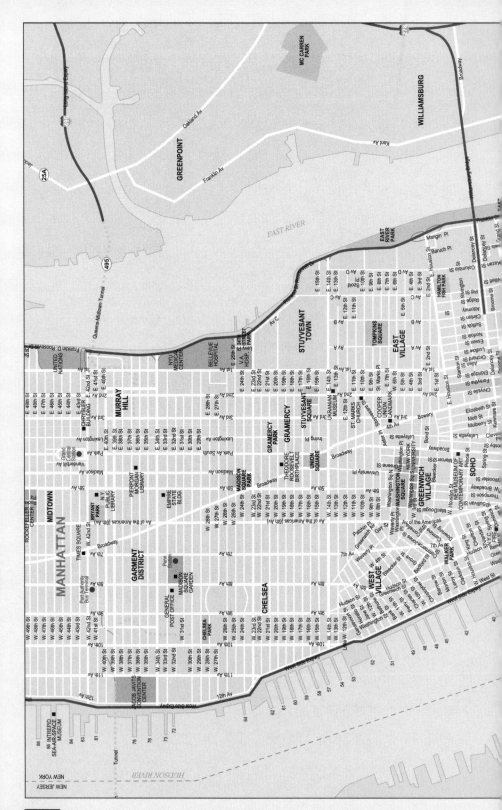

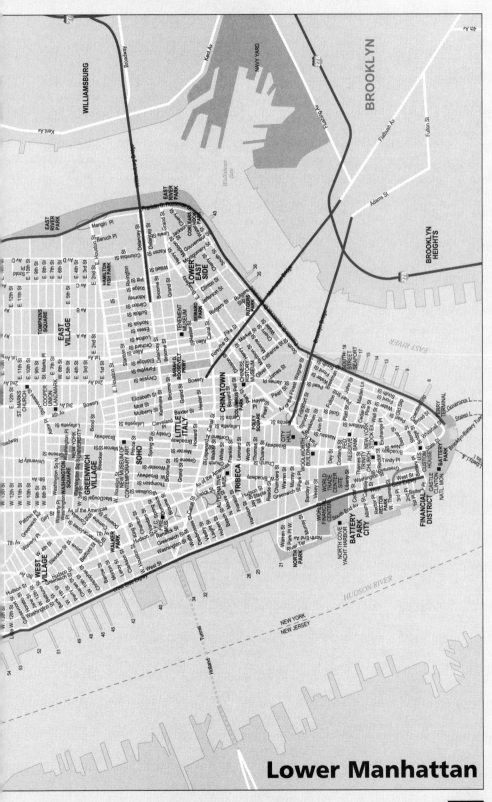

Lower Manhattan

Central Park

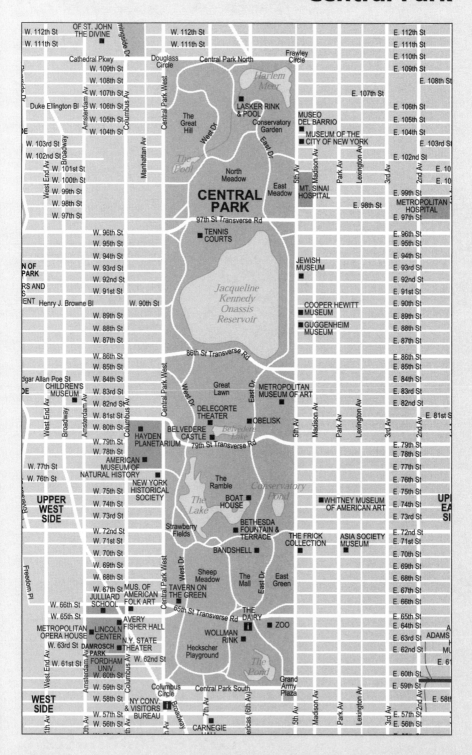

Index

shipping services, 193
theme restaurants, 90,
  250–52, 271–73
tipping, 244
on Upper East Side, 259–60
on Upper West Side, 261–62
restrooms, 200
Richard Rodgers Theatre, 229
Richmond County Bank
  Ballpark, 221
Ringling Brothers Barnum and
  Bailey Circus, 238
Riverside Park, 216
Rockaway Park Beach, 214–15
Rockefeller Center, 6, 14, 86–89,
  222
Roseland, 5
Rye Playland, 352–53

S
safety tips, 31, 43–44
St. James Theatre, 230
St. Patrick's Cathedral, 105–6
Saks Fifth Avenue, 195, 197–98,
  267
Sands Point Preserve, 348–49
Saturday Night Live, 238
Savoy Ballroom, 5
Schermerhorn Row, 108
Sephora, 207
Shakespeare Garden, 78, 126
Shea Stadium, 10, 155, 161,
  219–20
Sheep Meadow, 126, 213
Sheepshead Bay, 157, 159
shopping
  bargain shops, 203–5, 210–12
  book shops, 205–6

department stores, 194–98
discount stores, 198–200
flea markets, 202–3
malls, 203, 212
in New York, 193–212
secondhand shops, 203–5
shipping services, 193
souvenir stores, 208–9
specialty shops, 205–8
upscale shops, 200–202
Shubert Theater, 228
shuttles, 24–26
side trips, 341–53
sightseeing tours, 49–56
Six Flags, 351–52
Snug Harbor Cultural Center,
  190–91
SoHo, 36, 59
Sotheby's, 204
soul food, 290–91
South Street Seaport, 106–9
South Street Seaport Museum,
  107–9
Spanish cuisine, 282–83
sports, 118–21, 221–22
stadiums, 219–21
Staten Island
  attractions on, 187–91
  museums on, 190–91
  residents of, 155
  visiting, 163–64
Staten Island Botanical Garden,
  190–91
Staten Island Children's
  Museum, 190–91
Staten Island Ferry, 17, 82, 155,
  187
Statue of Liberty, 3, 80–82

We Have

EVERYTHING!

The Everything® Guide to Las Vegas
Jason Rich

1-58062-438-3,
$14.95 ($22.95 CAN)

Las Vegas is fast becoming America's choice for family vacations. With fabulous weather, great restaurants, and unbelievable attractions, there is something for everyone, all day, and all night. *The Everything® Guide to Las Vegas* is the one resource you need to help you with your vacation planning, and to guarantee that you won't miss a thing. It includes shows and attractions for every member of the family, restaurant listings in and out of the casinos, the best shopping and day trips, and much more!

The Everything® Guide to New England
Kimberly Knox Beckius

Whether it's "leaf-peeping" in the fall, skiing in the winter, taking historical tours in the spring, or spending leisure time at seaside resorts in the summer, New England is the perfect year-round travel destination. This comprehensive book offers many exciting places to go and things to see, from tracing the footsteps of our country's beginnings on Boston's historic Freedom Trail, to sampling local wines at one of Connecticut's vineyards, to enjoying the scenery at Maine's Acadia National Park.

1-58062-589-4,
$14.95 ($22.95 CAN)

Available wherever books are sold!

For Travel!

The Everything® Family Guide to Hawaii
Donald P. Ryan, Ph.D.

The Hawaiian islands have long been known as a premier travel destination. This island paradise is also gaining recognition for its family-friendly sites, high-quality accommodations, and exciting activities. *The Everything® Family Guide to Hawaii* provides readers with an easy-to-use guide to all the best hotels, shops, restaurants, and attractions in the Aloha State. This book features tips for finding the cheapest fares, traveling between islands, avoiding the tourist traps, and enjoying the unique culture and heritage of the Hawaiian people.

Lodging, restaurants, beaches, and must-see attractions for all eight islands

Donald P. Ryan, Ph.D.

1-59337-054-7, $14.95($22.95 CAN)

1-59337-137-3, $12.95 ($19.95 CAN)

The Everything® Family Guide to Washington D.C., 2nd Edition
Lori Perkins

The Everything® Guide to Washington D.C., 2nd Ed. captures the spirit and excitement of this unique city, from important historical showpieces such as the White House and the Smithsonian, to the best museums, galleries, and family activities. You'll find up-to-date reviews for tons of hotels and restaurants, guided tours, loads of attractions and activities, museums for every interest, and more!

To order, call 800-872-5627 or visit *www.everything.com*

The Everything® Travel Guide to The Disneyland Resort®, California Adventure®, Universal Studios®, and the Anaheim Area
Jason Rich

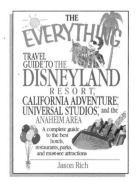

1-58062-742-0,
$14.95 ($22.95 CAN)

With millions of visitors each year, it's easy to see why Disneyland® is one of America's favorite vacation spots for families. Containing the most up-to-date information, this brand new expansive travel guide contains everything needed to plan the perfect getaway without missing any of the great new attractions. This book rates all the rides, shows, and attractions for each member of the family, allowing readers to plan the perfect itinerary for their trip.

The Everything® Family Guide to The Walt Disney World Resort®, Universal Studios®, and Greater Orlando, 4th Edition
Jason Rich

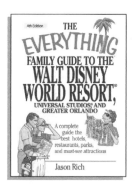

1-59337-179-9,
$14.95 ($22.95 CAN)

Packed with fun things to see and do, the Orlando area is the number one family vacation destination in the country. In this newest edition, travel expert Jason Rich shares his latest tips on how the whole family can have a great time—without breaking the bank. In addition to the helpful ride, show, and attractions rating system, the revised fourth edition contains a fully updated hotel/motel resource guide, rated restaurant listings, and the inside scoop on all the new additions.